GLOBALIZATION, ETHICS AND ISLAM

'An excellent example of co-operative scholarship between Muslims and Christians. Anyone who wishes to learn about a thoroughly orthodox, tolerant and eirenic Islam, as expressed by the early twentieth-century Turkish writer, Said Nursi, should read this book.'

Professor Keith Ward, Christ Church, Oxford, UK

'It can no longer be said that 'east is east and west is west and never the twain shall meet.' The world of Islam has penetrated the western world in ways that cannot be ignored. Inter-religious dialogue is essential and this book will do much to facilitate that dialogue. It is a brilliant read.'

Dr Tony Compolo, Founder and President of the Evangelical Association for the Promotion of Education, USA

'This is a welcome book: there are very few works on Said Nursi. It is obviously of great relevance in the post 9/11 period and will provide fascinating reading for scholars, academics and those interested in Islam, Turkey and in other fields of social science.'

Professor Lloyd Ridgeon, University of Glasgow, UK

Globalization, Ethics and Islam

The Case of Bediuzzaman Said Nursi

Edited by
IAN MARKHAM
Hartford Seminary, USA

and

IBRAHIM OZDEMIR
Ankara University Divinity School (llahiyat), Turkey

Routledge
Taylor & Francis Group
LONDON AND NEW YORK

First published 2005 by Ashgate Publishing

2 Park Square, Milton Park, Abingdon, Oxon OX14 4RN
711 Third Avenue, New York, NY 10017, USA

Routledge is an imprint of the Taylor & Francis Group, an informa business

First issued in paperback 2016

British Library Cataloguing in Publication Data
Globalization, ethics and Islam : the case of Bediuzzaman Said Nursi
1.Nursi, Said, 1873–1960—Political and social views 2.Nursi, Said, 1873–1960—Ethics 3.Nursi, Said, 1873–1960. Risale–i nur 4.Globalization—Religious aspects—Islam 5.Islamic ethics
I.Markham, Ian S. II.Ozdemir, Ibrahim
297.2'7'092

Library of Congress Cataloging-in-Publication Data
Globalization, ethics and Islam : the case of Bediuzzaman Said Nursi / [compiled by] Ian Markham and Ibrahim Ozdemir.
p. cm.
Includes index.
ISBN 0–7546–5015–4 (hardback : alk. paper)
1. Nursi, Said, 1873-1960. Risale-i nur. 2. Nurculuk—Doctrines. 3. Islamic ethics. 4. Globalization—Religious aspects—Islam. 5. Religious pluralism—Islam. 6. Islam—Relations. I. Markham, Ian. II. Ozdemir, Ibrahim.

BP252.G56 2004
297.8'3—dc22

2004025369

ISBN 13: 978-0-7546-5015-7 (hbk)
ISBN 13: 978-1-138-26275-1 (pbk)

Contents

PART III: Globalization

List of Contributors

Afsaruddin, Asma, Associate Professor of Arabic & Islamic Studies, University of Notre Dame, received her Ph.D. from Johns Hopkins University in 1993. She previously taught at Johns Hopkins and Harvard universities. Her fields of specialization are the religious and political thought of Islam, Qur'an and Hadith studies, and Islamic intellectual history. She is the author of *Excellence and Precedence: Medieval Islamic Discourse on Legitimate Leadership* (Leiden: E.J. Brill, 2002); the editor of *Hermeneutics and Honor: Negotiation of Female "Public" Space in Islamic/ate Societies* (Cambridge, Mass., Harvard University, 1999); and co-editor of *Humanism, Culture, and Language in the Near East: Studies in Honor of Georg Krotkoff* (Winona Lake, Ind.: Eisenbrauns, 1997). Her articles and book reviews have been published in the International Journal of Middle East Studies, Der Islam, the Journal of Semitic Studies, Harvard Middle Eastern and Islamic Review, the Journal of the American Oriental Society, and the Journal of Qur'anic Studies. She is currently serving on the editorial board of the Oxford Dictionary of Islam (Oxford University Press, forthcoming), is a member of the advisory boards of the Crescent University Foundation and the Michiana Institute of Islamic Studies, and is a fellow of the Center for the Study of Islam and Democracy.

Al-Roubaie, Amer, International Institute of Islamic Thought and Civilization (ISTAC), International Islamic University Malaysia (IIUM). Amer Al-Roubaie presently teaches economics at the International Institute of Islamic Thought & Civilization in Kuala Lumpur, Malaysia. Professor Al-Roubaie earned his Ph.D. in economics from McGill University in Montreal, Canada. His main area of research is economic development in the Middle East with emphasis on oil resources, the environment and labour migration. Recently, Al-Roubaie has written a book entitled *Globalization and the Muslim World* underlining some of the important challenges facing Muslims in the age of globalization. In addition he has published several other articles about the same subject. Prior to his current position, Professor Al-Roubaie taught economics in both Canada and the United States. At present he is writing another book related to the subject of globalization and its impact on Muslim societies.

Aries, Wolf D. Ahmed, Writer, Author, Germany. Ahmed Aries was born in Germany in 1938, and became a Muslim in 1953. He studied psychology, and is the director of an adult education college. He has done research on health education and has worked in publishing. He has participated in Islamic activities in Germany since 1972, and is at present a member of the German Islamic Council, and writes for the journal *Moslemische Revue*. He also teaches on Islamic subjects at Paderborn University.

Aydin, Necati, Furkan Aydiner is a Ph.D. candidate at Florida State University, majoring in the economics of education. He has a bachelor degree and a master degree in economics. Moreover, he had accomplished the coursework phase of two Ph.D. programs in economics before coming to FSU in January 1999. Currently, he is an Adjunct Professor of Economics at Florida A & M University, teaching courses such as the Introduction to Econometrics, Public Finance, Microeconomics, Macroeconomics, and Comparative Economic Systems. In addition, he works at the Center for Economic Forecasting and Analysis as an Economist. He is married with three daughters.

Brodeur, Patrice C., Ph.D., Canadian-born, is the Dean of Religious and Spiritual Life at Connecticut College where he has also been teaching for six years as an Assistant Professor of Religious Studies and conducted research as the Director of local Pluralism Project since 1999. His main area of interest is the contemporary study of Islam within the broader academic study of religion; with focus on contemporary Arab Muslim perceptions of religious others. This focus is framed by a broader set of interests that include the relationship between religion and applied religion as well as that between global and local religion(s). Both are used in his research and consulting work interreligious dialogue and cooperation for peace. He has published a number of articles in edited books as well in *The Journal of Ecumenical Studies* and *The Muslim World*, among others. He was the book review editor for *The Muslim World* from 1999 to 2002. Since September 11, 2001, he has actively participated in public debated at local, national and international arenas in the form of articles, lectures and interviews in a variety of media. Professor Brodeur holds an M.A. from the Institute of Islamic Studies at McGill University and a Ph.D. in the Study of Religion from Harvard University.

Hocaoglu, Durmus, Assistant Professor, University of Marmara, Turkey

Lee, Jemil Hee-Soo, Ph.D., Professor in the Department of Anthropology, Hanyang University, Haedang-dong, Seongdong-gu, Seoul, Korea, leading professor of Islamic Studies in Korea, BA/MA in Islamic History at Hankuk at the Istanbul University, Turkey (1988), Assistant Professor, Marmara University, Turkey (1988-1989), Visiting Scholar of the University of Washington (2003), Fieldwork in many Islamic countries between 1983-2003.

Leaman, Oliver, Professor of Philosophy, University of Kentucky, Professor Leaman graduated from the Department of Philosophy, Politics, and Economics at Oxford University in 1972. He received his Doctorate from the Philosophy Department of Cambridge University in 1979. Between 1976 and 1979 he taught in Khartum University, Sudan. Between 1990 and 1995, he was Lecturer in Islamic and Jewish Thought in the Department of Religious Studies in Lancaster

University, and at present is Professor of Philosophy in Kentucky University (USA) since August 2000. Professor Leaman has published numerous works and articles.

Markham, Ian S., Dean of Hartford Seminary and Professor of Theology and Ethics. He is the author of numerous books and articles including *Plurality and Christian Ethics* (Cambridge University Press 1994), *Truth and the Reality of God* (Edinburgh, 1999), *A World Religions Reader* (Oxford Blackwell, 2000) and most recently edited with Ibrahim Abu-Rabi' *September 11: Historical, Social and Theological Perspectives* (Oneworld 2002). He has degrees from the Universities of London, Cambridge, and Exeter in the United Kingdom.

Michel., Thomas, S.J., Professor, University of Notre Dame, Fr. Thomas Michel was born in St. Louis, Missouri, U.S.A., in 1941. After Arabic and Islamic studies in Egypt and Lebanon, he completed a doctoral dissertation on the thought of the 14th Century scholar Ibn Taymiyya and received a Ph.D. in Islamic Thought from the University of Chicago in 1978. Between 1978 and 1981, he taught at Sanata Dharma University in Yogyakarta, Indonesia. In 1981, he was appointed to the Asia Desk of the Vatican Pontifical Council for Interreligious Dialogue and in 1988, he became Head of the Office for Islam in the same Vatican department. Between 1994 and 1996 he served as Executive Secretary of the Office for Ecumenical and Interreligious Affairs of the Federation of Asian Bishops' Conferences (FABC-OEIA), in Bangkok, Thailand. He is now Secretary of the Jesuit Secretariat for Interreligious Dialogue in Rome, Italy, and Ecumenical Secretary for the Federation of Asian Bishops' Conferences. He has taught at Northwestern and Columbia Universities in the U.S.A., at Sanata Dharma University and Driyarkara Institute of Philosophy in Indonesia, at St. Paul's Major Seminary, Dansalan College, and Euntes Asian Center in the Philippines, at Ankara, Dokuz Eylül, Selcuk, and Harran Universities in Turkey, at the Pontifical Institute for Arabic/Islamic Studies in Rome, at St. Peter's Major Seminary in Malaysia, at St. Paul's Seminary in Albania, and at the University of Birmingham, in England. In 2000, he delivered the D'Arcy Lectures at Oxford University in Oxford, England, on Christian-Muslim relations. Fr. Michel is on the Academic Council of the "Center for Muslim-Christian Understanding" of Georgetown University, Washington, USA. He is on the International Advisory Board of the Khalidi Library, Jerusalem and the Editorial Board of the journal Islam and Christian-Muslim Relations in Birmingham, UK. He is on the International Advisory Panel of the International Movement for a Just World in Kuala Lumpur, Malaysia and the International Advisory Committee of the Center for World Thanksgiving, Dallas, Texas, USA and on the Advisory Board of the Centre for Civilizational Dialogue at the University of Malaya in Kuala Lumpur, Malaysia.

Mirza, Mahan Hussain, Yale University. Mr. Mahan H. Mirza is an MA student at the Hartford Seminary. Although his background is mechanical engineering and he has worked for Siemens as a design engineer, he has shown dedication to undertaking Islamic Studies with particular emphasis on Christian-Muslim Relations. He has spent two years in Pakistan studying Islamic revival from an intellectual perspective, keeping in mind the tensions between tradition and modernism. He intends to continue his studies in pursuit of a Ph.D. at Yale University.

Ozdemir, Ibrahim, Assistant Professor, University of Ankara, Turkey. Dr. Özdemir graduated from the Theology Faculty of Ankara University in 1985, and in 1988 was awarded a Master's degree by the Philosophy Department of the Middle East Technical University. In 1996 he received his Doctorate from the same department. He at present lectures in the Theology Faculty of Ankara University. He has published numerous articles. Among his other published works are: *Çevre Sorunları ve İslam* (Environmental Problems and Islam) (together with Münir Yükselmiş), 1995; *The Ethical Dimensions of Human Attitudes Towards Nature*, 1997; *Çevre ve Din* (The Environment and Religion), 1997.

Reed, Fred A., Writer and Translator Living in Montréal, Canada. In 1994, Fred A. Reed's *Persian Postcards: Iran after Khomeini* was published by Talonbooks, Vancouver, Canada. In 1996, his impressionistic survey of the southern Balkans, *Salonica Terminus,* accurately predicted the 1999 war in Kosovo. His third book, *Anatolia Junction,* published in 1999, is an in-depth examination of the Islamic movement in Turkey focused on the life and career of Bediuzzaman Said Nursi, one of the outstanding figures of modern Muslim thought. A Turkish translation of the book appeared in late 2002. In 2000, Talonbooks published Massoumeh Ebtekar's *Takeover in Tehran,* the first eye-witness account of the 1979 U.S. Embassy hostage-taking incident, written in collaboration with Fred Reed. His fifth book, *Shattered Images*, an examination of the rise and fall of the Iconoclast movement set in Syria, was published in 2003.

Fred A. Reed ranks high among Canada's literary translators. In 1991, his translation of Thierry Hentsch's *L'Orient Imaginaire* (Imagining the Middle East, also translated into Turkish) won the Governor General's Award for translation. In 2001, he won this prestigious award for the second time, along with David Homel, for their translation of Martine Desjardin's *Le Cercle de Clara* (Fairy Ring). He has translated works by Nikos Kazantzakis, Kostas Mourselas, Giorgos Ioannou and Pavlos Matesis from Greek into English. He is considered his country's foremost authority on Islamic Iran, has visited the Islamic Republic 25 times since 1984, and has reported extensively on Iranian, Balkan, Turkish and Middle Eastern affairs for *La Presse*, Canada's largest French-language newspaper. Recently, he worked as head researcher for *Salam Iran*, a documentary by Jean-Daniel Lafond.

Vahide, Sükran, Writer-Author, Turkey. Sükran Vahide was born in England, and in 1980 graduated from the Persian Department of School of Oriental Studies in Durham University. In 1981 she became a Muslim after reading English translations of the *Risale-i Nur*. She has translated a large part of the *Risale-i Nur* into English, and continues to write and do research on it.

Voll, John Obert, Professor (Ph.D.), University of Georgetown. Professor Voll graduated in 1958 from Dartmouth University. In 1960 he was awarded a Master's degree by Harvard University, and in 1969 received his doctorate from the same university. He at present teaches Georgetown University, Washington D.C., and is Professor of Islamic history in the Centre for Muslim-Christian Understanding. He has published numerous books and articles.

Acknowledgements

The editors wish to acknowledge the help of the *Nur* community in the writing of this book. We are especially grateful to the support of Faris Kaya, Director of the Istanbul Ilim ve Kultur Vakfi.

We are also grateful to Ibrahim Abu-Rabi' and Abdullah T. Antepli, who assisted in the editing. Yvonne Bowen turned the text into camera-ready copy. She worked tirelessly on the manuscript.

Finally, we wish to acknowledge our debt to the one God that both Christians and Muslims worship. Ultimately everything we do should honor God.

Ian Markham
Ibrahim Ozdemir

Introduction

If you want to know about Islam, then find a Muslim who is willing to explain the religion to you. On one level, this seems so obvious. It is a principle of basic enquiry: learn from the people who are most informed. And in the case of a religious tradition, the person most informed is the one who lives inside the tradition. Granted there are some Muslims who do not speak Arabic or do not know about the history of the Ottoman empire, but for understanding a religion – how it is lived – a Muslim is always better than a non-Muslim (even a non-Muslim scholar of Islam) and a Muslim scholar of Islam is probably best of all. With the latter, you get the perfect combination of learning with participation.

The academy has learnt this basic lesson the hard way. We now know that certain orientalists have given us a distorted image of Islam. And even at the more basic level: we know how Catholics distort the description of Protestant beliefs and vice versa. The Revd. Ian Paisley (a leading Unionist politician in northern Ireland), for example, is not the best person to ask if you want to understand the Roman Catholic Church; and Bishop John Shelby Spong (the most liberal Bishop in the Episcopal Church) is not the best person to explain the beliefs and worldview of evangelical Baptists. The problem in both cases (Paisley on Catholics and Spong on Baptists) is that the entrenched opposition makes it inevitable that distortions will occur. At the very least there will be an emphasis on certain elements that the opponent finds unattractive; but in addition it is likely that the interpretation will be distinctive. It is so often the case that opponents interpret this or that doctrine or idea in ways that the proponents of those doctrines do not recognize.

Naturally once one is informed about a different tradition, then there is an entitlement to comment. But this commentary is only permitted once one has understood a tradition in a way that the adherents of that tradition would recognize and appreciate.

So the basic principle that we seek to listen to the representatives of a position to explain their position has been established right across the academy. It is observed almost universally, save for one area: in America today the experts on Islam – the 'experts' that everyone in the academy reads – are the opponents.

The best example of this is the work of Daniel Pipes. Pipes' books on Islam have become bestsellers. His *Militant Islam Reaches America* is typical. It is a vitriolic treatment of Islam that distorts, misrepresents, and therefore offers a faulty analysis of his subject matter.

Starting with the distortions and misrepresentations, Pipes complains that Muslims hope, trust, and strive for Islam to be the 'dominant world religion'.[1] He speaks in apocalyptic terms about Islamic aspiration to convert America. So he writes:

> There are three possible means to increase Muslim numbers to achieve this dream: immigration, reproduction, and conversion. Sensing that overwhelming the country with immigrants would provoke a backlash and that reproduction will take a long time, Islamists focus most of their efforts on conversion. Indeed they see converting Americans to Islam as the central fact of Muslim life in the United States. . . . Many Muslims attest to the sense of responsibility in their daily lives that comes from being an "ambassador for Islam," always mindful of the importance of winning new adherents to Islam.[2]

The desire to convert is a natural human desire. Of course, Muslims would like to see more converts; this is also true of Roman Catholics and Evangelicals. This is part of the nature of Islam and Christianity; they both share a universal mission to the world. And plenty of political traditions are seeking to 'convert' the world to their worldview: friends of Israel – like Daniel Pipes – are trying to convert the world to support Zionism. And neo-conservatives in the United States are trying to promote their political commitments to capitalism and liberty. The fact that Muslims are the same is not a matter of fear or surprise; it is just inevitable.

Pipes does not simply distort the emphasis but then ignores the other half of the Islamic story. Islam, unlike Judaism and Christianity, has a Qur'anic obligation to respect Christians and Jews (e.g. sura 2:62). The Qur'an explicitly states that although God could have created one religious community, God did not do so (see sura 42:8). The diversity of religion is intended by God.

The faulty analysis generated by such distortions emerges when he identifies the three major Islamic responses to the dilemma and challenge of modernity. Pipes writes:

> Muslims have developed three major responses: secularism; reformism; and fundamentalism. Secularism holds that Muslims can only advance by emulating the West. Yes, Islam is a valuable and esteemed legacy, but its public dimensions must be put aside so that it becomes a private faith. . . Reformism, which offers a murky middle, is very popular. ... [R]eformers reread the Islamic scriptures in a Western light. ... Though intellectually bankrupt, this is politically very useful and explains why reformism is very widespread. The third response to the modern trauma is fundamentalism, also known as Islamism or militant Islam.[3]

---

[1] Daniel Pipes, *Militant Islam Reaches America*, (New York and London, W. W. Norton and Co 2002), p. 14.
[2] Ibid. p. 118.
[3] Ibid. pp. 6-7.

Pipes is an avowed secularist; he believes that 'moderate Islam' depends on opting for the first response. Religion must have nothing to do with society; it must be confined to the realm of the private. Pipes ignores totally the wholly legitimate complaint by Christians that this is undemocratic usurping of the public square by the secular agnostics. As Richard John Neuhaus famously argued, if the public square becomes a naked, value-free space, then the religious sensitivities of perhaps the majority of its citizens are being disregarded.[4] Granted minorities need protecting, but if a majority in a culture wants a certain shape and worldview in the public square then that is not necessarily a totalitarian aspiration. Pipes is adamant – anyone who wants to offer the wisdom of the Qur'an to the public square is a totalitarian. It is absurd for Pipes to write: 'Seeing Islam as the basis of a political system touching every aspect of life, Islamists are totalitarian.'[5] For Pipes the only good Muslim is the secular Muslim. His hero is Mustafa Kemal Atatürk in Turkey; indeed aggressively secular Turkey is the model as far as Pipes is concerned. Pipes is deeply suspicious of any Muslim who is committed to his or her tradition. If we allow ourselves to be infected by the Pipes worldview, then perhaps we are in for a long, desperate battle between Islam and the West, which may indeed costs many thousands of lives.

This book is intended to be a corrective to the Pipes worldview. The book partly agrees with Pipes in two respects. First, Turkey has within its rich history a form of Islam that is committed to non-violence and constructive engagement with the West and with Christians and Jews. So Pipes is right to say that Turkey can provide a model, but that model is not located so much in its aggressive commitment to secularism. Second, there is a problem with militant Islam. But we need to be careful about who we identify with this militant Islam and the solution to it is not and cannot be to require all Muslims to become secular.

This collection of essays is an introduction to the Ottoman/Turkish thinker Bediuzzaman Said Nursi (1876-1960), who was born in the Eastern Kurdish part of the Ottoman Empire. The themes of the book are grouped around 'ethics' and 'globalization'. To treat these two topics properly, we will also have essays on non-violence and modernity. Each chapter looks at the thought of Said Nursi and explores an issue from a certain vantage point.

Said Nursi is an extremely significant Muslim thinker for several reasons. First, he is a mainstream, conservative Muslim. The temptation for non-Muslims is to find a liberal secular Muslim as a conversation partner. But the fact is that the majority of Muslims are not secular and liberal. Almost all Muslims believe that the Qur'an is infallible; the western tradition of 'textual criticism' has not developed and is unlikely to develop amongst mainstream Islam. Said Nursi is a mainstream Muslim: he believes that the Qur'an is the infallible Word of God. He believes that Muhammad is the final prophet of God. It is because of these basic commitments that the teaching of Nursi relates to other traditional Islamic traditions.

[4] See Richard John Neuhaus, *The Naked Public Square*, (Grand Rapids, Eerdmans, 1984).
[5] Daniel Pipes, *Militant Islam reaches America*, p. 39.

It is this that leads to the second reason why Nursi matters. His commitment to a constructive engagement with the West, coupled with a positive view of the conversation with Judaism and Christianity, arises from his commitment to mainstream Islam. He is an appropriate challenge to the widespread assumption that only liberal secular religious adherents are tolerant of diversity.

The third reason is that Nursi represents a form of Islam that is growing. M. Hakan Yavuz suggests that the 'number of adherents of the *Nur* movement, known as Nurcular, varies between five and six million believers.'[6] Twice a week many of these believers meet in 'Nurcu textual reading circles, known as *dershanes*'.[7] Currently there are approximately 5,500 such groups – all meeting to reflect on Said Nursi's *magum opus* the *Risale-i Nur*. Given Nursi's primary theme is the need for a deeper sense of Islam in the individual Muslim's life, this is a powerful Islamic renewal movement.

The fourth reason is that Nursi had a strong commitment to non-violence. The distinguished Jesuit theologian Thomas Michel summarizes up this aspect of Nursi's work very well, when he writes:

> Said Nursi's opposition to war as an inhumane and ultimately useless endeavor was highly controversial in his time, for in any nation all citizens are expected to support whatever wars are decided and carried out by their governments, and anyone opposing war is accused of being disloyal. ...Critics claimed that war against British and Italian incursions provided an opportunity to revive Islamic zeal and to assert the moral strength of the nation. They charged Said Nursi, who proposed prayers for peace and negotiated settlement as indirectly supporting the invaders' aims. In response, Said Nursi held that he wanted release from the attacks of aggressors, but not by using the same methods which the attackers were employing. In other words, he rejected the practice of opposing force by force. Religion teaches people to seek truth and uprightness, not to try to achieve their aims by use of force.[8]

With Pipes presenting all traditional Muslims as potential Islamic militants determined to bring down the West, it is important that we know about this alternative stream.

Through this distinguished set of essays, the reader will discover the extraordinary world of Said Nursi. We are learning about Islam from a very distinguished Muslim. Naturally as one becomes informs, so one is then welcome to the table; we can join the conversation. So in this book one will find Islamic scholars are joined by Christians and a Jewish scholar to reflect on the nature of Islam and the particular achievement of Said Nursi.

---

[6] M. Hakan Yavuz, *Islamic Political Identity in Turkey* (Oxford: Oxford University Press 2003), p. 11.

[7] Ibid. p. 11.

[8] Thomas Michel, S.J. *Reflections on Said Nursi's Views on Muslim-Christian Understanding*, (Istanbul:Soz Bosim Yayin 2003), pp. 42-3.

It is not that non-Muslims should be silent; instead non-Muslims should simply accept the cardinal rule that participation depends on being informed. The rant of those who are seeking to create fear, misunderstanding, and hate must be resisted. Study of the thought and ethics of Said Nursi should be encouraged.

Ian Markham
Ibrahim Ozdemir

PART I
NON-VIOLENCE AND PEACE

Chapter 1

Bediuzzaman Said Nursi and the *Risale-i Nur*

Sükran Vahide

The Old Said 1876/7-1918

Nurs

Bediuzzaman Said Nursi was born in 1876 or 1877[1] in Nurs, a small hamlet of some twenty houses in the province of Bitlis in eastern Anatolia. His father, Mirza, had a small holding of land, and his mother, Nuriye, was from the neighbouring village of Bilkan. On both sides they were a family of Sayyids.[2] Said was the fourth of seven children. The first event mentioned in his 'official' biography[3] is his leaving home at the age of nine to begin his studies. He had been impressed at the way his elder brother, Abdullah, had come to excel over his fellows in the village as a result of his studies, so accompanied him when he returned to the *medrese* (religious school) of Molla Mehmed Emin Efendi in the nearby village of

[1] There are some discrepancies between the dates given for his birth in the available sources, but the majority give it as 1293 according to the Rumi calendar, then in use int he Ottman Empire.

[2] Despite there being no explicit claims to being a Sayyid, that is, a direct descendant of the Prophet, in Nursi's work, there are several first-hand reports of his stating this verbally. See, Salih Özcan in Necmeddin Şahiner, *Son Şahitler Bediüzzaman Said Nursi Anlatıyor* [hereafter, *Son Şahitler*] (Istanbul: Yeni Asya Yayınları, 1986) iii, p. 129; Muhiddin Yürüten, in *Son Şahitler*, iii, p. 74; Hüseyin Aksu, in *Son Şahitler*, i (2nd edn.) (Istanbul: 1980) p. 242-3. The two former record that Nursi said both of his parents were from a line of Sayyids. Nursi told Salih Özcan that his mother was "Husaynî," and his father, "Hasanî." It was probably the political implications which deterred Nursi from mentioning the matter in his written works. However, there is no record of his family being known as a Sayyid family.

[3] The biography prepared during the last years of Nursi's life by some of close students. It was first published in 1958 under the title of *Risale-i Nur Külliyatı Müellifi, Bediüzzaman Said Nursi, Tarihçe-i Hayatı, Mesleki, Tercüme-i Hâli* [hereafter, *Tarihçe*] (Istanbul: Sözler Yayınevi, 1976).

Tağ. However, the young Said fought with another student and after a short while returned home. This pattern was to recur over the next five years. For despite his tender years, Said held himself in great esteem and could not endure to be dominated or dictated to in any way. He moved from *medrese* to *medrese* continuing his studies, falling out either with his peers or his elders, and spending intervals in Nurs. Here he was taught by Abdullah, whenever he visited.

From the few references to his childhood in Nuri's later writings, one can catch brief glimpses of the independently-minded boy who, with his self-esteem, as though acted in unconscious prescience of his future service fame and calling in life[4]. Among the events of that time, his biography recounts a dream he had in which the Prophet Muhammad told him that knowledge of the Qur'an would be given him on condition he asked no questions of anyone. He made this a rule of his life and subsequently became famous for never asking questions of other scholars.

Doğubayezid — 1891

Said's dream fired him with enthusiasm to pursue his studies. As previously, he moved from *medrese* to *medrese*, unable to find what he was seeking. Eventually he set off for Doğubayezid and the medrese of Shaykh Muhammad Jalali. It was 1309H/1891. Up to this time he had studied only the principles of Arabic grammar and syntax. Now, his extraordinary power of memory and faculty for absorbing knowledge emerged, and in unprecedented manner he completed in six months the course of study, which normally continued over fifteen or even twenty years. This seemingly impossible feat he achieved by extracting the substance of each heavily annotated and glossed work in the syllabus, then passing on to the next. He is said to have read in this way around a hundred works in the three month period, digesting in twenty-four hours even the most difficult works of two hundred pages and more. Said's purpose in following this course, despite the displeasure of the *medrese's* principal of the medrese, was to point out what he had instinctively felt since he began his studies, namely his dissatisfaction with the existing educational system, and his realization of the need for its reform.

At the same time as plunging himself into this intensive study — at nights even retiring into the mausoleum of a local saint — Said started to practice extreme self-discipline, in emulation of the *Ishraqiyyun* philosophers. Shaykh Muhammad Jalali must have recognized his exceptional student's talent, for at the end of the three months he awarded him his diploma (*ijazet*), confirming that he had completed the course. Said had now earned the right to wear the scholar's turban and gown. Although he declined this, feeling loath to wear at his young age the dress of the respected teachers and shaykhs, he was now known as Molla Said-i Meşhur, Molla Said the Famous. He was still only fourteen or fifteen years of age.

---

[4] See Bediuzzaman Said Nursi, *Sikke-i Tasdik-i Gaybî* (Istanbul: Sinan Matbaasi, 1960) p. 116; Nursi, *Emirdağ Lahikası* (Ist., Sinan Matbaası, 1959) i, pp.52-3.

Molla Said's fame spread after he left Bayezid for Şirvan and his brother Abdullah, for he now engaged other religious scholars in debate whenever the opportunity arose. Besides invariably emerging victorious from these encounters, he became an object of wonder by virtue of his success at answering every sort of question and test set him by the masters and shaykhs of the *medreses*. It was at this time that he was first given the name of Bediuzzaman (Wonder of the Age), by the eminent Molla Fethullah Efendi of the Siirt *medrese*.[5]

As Said's fame grew so did his difficulties. As he moved from place to place — Sirvan, Siirt, Tillo, Cizre and the Miran tribe, Mardin, and Bitlis— often on the orders of the authorities, he had many adventures, some resulting from the plots of rivals and enemies. It was at this time too that he started to gain popularity as a teacher.

Molla Said's other exceptional qualities become clear from his activities at this time. His personal courage and daring, which exceeded even those of the Kurdish tribesmen, were legendary and well-attested, as were his moral courage, and boldness in upholding right and confronting tyranny. Such charismatic qualities were necessary to command the respect of the tribes and their leaders, among whom he began to act as mediator.[6] It should be mentioned that although in later years, particularly as the New Said when he wanted to direct attention away from his own personality to the *Risale*, Nursi virtually discounted such powers (*kerâmet*) or else attributed them to the Qur'an, from this time he began to be known among the people as a 'veli' or saint.

Also, it was from his very early years of *medrese* life that Said began to practise the self-sufficiency that was to be his mark throughout his life, even in times of extreme need. Contrarily to normal practice among the *medrese* students of eastern Anatolia, who had their daily needs met by local villagers or by *zakat* (the publication tax), the young Said displayed complete independence, accepting nothing from others, even gifts, unless he was able to give something in return. Similarly, when he later had his own students, he did not permit them to accept charity. Often he would meet their needs himself.[7] This was to impress on them the need to work for God's pleasure alone. He also always remained detached from the world and its vanities, owning virtually no property or possessions.

---

[5] See Şükran Vahide, *The Author of the Risale-i Nur, Bediuzzaman Said Nursi* (2nd ed.) (Istanbul, Sözler Publications, 1998), p. 12. Also, Vahide, Islam in Modern Turkey: An Intellectual Biography of Bediuzzaman Said Nursi (Albany: State University of New York Press, 2005) forthcoming.

[6] For the social and demographic background to life in south-eastern Anatolia in that period, see, Serif Mardin, Şerif, *Religion and Social Change in Modern Turkey, The Case of Bediüzzaman Said Nursi* (New York, SUNY Press, 1989), pp. 42-54.

[7] See Nursi, *Emirdağ Lahikası*, ii, p. 187.

Mardin — 1892

It is recorded that Molla Said first became involved in politics when visiting Mardin at this time. It is not clear precisely what this entailed, but it is known that he encountered two students, one a follower of Jamal al-Din al-Afghani[8] and the other a member of the Sanusi order. Also, in one of his later works he makes an allusion to a work of Namık Kemal in connection with this visit. It may be surmised, therefore, that here he first became acquainted with the major political issues facing the Ottoman Empire and Islamic world, and became involved with them. This seems likley in view of his later opposition to 'despotism' and support for 'freedom and constitutional government' on the one hand, and Islamic Unity (*Ittihad-ı Islam*) on the other.

Bitlis — 1892/3

Despite being expelled from Mardin for his activities and deported to Bitlis under guard, from this time, 1892 or 1893, until he left for Istanbul in November 1907, Nursi won the support of first the Governor of Bitlis, Ömer Pasha, then the Governors of Van, Hasan Pasha and Tahir Pasha, and when in those centres was given accommodation in their residences. He took advantage of these amenities to pursue his studies.

While in Bitlis, with his maturing years, we are told that Molla Said began to lose the 'inspirational' quality of his knowledge, called *sunûhat*. Up to this time, understanding had come to him without undue exercise of the reason. He had not studied the texts in depths. So now, in order to maintain his position among the *'ulama*, he embarked on comprehensive study of all the Islamic sciences, committing to memory in the two years he was in Bitlis around forty basic works on logic and the Arabic sciences on the one hand, and Qur'anic exegesis (*tafsir*), Hadith, *fiqh*, and theology (*kalam*) on the other. Among these was a work on the principles of Hanafi *fiqh*, called *al-Mirqat*. This was a subject he had not previously studied since the people of eastern Anatolia all followed the Shafi'i school. A second and major reason he undertook this study was to prepare himself to reply to criticisms of Islam made by works of Western origin and to dispel the doubts they had given rise to.

A further important personal quality of Molla Said is to be learnt from a letter replying to slanders made against him in the 1940s. In this letter, he recalled that although he stayed for two years in the Governor's residence in Bitlis when he was in his late teens, at the end of his stay he was unable to tell apart the eldest three of the Governor's six daughters, he had paid them so little attention. When questioned about this, he had replied: "Preserving the dignity of learning does not allow me to look at them."[9]

---

[8] That same year, in 1892, Sultan Abdulhamid had brought Afghani to Istanbul in connection with his Pan-Islamic policies.

[9] Nursi, *Emirdağ Lahikası*, i, p. 257.

Nursi's Attitude Towards Sufism

Although up to this time, Nursi had received instruction from the leading Sufi shaykhs of the area, he never followed any one of them exclusively, or joined one of the tariqah. The reason he gave for this was his preoccupation with his studies.[10] Şerif Mardin describes the rise of the Khalidi Naqshbandi Order in the nineteenth century in eastern Anatolia, and its supplanting the previously popular Qadiri Order.[11] It appears that the majority of shaykhs in the time of Nursi's youth were Khalidis, including those named in his biography.[12] However, from his childhood and contrarily to everyone else in the neighbourhood, including his family, who followed the Naqshi (Khalidi) Order, Said was drawn to Shaykh 'Abd al-Qadir Gilani (Gawth al-A'zam), under whose spiritual patronage and protection he felt himself to be throughout his life.[13] He similarly had close spiritual links with the Naqshbandi Shaykh Ahmad Sirhindi (Imam-i Rabbani), reputedly Regenerator of the Second Millennium, Shaykh Ahmad Sirhindi (Imam-ı Rabbani), to whose influence on his life and thought he made frequent references.[14]

Although in the *Risale*, Nursi did not afford the place to Mawlana Khalid,[15] the Regenerator who followed Sirhindi, that he did to Sirhindi himself, it might be recalled that as the New Said, when he had left aside virtually all books other than the Qur'an, a work he constantly read[16] for its supplications and as a source of reflective thought, was *Majmu'at al-Ahzab* by Gümüşhaneli Ahmed Ziyaeddin (d. 1893), a prominent shaykh of the Khalidi Order. The three-volume work contains such supplications as *Jawshan al-Kabir*, and clearly at least played a part in moulding the New Said's spiritual life. Moreover, probably in 1940, when in Kastamonu, he was given Mawlana Khalid's gown by the granddaughter of one of his *khalifas*. Nursi accepted it, saying that Mawlana Khalid had dressed him in his own gown over a hundred year distance.[17]

Nevertheless, as will be pointed out later, Nursi was always at pains to emphasize that in his view the modern age was not the age of Sufism. He frequently compared and contrasted the Qur'anic way to reality (*haqiqat*), which

---

[10] Nursı, *Sikke-i Tasdik-i Gaybî*, p. 116.

[11] See Mardin, pp. 51-60.

[12] See Abdülkadir Badıllı, Abdülkadir, *Bediüzzaman Said-i Nursî, Mufassal Tarihçe-i Hayatı* (Istanbul, Timaş Yayınları, 1990) i, pp. 100-103.

[13] *Sikke-i Tasdik-i Gaybî*, p. 116.

[14] See for example, Nursi, *The Rays Collection* [Engl. trans.] (Istanbul: Sözler Publications, 1998), p. 188; *Bediuzzaman Said Nursi, Letters 1928-1932* [Engl. Tr. Sükran Vahide] (Istanbul: *Sözler* Publications, 2nd. edn., 1997), pp. 418-19.

[15] For interesting parallels between Mawlana Khalid and Nursi, see, Nursi, *Sikke-i Tasdik-i Gaybî*, pp. 14-16.

[16] Mustafa Sungur, in *Son Şahitler* (New ed., 1994) iv, pp. 31-2.

[17] Nursi, *Kastamonu Lahikası* (Ist., Envar Neşriyat, 1994), pp. 96-7; Vahide, *The Author of the Risale-i Nur*, pp. 256-7.

he opened up, described below, with the Sufi way (*tariqat*), in order to illustrate the differences.

Van — 1895/6

The Governor's residence in Van under the appreciative direction of Tahir Paşah provided Nursi with a favourable environment to continue his studies and gain wider experience. For here he had the opportunity to mix with government officials and people of different walks of life, including those conversant with modern science and learning. Tahir Pasha was a patron of learning and owned an extensive library, so too he encouraged discussion, debate, and contests of knowledge.

It was here that Nursi realized that in its traditional form, theology (*kalam*) lacked the capacity to answer the doubts and questions raised by science and modern advances in knowledge. In consequence, uniquely among the *'ulama* of eastern Anatolia at that time, he took up the study of modern science, and by himself studying the relevant books, in a short time mastered all the sciences current at that time, including philosophy.

Nursi's new familiarity with modern science led to a development in his ideas on educational reform, and in his teaching methods. He had his own *medrese* in Van, at the foot of the citadel, called the Horhor Medrese. Here he put his ideas into practice, and taught his students, who sometimes numbered as many as sixty. His method was based on the combined teaching of the religious sciences and the modern sciences.[18]

It was at this time too that Nursi first had the idea of founding an Islamic university in the Eastern Provinces that would be the embodiment of his ideas on educational reform. He named it the Medresetü'z-Zehrâ, after al-Azhar in Cairo, as it was to be its sister-university in the eastern Islamic world. He considered its educational, unifying, and reconciling role to be so important in that backward and poverty-striken corner of the Empire that it became one of the main aims of his life, in that period taking him to Istanbul on several occasions. He even described it as "the most important matter" of his biography.[19]

In a later work, Nursi noted that in 1318/1901-2, he made the transition "from teaching to writing."[20] He gives no clue as to which works he produced at that time, but in his nephew's biography, published in 1919, two treatises are mentioned, both of which were later lost in a fire. One was a treatise on algebraic equations, and the other, a short piece on arithmetical problems and reckoning.[21]

An incident occurred around the turn of the century which was decisive in giving him direction. He learnt through Tahir Paşha who had read a report in the newspapers, of the explicit threats to the Qur'an and Muslim community made by

---

[18] *Tarihçe*, p. 45.

[19] *Emirdağ Lahikası*, ii, p. 37.

[20] Nursi, *Şuâlar* (Istanbul: Envar Neşriyat, 1994), p. 698.

[21] Abdurrahman, *Bediüzzaman'ın Tarihçe-i Hayati* (Istanbul: Necm-i İstikbal Matbaasi, 1335 [1919]), p. 33.

the British statesman, Gladstone. Said was severely shaken and experienced a complete turnabout in his ideas. He realized that he should make all the sciences and knowledge he had acquired means to understand the Qur'an and prove its truths, and that "the Qur'an alone should be his aim, the purpose of his learning, and the object of his life;" he should use his knowledge to defend the Qur'an.[22] At the end of his life he wrote that he had found two means of doing this: one was the Medresetü'z-Zehrâ, and the other was the *Risale-i Nur* [henceforth, *Risale*].[23] The latter was realized only on the emergence of the New Said after the First World War. Until that time, as he himself admitted, he was in part deflected from his goal by the compelling events of the times.

Istanbul — November 1907

Armed with a letter from Tahir Paşha, dated 3 Teşrin-i Sani 1323 (November 16, 1907), Nursi set off for Istanbul, presumably arriving there towards the end of the month, or in December. As soon as he arrived, he sought ways of publicizing his ideas on educational reform in the Eastern Provinces, and obtaining official support. To establish his reputation, he first settled in an inn in the Fatih district that accommodated a number of the leading intellectual figures of the day. Here he hung a notice on his door that was indeed to attract attention: "Here all questions are answered, all problems solved, but no questions are asked." Numbers of students and scholars visited him and were amazed at his extraordinary ability to answer correctly whatever questions they had prepared.[24] He not only soon became well-known, but also respected by the Istanbul *'ulama*, for they sought his assistance in connection with questions asked of them by the Commander-in-Chief of the Japanese Army.[25]

Nursi thus found the opportunity to publicize the problems of the East. Similarly, within a short time, he was successful in presenting a petition to Sultan 'Abdülhamid setting out concisely his ideas for their solution.[26] He noted gratefully moves to construct a number of new secular schools (*mekteb*) in the region, but pointed out that if the teaching was only in Turkish and there was no provision for religious instruction, they would be of little benefit for the local population. His proposal was for three educational establishments strategically placed in the centres of various tribes, which would teach both the religious sciences and the modern sciences, and would be known by the familiar name of 'medrese.' Nursi predicted a ghastly future for the people of the area if such steps were not taken.

[22] *Sikke-i Tasdik-i Gaybî*, p. 76.
[23] Nursi, *Emirdağ Lahikasi*, ii, p. 195.
[24] Necmeddin Şahiner, *Bilinmeyen Taraflariyle Bediüzzaman Said Nursi* (12th edn.) (Istanbul: Yeni Asya Yayinlai, 1996), pp. 91-5; Vahide, *The Author of the Risale-i Nur*, pp. 38-41.
[25] *The Rays Collection*, pp. 380-1.
[26] Şahiner, *Bilinmeyen*, pp. 95-7.

Moveover, it would make over to the Government the huge manforce of the region, that was then being wasted on internal conflict.

However, as was inevitable at that time of repression, Nursi's activities had not gone unnoticed. He had won rivals among the *'ulama*, jealous at his success. He was certainly kept under surveillance, and was critical of the Sultan. The petition he presented was later published in the first number of the newspaper, *Şark ve Kürdistan Gazetesi*, November 19, 1908, which noted in the introductory paragraph that in consequence he became "the target of many misfortunes." Whatever the reason, Nursi was sent before the Yildiz Palace Court Martial, and from there sent to Toptaşi Mental Asylum. He eventually managed to have himself released on the strength of "a conversation" he held with one of the doctors, who then wrote a favourable report. He was still held in custody, however.

In the course of describing to the doctor the true reasons for his incarceration in Toptaşi, Nursi outlined his proposals, details of which he had doubtless explained to the Sultan. A brief summary is included here:

Besides the combined teaching of the religious and modern sciences, mentioned above, the heart of Nursi's proposals lay in the reconciling and bringing together in the Medresetü'z-Zehrâ and its sister establishments, of "the three main branches" of education: the *medreses* or traditional religious schools, the *mekteb*s or new secular schools, and the *tekkes* or Sufi establishments. He believed the divergence and even conflict between the three to be a major cause of the backwardness of Islamic cilivization. For Islam to function efficiently, mutual consultation had to be established between those "three divisions of the army of Islamic education."[27] To restructure the *medreses* in this way would be to put into practice "the rule of the division of labor."[28] It would also allow the students to specialize in subjects for which they had an aptitude, a question to which Nursi attached the greatest importance, and which constituted a radical break with traditional methods.

A further point to mention is Nursi's opposition to what he called "scholastic despotism." He posited that the 'democratization' of the *medrese* system would provide a powerful incentive for students to progress.[29] Nursi's proposals, only the main points of which have been mentioned here, were thus comprehensive, realistic, and far-sighted. They were also modern in their approach. Although they did not meet a favourable response on this occasion, Nursi finally secured funds from Sultan 'Abdulhamid's successor, Sultan Reşad. The foundations of the Medresetü'z-Zehrâ were even laid on the shores of Lake Van, but its construction had to be abandoned on the outbreak of the First World War.

---

[27] Nursi, *Münâzarat* (Istanbul: *Sözler* Yay., 1977), p. 76.

[28] Nursi, *Muhâkemat* (Istanbul: *Sözler* Yay., 1977), pp. 46-7.

[29] Nursi, "Bediuzzaman Kürdi'nin Fihriste-i Makasidi ve Efkârının Programı" in *Volkan* Nos. 83-4, in Ertuğrul Düzdağ, (ed.), *Volkan Gazetesi* 1908-1909 (Istanbul: İz Yayincilik, 1992), pp. 402-3, pp. 407-8.

The Constitutional Revolution of 1908

Nursi supported constitutional government and freedom from despotism because in his view they were the primary condition for progress in all fields.[30] Similarly to Namık Kemal and many thinkers of the day, Nursi believed that in principle, constitutionalism and the concepts it comprised, such as the sovereignty of the nation, equality before the law, the rule of law, and consultation, were entirely in conformity with the Shari'a. His endeavours in this cause were on the one hand to dispel anxieties concerning it, and on the other, to insist on the freedom it brought being based on and limited by the Shari'a. Otherwise, he argued, it would only bring down on the Ottomans a tyranny worse than they had previously suffered.

Among his activities in the first days of the Constitution was the speech he delivered firstly in Beyazid in Istanbul, and two or three days later in Salonica, entitled "Address to Freedom."[31] In addition to informing the people at large of the meaning of constitutionalism and of its importance for them, Nuri's emphasized the need to adhere to Islam and its morality in the new era. Only in this way could they advance and establish true civilization.

Nursi even saw support of consitutionalism to be a religious obligation, for so long as it was within the sphere of the Shari'a, it was "the means of upholding the might of Islam and exalting the Word of God." For in his view, in the modern age, upholding the Word of God (*ilâ-yı kelimetullah*), with which every believer is charged, is dependent on material progress, and since freedom and constitutionalism were the way to achieve progress, it was encumbent on all to work for them.[32]

Nursi lived a very active life at this time, employing every means to illuminate every section of society concerning these questions. He exploited his good name and reputation to the full to have his ideas accepted. He published articles in many of the newspapers of the day. He addressed meetings and gatherings. He joined a number of religiously oriented societies, one of which was *Talebe-i 'Ulum Cemiyeti* (Society for Students of the Religious Sciences),[33] another of which was *Ittihad-ı Muhammedî Cemiyeti* (Muhammadan Union).

Following the initial jubilation at the proclamation of the Constitution, there was rapid disillusionment among the people as political conditions deteriorated and the incipient conflicts of interest between the various groups and classes surfaced and led to political violence and bitter battles in the press in particular. Despite his initial support for the Committee of Union and Progress (CUP), Nursi became a fierce opponent of it, combatting especially the corrupting social consequences of their misrule. It was in the cause of unity, as well as to prevent a society bearing the Prophet's (PBUH) name being made a tool of narrow

---

[30] See Vahide, *The Author of the Risale-i Nur*, pp. 59-64.

[31] Nursi, *Âsâr-ì Bedi'iye* (n.p., n.d.), pp. 347-356.

[32] Nursi, 'Hakikat,' in *Volkan* No: 70, pp. 337-8.

[33] *Volkan* No. 95, p. 461.

political interests, that he joined the Muhammadan Union.[34] Although it was with this intention that he became active in the Society, publishing fifteen articles in its press organ, *Volkan*, it was because of his involvement that he was arrested following the famous March 31 Incident and sent before the Court Martial. All his articles in the paper reiterate his views on education and 'Islamic' freedom and constitutionalism, or explain the unifying role of the Society, answering doubts and anxieties about it. Its aim, through the revival of the *Sunna* and moral renewal, and strengthening the bonds of unity between all Muslims, was to activate the vast potentiality of the Umma and urge it towards the way of progress.

Nursi played no part in the revolt which broke out on March 13, 1325 (April 13, 1909). As in a number of previous incidents,[35] he played a pacifying role. In his celebrated defence in one of the military courts set up afterwards, which he later published under the title, *İki Mekteb-i Musibetin Şehadetnamesi veya Divan-ı Harb-i Örfî ve Said-i Nursî* (The Testimony of Two Schools of Misfortune or The Military Court and Said Nursi), he described his movements during the revolt and how he had persuaded eight battalions of soldiers to give up their insurrection and return to barracks. Nursi was acquitted and freed by the court, despite the unfearing boldness with which he faced he all-powerful, autocratic pashas presiding over it, even attacking the CUP's betrayal of constitutionalism.

Nursi had been disillusioned by what he had seen and experienced in Istanbul, causing him to declare that he was "resigning from civilization." Because, he wrote: "True civilization serves mankind's progress and development, and the realization of man's potential. In this regard, therefore, to want civilization, is to want humanity."[36] He remained only a short while after this, then set out for his native East.

Eastern Anatolia — 1910

Nursi's disillusion did not lead him to despair, however; on the contrary, he returned to persuade the tribesmen and people of his native East to accept the constitutional government, and so to secure both their own futures and that of the Ottomans. It seems most likely that Nursi set out on his journey in early 1910. He travelled by sea to Batum, calling in at various Black Sea ports, from where he travelled to Tiflis, the capital of Georgia. Here his famous encounter with the Russian policeman took place, during which, contrary to the pessimistic view of the Islamic world the policeman voiced, Nursi predicted its future ascendancy.[37]

From there he travelled to Van and his medrese, and from there set out on his tour of the tribes, also addressing gatherings in the towns. In the autumn of

[34] Nursi, *İki Mekteb-i Musibetin Şehadetnamesi veya Divan-ı Harb-i Örfî ve Said-i Nursî* (Istanbul: Sözler Yayinevi, 1975), p. 20.
[35] See Vahide, *The Author of the Risale-i Nur*, pp. 67-71.
[36] Nursi, *Divani-i Harb-i Örfî*, p. 39.
[37] Nursi, *Sünûhat* (Istanbul, Sözler Yayinevi, 1977), pp. 63-4.

1910, he travelled south, possibly spending that winter in Damascus. For the following spring, by which time he was well-known there, on the insistence of the *'ulama*, he addressed a gathering of thousands in the Umayyad Mosque. This was subsequently published under the title of *Hutbe-i Şamiye* (The Damascus Sermon). This and the other works he produced at this time he offered as "prescriptions" for the ailments afflicting the Islamic world, as is reflected in their titles. These included, in Arabic, *Reçetetü'l-Avam* (Prescription For the Common People) and *Reçetetü'l-'Ulema* (Prescription For the *'Ulama*). He also wrote expanded Turkish versions of these, called *Münâzarat* and *Muhâkemat*, respectively. The former consists of his answers to the questions put to him during his journey around south-east Anatolia. The works were published in Istanbul in 1911, with the exception of *Münâzarat*, which was published in 1913. *Hutbe-i Şâmiye* was printed twice in Damascus following the sermon, due to popular demand. Its various Istanbul editions had addenda entitled *Deva'ü'l-Ye's* (The Cure For Despair) and *Teşhisü'l-'Illet* (Diagnosis of the Complaint). The sermon consists of six 'Words' taken from "the pharmacy of the Qur'an" which constitute the cure for "the six dire sicknesses" Nursi had diagnosed as arresting the development of the Islamic world. Its main message was one of hope, for despite the seeming hopelessness of the Islamic world at that time, Nursi argued that the foreseeable future would see the rise of the Qur'an and Islamic civilization.

Istanbul — Late Spring 1911

Nursi returned to Istanbul shortly after giving the sermon, travelling by boat from Beirut. What he had seen on his travels had reimpressed on him the urgent necessity of founding the Medresetü'-Zehrâ and similar establishments in Turkey's eastern provinces. He had returned with the intention of obtaining official backing and funds for the project.

He was soon to find the opportunity, for at the beginning of June 1911 he was invited to join Sultan Mehmed Reşad's Rumeli journey, as the representative of the Eastern Provinces. The trip lasted three weeks, from the 5th to the 26th June, and in the face of growing nationalism, was intended to rekindle feelings of loyalty for the Ottomans among the peoples of Albania and Macedonia. In Skopje and Kosova plans were discussed to found universities. Nursi explained his project, stating that because of its position in the centre of the Islamic world, its need was even greater. When with the Balkan Wars the following year the region was lost to the Empire, Nursi applied for the 20,000 gold liras allotted to Kosova's proposed university. His request was granted. He then returned to Van, and the foundations of the Medresetü'z-Zehrâ were finally laid at a site on the shores of Lake Van at Edremit. It is not known exactly when this took place, but it is likely to have been in June of 1913, for there was busy telegraph traffic at that time between Tahsin Paşha, the Governor of Van, and Istanbul on the subject of its funding.[38]

[38] Necmeddin Şahiner, *Bediüzzaman Üniversitesi, Medresetü'z-Zehra* (Istanbul: Timaş Yayınları, 1996), pp.118-133.

Van — 1913

Whenever in Van, Nursi continued to teach his students. A work on logic from that time has come down to us, which consists of his expositions of a work called *Burhan al-Galanbawi fi'l-Mantiq*, written by one of his students on the margins of the work.[39] This was Molla Habib, Nursi's much loved student who acted as his scribe on the front at Erzurum, writing down the celebrated Qur'anic commentary *Isharat al-I'jaz (* Signs of Miraculousness*)*[40] as Nursi dictated.

Nursi was already a legendary figure in Eastern Anatolia, and his reputation was reinforced by the extraordinary courage and self-sacrifice he and his students displayed in the face of Russian and Armenian aggression during the War. Besides training his students' minds, he trained them in warfare and the use of firearms, so that they became the terror of the Armenian revolutionaries, particularly in 1915. He was detailed by Enver Pasha to raise and command the militia force of the region, which consisted of four to five thousand men. This he led on the Caucasian front against the second Russian invasion in January 1916. It was at this time, in the arctic winter conditions, that he wrote *Isharat al-I'jaz*, dictating while riding around the trenches on horseback, raising the morale of his men under the heavy Russian shelling.

Nursi was finally taken prisoner after the fall of Bitlis, having performed memorable services in the jihad, for which he was subsequently awarded a War Medal. The majority of his students had fallen in battle, including Molla Habib. He was sent by way of Tiflis and Kologrif to a camp in the town of Kosturma on the Volga, where he was held till he managed to escape in the spring of 1918. He returned to Istanbul by way of Petersburg, Warsaw, and Vienna. His captivity had lasted two years and three months.

Istanbul — June 1918

Nursi arrived back in Istanbul to a hero's welcome. He was applauded by Enver Pasha for his services, and was nominated by the army for membership of the *Darü'l-Hikmeti'l-İslâmiye*. The *Darü'l-Hikmet* was a learned institution attached to the Shaykh al-Islam's office which had been recently founded to find solutions for the problems facing the Islamic world and to answer attacks on it; to issue

---

[39] Nursî, *Ta'liqat 'ala Burhan al-Galanbawi fi'l-Mantiq* (facsimile edn.) (Istanbul: Sözler Yayınevi, 1993).

[40] Another of Bediuzzaman's students, Müküslü Hamza Efendi, described the work as follows: "... up to the present, no other *tafsir* has been written according to this method (*minhaj*)... it proves that, with its word-order being miraculous and concepts, truth and reality, the Qur'an is entirely in conformity with the physical sciences, and is their guide." See *Asari Bedi'iye*, p. 674. English tr. Sükran Vahide, *Sings of Miraculousness: The Inimitablity of the Quar'an's Conciseness* (Istanbul: Sözler Publications, 2004).

educational publications; and to uphold Islamic morality.[41] Nursi remained a member until he departed for Ankara four years later.

Nursi himself had been severely shaken by the rigours of the war and his years of captivity, and by the Ottoman defeat which followed it. But despite his inner turmoil, which was finally resolved with the emergence of the New Said, besides his duties in the *Darü'l-Hikmet*, he wrote and published no less than nineteen works. He also combatted the occupying forces and their divisive influence with his pen, and supported the independence movement. He was active in other fields too, such as with the founding of the Green Crescent Society, and in the *Cemiyet-i Müderrisin* (The Medrese Teachers' Association). He opposed the *fatwa* issued by the Shaykh al-Islam in March 1920 under the constraint of the British, which condemned as rebels the nationalist groups in Anatolia, and supported the counter-*fatwa*.[42] Although summoned to Ankara on several occasions, he remained until the last months of 1922, in order to pursue his struggle in Istanbul.

The Emergence of the New Said — 1920-1

Nursi described in his works of the period, and in the *Risale*, his inner struggles and the crystalization of his ideas that was their consequence. At a number of critical junctions earlier in his life he had resolved to dedicate himself to the defence of the Qur'an but had been distracted by the course of events. Now, what drove him to resume his search for an effective way of doing this was that the philosophy on which had placed so much store, as well as his learning, afforded him no consolation or "light" in the face of his vivid realization of the realities of death and the transience of things. On the contrary, they plunged him further into materiality and "darkness."[43] It was only after retreating into solitude and suffering a spiritual crisis that through the assistance of Shaykh 'Abd al-Qadir Geylani's *Futuh al-Ghayb* and Shaykh Ahmad Sirhindi's *Maktubat* he came to the realization that he should take the Qur'an as his sole guide.[44] He had unfolded to him a previously "untravelled" way to reality. In contrast to the ways of scholarship, represented by the intellect, and of Sufism, represented by the heart, this Qur'anic way was characterized by its being traversed through "an alliance of the intellect and heart."[45] It was also marked by being a way of reflective thought on the universe in the manner enjoined by numerous Qur'anic verses, by means of which it "opens up a window onto knowledge of God in everything."

---

[41] Albayrak, Sadık, *Son Devrin İslam Akademisi, Dar-ül Hikmet-il İslamiye* (Istanbul: Yeni Asya Yayinlari, 1973), pp. 7-9.

[42] Nursi, 'Tulu'at', in *Asâr-ı Bedi'iye*, pp. 105-6.

[43] Nursi, *The Flashes Collection* [Engl. trans. Sükran Vahide] (Istanbul: Sözler Publications, 1995), pp. 305-6.

[44] Nursi, *Letters*, pp. 418-19.

[45] Nursi, *al-Mathnawi al-'Arabi al-Nuri* [ed. Tahqiq: Ihsan Qasim al-Salihi] (Istanbul: Sözler Yayinevi 1994), p. 170, p. 318.

Nursi explained that the basis of this way or method was the manner in which things are considered; that is, the Qur'anic way of looking at beings not for themselves, but for what they signify (*mânâ-yı harfî*), as opposed to 'philosophy,' which considers things to signify only themselves.[46] It was this realization that led him to make the admission that in his forty years of life and thirty years of study he had learnt only "four words and four phrases."[47]

Ankara —November 1922

Nursi continued with his various activities in Istanbul until he finally consented to leave for Ankara. The date is not known of his departure, but on November 9, 1922 he was given an official "welcoming" in the Grand National Assembly. Against all odds, the Turks had won the war of independence, it was a time of rejoicing. Yet Nursi was dismayed to find a generally lax attitude towards religion and the practice of it, and even the spread of atheistic ideas. He had come to Ankara to persuade the leaders of the new republic to make the Qur'an and Islam the basis of their government, to work to establish Islamic civilization and make it a centre of Islamic unity.[48] In the five and half months he remained there, he endeavored to spread these ideas among the deputies, and to encourage them to perform the five daily prayers and other religious obligations, even braving Mustafa Kemal's wrath at his doing this. The circular he wrote dated January 19, 1923 and read to the deputies resulted in an increased in the numbers who prayed regularly, so that a larger room had to be assigned to the purpose. He wrote a short treatise in Arabic called *Zeylü'l-Zeyl*, disproving naturalism and atheistic philosophy, which he later made the basis of the Twenty-Third Flash, *Treatise On Nature*.[49]

Nursi also attached importance to the principle of consultation and forming of corporate bodies to solve the problems of the Islamic world. It was his view that the modern world is the age of the social collectivity rather than of the individual, and that such collectivities give rise to "collective personalities," the capacity of which for both good and evil is unlimited. In connection with this, in his address to the deputies, he told them that just as they now represented the Sultanate — due to the power invested in them by the nation, so they should represent the Caliphate. That is to say, because of the magnitude and complexity of the problems facing the Islamic world, the Caliph could perform his function efficiently only by relying on a body similiar to the Assembly. Such a collective personality would be better able to execute the injunctions of the Shari'a. This was

---

[46] For discussion of this see Yamine B. Mermer, "The Heremeneutical Dimension of Science: A Critical Analysis Based on Said Nursi's *Risale-i Nur*." *The Muslim World*, Special Issue: Said Nursi and the Turkish Experience, Vol. LXXXIX Nos.: 3-4 (1999), p. 273 ff.

[47] Nursi, *Mesnevi-i Nûriye* [Turk. trans. Abdülmecid Nursi] (Istanbul: Sözler Yayinevi, 1980), p. 46.

[48] *Tarihçe*, p. 129.

[49] Şahiner, *Bilinmeyen*, pp. 255-64.

an added reason the deputies should be scrupulous in performing their religious obligations and answering the nation's religious needs.[50] Nursi was successful while in Ankara in persuading the Assembly to support his Islamic university in the East, the Medresetü'z-Zehrâ. Of the two hundred deputies addressed on the question, one hundred and sixty-seven endorsed the decision to set aside 150,000 liras for the project.

Notwithstanding Nursi's fierce altercations with Mustafa Kemal, Kemal offered him various posts and benefits, all of which he declined. He told him: "The New Said wants to work for the next world and cannot work with you. But he won't interfere with you either."[51] However, the true reason was that he had understood that the new leaders were not to be combatted in the realm of politics, but with "the immaterial sword of the Qur'an's miraculousness." So he left Ankara for Van, where he retired from public life altogether. The train ticket for the journey was issued on 4/17/39; that is, April 17, 1923.

Van — April 1923

It was the first time Nursi had returned to Van since the retreat before the advancing Russians in early 1916, when he and his students had valliantly defended the straggling stream of its fleeing inhabitants. It proved a harrowing experience for him. He visited his *medrese*, now in ruins, and recalled his students, most of whom had been killed. The town itself had been virtually razed.

Nursi passed the greater part of the next twenty-one months in retreat on a mountain to the south-east, spending only the winters in the town, in the Nurşin Mosque. He would also come down to the mosque on Fridays, to give the *khutba*. Some of those who followed his sermons have recorded that they differed from what they were accustomed to hear from him, with his concentrating on the fundamental tenets of belief, such as divine unity and the resurrection of the dead.[52] It has also been recorded that some of the things he taught his students at this time, were subsequently included in the *Risale*.[53] There is no record of his writing any works during this period. It appears to have been a time of deep thought and preparation.

An outward sign of Nursi's inner changes was his giving up the colourful dress of the region for clothes of a more sober nature. Up to this time, no persuasion or anything had induced him to change it. Again, in later years, when so many had fallen victim to the new dress laws, he resolutely refused to discard the dress of Islam, persisting in wearing it to the end of his days.

The events that began in February 1925 with the uprising in eastern Anatolia against the Ankara Government were to have far-reaching consequences

---

[50] *Tarihçe*, p. 125-7. See also, *Sünûhat*, pp. 36-40, where Nursi advocates the setting-up of a learned body to tackle the problems facing the office of Shaykh al-Islam.

[51] *Tarihçe*, p. 195.

[52] Hamid Ekinci, in Sahiner, *Son Şahitler*, i, p.200.

[53] İsmail Perihanoğlu, in Sahiner, *Son Şahitler*, ii, pp. 26-7.

both for Nursi himself and for the country as a whole. For the Government made it the pretext for giving itself the dictatorial powers it was seeking to eliminate opposition of all kinds, and to disperse any potential alternative centres of power. Before the revolt, Nursi had been approached by various leaders and tribal chiefs who sought his support and to profit from his considerable influence. Shaykh Said, the instigator of the revolt, also invited Nursi to join it, by means of a letter. It seems certain that although various interpretations have been put on it, it was a revolt against the abolition of the Caliphate and ensuing secularist measures. For although the National Assembly in Ankara had voted to retain the Caliphate on abolishing the Sultanate on November 1, 1922, around the time Nursi was in Ankara, it subsequently abolished it completely, on March 3, 1924. This was followed by a series of other measures aimed at removing the power of the *'ulama*: the office of the Shaykh al-Islam and Ministry of the Shari'a were also abolished, and the *medreses* (religious schools) closed.

This is corroborated by Nursi's replies to the leaders who sought his support. He told them that such action, and "to make brother fight brother," was absolutely opposed to the Shari'a; it was not possible to demand the Shari'a by contravening it. In his reply to Shaykh Said, he also said: "The sword is to be drawn against external enemies, it may not be used internally. Our only salvation at this time is to offer illumination and guidance through the truths of the Qur'an and belief; it is to get rid of our greatest enemy, ignorance."[54]

Some of the tribal leaders heeded his advice and did not take part, thus saving many lives in the Van area.[55] Nevertheless, Nursi was taken from his retreat on Mount Erek and arrested along with many others, and sent into exile. The lengthy caravan of several hundred souls trekked out of Van on 25 March 1925. From Erzurum, they were taken to Trabzon, where they boarded the boat for Istanbul. Nursi was questioned in Istanbul concerning the revolt along with four others, and cleared, while they were sent to Diyarbekir and the arbitrary justice of the 'Independence Tribunal;' three of them met their end on the gallows.[56] From Istanbul Nursi travelled by boat to Antalya, from where he was taken to the small town of Burdur.

Burdur — May/June 1925

It seems most probable that Nursi arrived in his first place of exile in May or June of 1925 and remained here for six or seven months, before being moved on to Isparta, and then to Barla towards the end of February the following year.

Nursi started writing again during this period, producing a number of pieces in Arabic which he added as addenda to the treatises *Şemme* and *Şu'le*, two of the last treatises he had written in Istanbul in 1922. He subsequently rewrote

---

[54] Şahiner, *Bilinmeyen*, p. 269.

[55] Kartal Kinyas, in Sahiner *Son Şahitler*, ii, p. 17.

[56] Necmeddin Şahiner, *Said Nursi ve Nurculuk Hakkında Aydınlar Konuşuyor* (2nd edn.) (Istanbul: Yeni Asya Yayınları, 1979, pp. 165-7.

these addenda in Turkish, arranging them in book form in sections entitled, First Lesson (*Ders*), Second Lesson, and so on. It was most probably these that formed the basis of the daily 'ders' or instruction he gave in the mosque where he stayed, every day after the afternoon prayer. These were the first fruits of his period of deep thought and contemplation in Van, that were to find full expression in the *Risale*. He described the work as "an index, list, and seed of the *Risale*," and said it was the first instruction the New Said received "directly from verses of the Qur'an."[57]

The popularity of Nursi's talks in the mosque perturbed the authorities finally prompting them to send him to the provincial centre of Isparta, from where after a brief stay, on the orders of Ankara, he was sent to the tiny, isolated village of Barla in the mountains to the north-west of Lake Eğirdir. It was around the middle of February that he was taken there by sailing-boat, for until the 1950s there was no road, or modern convenience of any sort.

Barla — February 1926

Nursi was not guilty of any crime or misdemeanour that he should have been exiled to western Anatolia and then sent alone to the remote village of Barla. It was, in the words of the police inspector who had interviewed him in Istanbul, merely "a precautionary measure." And the fact is that in the four major trials of 1934, 1944, 1948, and 1952, except in one instance related to Islamic dress, the courts were compelled to acquit both himself and his students on all charges. Yet Nursi continued to be held under close surveillance, often in most constraining conditions, subject to the arbitrary harassment and mistreatment of minor officials.

The intention of the founders of the Turkish Republic was to do away with the institutions of the past and reconstruct life and society on the "modern" Western pattern. Their ideal was to import Western models for every area of life and graft Turkey with Western civilization. In this they had been most influenced by Ziya Gökalp's ideas on nationalism, and Abdullah Cevdet's writings on biological materialism, and on social reform, many aspects of which they applied directly. These included the enforced adoption of Western-style headgear and dress, the closure of the Sufi *tekkes*, the founding of a modern educational system, language reform, the adoption of the Latin alphabet and the Western calendar and form of time-keeping. This "cultural revolution" was underpinned by economic reforms, industrial development, and radical changes in education. The unified, centralized "national" educational system was based on "universal, humanist, secular, positivist" principles, and aimed to develop "national consciousness."[58] A string of laws were passed implementing these reforms. Finally, in 1937, the six principles of Kemalism, and of the party he founded, the Republican People's Party, [henceforth, RPP] were written into the Constitution; thus legalizing its absolute monopoly of power. Programmes of mass education in these principles,

---

[57] Nursi, *Nur'un İlk Kapısı* (Istanbul: Sözler Yay., 1977), pp. 6-7.

[58] See Sina Akşin, (ed.), *Türkiye Tarihi* (Istanbul: Cem Yayinevi, 1989), iv, pp. 471-4.

the most important of which were secularism, nationalism, and étatism, were introduced. Thus, it was hoped to finally root out the Islamic past and pave the way for the total adoption of a secular form of Western civilization.

Nursi was not unprepared for these developments, as we have seen. He perceived the way Turkey's new leaders were going to take when in Ankara in 1922, and declined to work with them. So too he realized that any attempt to combat them in the realm of politics would be fruitless. And, indeed, within a short period of time, all political opposition was suppressed and those who attempted it, eliminated; just as overt or active opposition to the reforms was suppressed. Nursi's response was unique, he replied with "decisive proofs of the truths of belief?" For in his veiw, the Qur'an was truth and reality, while the materialist philosophy it was to supplant with was "based on principles of futility," and that man's true happiness and progress were to be achieved only through the former. Thus, he began to write treatises that by offering what he claimed were irrefutable proofs of the main tenets of belief and demonstrating the logical absurdity of materialist philosophy, made it possible to gain belief so firm and certain it could withstand any doubts caused by science or philosophy. Rather than being one of opposition, therefore Nursi's struggle was to write such treatises, and to have them written out and disseminated at a time, after 1928, there were no printing-presses and the writing of religious material was forbidden. He embarked on the constructive, positive struggle he called "*cihad-i mânnevî*, by which he meant a moral, non-material struggle, or "*jihad* of the word."

The *Risale-i Nur*

The first major treatise Nursi wrote in Barla was about the resurrection of the dead and the hereafter. He wrote it in 1926, the first spring he was there. He designated it the Tenth Word among the pieces he subsequently put together with the title of *Sözler* (The Words), the first volume of the *Risale*. There are probably more references in his writings to this piece and the writing of it than to any other part of them, so we shall use it as an example to describe his aims and method.

Firstly, it should be mentioned that the resurrection of the dead and the life of the hereafter were openly denied by at least the two thinkers mentioned above, whose ideas were very influential at the time.[59] Nursi himself said that the writing of the Tenth Word coincided with official moves to spread atheistic ideas denying resurrection among the people.[60]

In later years Nursi described the writing of the Tenth Word to his students. Blossoming almond trees had recalled to him the verse: "So look to the signs of God's mercy, how He gives life to the earth after its death; indeed, He it is Who will life to the dead, and He is powerful over all things" (30:50), which he then recited over and over again as he walked among the fields and orchards by

---

[59] See Necmeddin Şahiner, *Haşır Risalesi Nasıl Yazildı?* (Istanbul: Zafer Yayinlari 1997), pp. 23-4, pp. 31-3.

[60] Nursi, *Barla Lahikasi* (Istanbul: Sinan Matbaasi, 1959), p. 171.

Lake Eğirdir. That evening the Tenth Word 'came' to him and he dictated it, while his student Şamlı Hafiz Tevfik wrote it down.[61] Nursi said that most of his works were "bestowed" on him in this way, of a sudden. It was in consequence of this that the writing of even the most difficult of his treatises was extremely quick, despite being dictated out in the countryside in all weathers.

If the subjects of the treatises came to Nursi by way of inspiration, the method by which he presented and elucidated the truths they contained was clearly the fruit of both much thought, and his long years of concern with education and teaching. Here we shall point out a few elements of that method:

Firstly, is his frequent use of allegorical comparisons (*temsil*). As with all parts of the *Risale*, the Tenth Word in part consists of such comparisons. In a note at the head of the piece, he says that the reasons for his writing in this form are firstly, "to facilitate comprehension," and secondly, "to show how rational, appropriate, well-founded, and coherent are the truths of Islam... each story is like an allusion pointing to its concluding truth."[62] In the Twenty-Eighth Letter Nursi describes the allegories as "a single ray from the allegories of the Qur'an," and goes on to say that they bring distant truths close like a telescope, collect together diffuse matters, and are means of reaching the highest truths, like stairs.[63] In truth, these allegorical comparisons, which are often employed as an introduction in the first section or "station" of a treatise, attract and hold the attention, and preparing the mind make easily comprehensible truths that might otherwise be difficult to grasp. They are a significant factor explaining the widespread popularity and continuing success of the *Risale*.

A second element of the *Risale*'s original method of expounding the Qur'anic teachings are comparisons, sometimes allegorical, between the "wisdom" (*hikmet*) of the Qur'an and of philosophy. This aspect, which is also represented in the Tenth Word, is fundamental to the *Risale* and is related to its historical function. For in one respect, the *Risale* may be said to be a refutation of materialist and naturalist philosophy. The Twenty-Third Flash, the *Treatise On Nature*, deals with this specifically.

A third element of the method is the use of logical proofs and reasoned argument. Virtually every statement is supported by proof, demonstrating its necessity and very often proving the absurdity of the corresponding explanations of philosophy. These proofs, supported by reasoned argument and illustrated by the allegorical comparisons mentioned above, offer explanations of the teachings of the Qur'an that Nursi hoped would be persuasive as to be readily acceptable by everyone.

---

[61] According to the 'Fihrist' of *Mesnevi-i Nuriye*, it was actually an Arabic piece, *Lâsiyyemalar*, later included in Mesnevi, that was written in this way. As with other pieces written in Burdur and Barla up to this time, Bediuzzaman used the Arabic piece as the basis of a Turkish version. See, *Mesnevi-i Nûriye* (Istanbul, Envar Neşriyat, 1994), p. 261.

[62] Nursi, *The Words* [Engl. tr. Sükran Vahide] (Istanbul: Sözler Publications, new ed., 1998), p. 59.

[63] Nursi, *Letters*, pp. 443-4.

A further element is reflective thought on the universe, the distinguishing mark of the way of the New Said. A letter which Nursi wrote while in Barla both shows how the twelve "Truths" constituting the main part of the Tenth Word have been tackled, and throws light on one type of reflective thought in the *Risale*:

> Each of the twelve Truths proves three things at the same time. Each proves both the existence of the Necessarily Existent One, and His names and attributes, then it constructs the resurrection of the dead on these and proves it. Everyone from the most obdurate unbeliever to the most sincere believer can take his share from each Truth, because in each, the gaze is turned towards beings, works. Each says: 'There are well-ordered acts in these, and a well-ordered act cannot be without an author. In which case it has an author. And since the act has been carried out with order and balance, its author must be wise and just. Since he is wise, he does nothing in vain. And since he acts with justice, he does not permit rights to be violated. There will therefore be a great gathering, a supreme tribunal.' The Truths have been tackled in this way. They are succinct, and thus prove the three things at once.[64]

Nursi said that as an instance of divine grace, the Tenth Word explains clearly "to ordinary people and even children" truths of belief before which even a genius like Ibn Sina had confessed his impotence.[65] He sent the manuscript to Istanbul with a Barla merchant to be printed by one of his old students, Müküslü Hamza Efendi. A thousand copies were printed and brought back to Nursi, who corrected them, before distributing them. He sent a number of copies to Ankara to be given to the deputies in the Assembly and other officials.

Thus began Nursi's counter-offensive against the moves to deprive the Muslim people of Turkey of their faith. In the eight and half years he was in Barla, he completed the first two collections of the *Risale*, *Sözler* (*The Words*) and *Mektûbat* (*Letters*), and wrote a greater part of *Lem'alar* (*Flashes*), a total of 119 pieces. Among them are pieces explaining and proving in the manner described above all the main truths of belief. Especially noteworthy are the Twenty-Second and Thirty-Second Words, and Twentieth and Thirty-Third Letters, on the divine existence and unity; the Twenty-Fifth Word, which proves that the very matters of the Qur'an that had been attacked by its enemies are sources of its "eloquence" and "miraculousness;" the Nineteenth Letter, on the miracles of Muhammad; and the Twenty-Ninth Word, on the angels, the immortality of man's spirit, and the resurrection of the dead.

Life in Barla

Nursi's life in Barla was for the greater part solitary, only by degrees did he attract the students who were to assist him as scribes, and by writing out and distributing

---

64 Nursi, *Barla Lahikası*, p. 160.

65 Nursi, *Letters*, p. 438.

the treatises as they were written. As always, he lived the simplest of lives. His frugality was such that throughout the years of his exile, he supported himself from his savings and salary while a member of *Darü'l-Hikmet.* Of that salary he had kept only a small percentage to meet his own needs, the rest he had used to print his works and distribute them free of charge.[66] He persisted in practising his rule of never receiving gifts or food without giving something in return.

In their banishing Nursi to what they considered to be the back of beyond, the Ankara authorities had in fact served the purposes of divine wisdom. For the remoteness, as well as the great beauty of the mountainous region provided Nursi with an environment conducive to the contemplation on the natural world, "the book of the universe," which was fundamental to his thought. In the summer months he would spend weeks on end on Çam Dağı, a mountain three hours distance from Barla, on the summit of which he had two tree-houses made. There, with the broad sweep of the landscape far below him, he would pray and reflect, write, and correct the handwritten copies of his works.

There was no respite in the harassment Nursi suffered. In fact it increased proportionately to the increase in his students and spread of the *Risale.* After the introduction of the Latin alphabet and banning of the Ottoman/Arabic script at the end of 1928, the authorities stepped up their pressure, and the *Nur* students were subject to having their houses raided, and to imprisonment and ill-treatment. Nevertheless, inspired by Nursi and looking on his writings as a divine bounty at that time, the students were unflagging in their efforts to write out, read, and disseminate them. The local District Officer and teacher continually pestered Nursi.[67] It was probably the misinformation they supplied that eventually alarmed the authorities, causing them to have him moved back to Isparta. He was taken there around the end of July 1934.

Isparta — July 1934

Nursi spent nine months in Isparta and was kept under strict surveillance, with a policeman posted permanently at his door. He lived in a house rented from one of his students. Husrev and Re'fet Bey, two of his closest students in Isparta, visited him whenever they could, assisting him as scribes and writing out copies of the *Risale-i Nur.* He wrote three parts here: the Nineteenth, Twenty-Fifth, and Twenty-Sixth Flashes, called *On Frugality, Message For The Sick, and Treatise For The Elderly.*[68] He was unable to complete the latter due to his arrest and imprisonment.

---

[66] See unpaged addendum to Abdurrahman's *Tarihçe*; *The Flashes Collection*, p. 192; *Letters*, pp. 88-90.

[67] See Nursi *Letters*, p. 425; Şahiner, *Bilinmeyen*, p. 308; Mehmed Sözer, in *Son Şahitler*, ii, p. 212.

[68] Şahiner, *Bilinmeyen*, p. 314.

Eskişehir — April 1935

On April 25, 1935 the arrests started, with some of Nursi's students being taken into custody. Nursi himself and some others were arrested two days later. It was evident from the way things developed that the whole affair had been orchestrated. The Government was alarmed by false reports. Nursi and a number of his students were arrested — eventually 120 were rounded up from a number of provinces including Van. A campaign was started in the press with sensational news of a "countrywide network of reactionaries." Rumours were spread that Nursi and the others were to be executed. The Home Affairs Minister Şükrü Kaya and the Commander-in-Chief of the Gendarmerie immediately set out for Isparta with a detachment of a hundred gendarmes and fifteen to twenty policemen, although there was a miliary division permanently posted there,[69] as though taking under control a major uprising. Soldiers were posted at key points in the area. An air of general panic was generated. As Nursi later pointed out in his defence, the plan had been to create an incident similar to that at Menemen 1930.[70] However, on this occasion there was no reaction to the provocation, and the plan came to nothing.

Although on the two subsequent occasions Nursi and a large number of his students were tried and suffered terms of imprisonment they were not preceded by campaigns of this proportion. The general purpose was the same: to intimidate the population and scare them away from religion; and to publicly humiliate religious figures such as Nursi, and to ridicule them, so as to make the people look coldly on them. For as is shown by the indictments in all the trials, despite the pressure brought to bear on the courts and judiciary to convict Nursi and his students whatever the truth of the matter, the state prosecutors could find nothing concrete with which to charge them. The charges were all baseless, and the same, on each occasion. They included: "exploiting religion with the idea of political reaction, with the intention of launching an enterprise that might breach public security;" founding a secret political organization; giving instruction in Sufism; opposing the principles of secularism and republicanism, and the reforms; and the possible disturbance of public order. The fact is that the Government put a political meaning on Nursi's activities, was accusing him of conspiring to bring down the regime and the system it had set up. Despite what might appear today to be mostly innocuous charges, certainly in the Eskişehir trial, the prosecution was calling for the death penalty anyway for Nursi, and perhaps also for his closest students.[71]

Thus, Nursi and a hundred and twenty of his students were put in Eskişehir Prison, where they were kept in appalling conditions. While the students were crowded together in wards, Nursi was kept in solitary confinement. He was denied virtually all rights. Nevertheless, during the eleven months he was held in the prison, he wrote six major treatises, including his defence speeches. These were the Twenty-Seventh to the Thirtieth Flashes, and the First and Second Rays. The

---

[69] *Tarihçe*, p. 212.
[70] *Tarihçe*, p. 202.
[71] *Tarihçe*, pp. 191-2.

Twenty-Eighth Ray consists of the letters and notes he wrote his students in the prison, offering them solace and guidance. For he was greatly distressed at the difficulties caused to them and their families by this unjust imprisonment. With the other treatises too, he hoped to maintain their morale and keep them occupied by reading them and writing out copies. Nursi called prison "Medrese-i Yusufiye," the School of Joseph, recalling the Prophet Joseph, the patron of prisoners, and that prison is essentially a place of training and education.

When it came to Nursi's defense, his chief concern was to defend firstly the *Risale*, and secondly, to have his innocent students acquitted, for which reason, he said, he couched his defence in very mild terms. He was largely successful on both counts. For when the court passed judgment on August 19,1935, it acquitted a total of ninety-seven of the students, a number had anyway been released after two months, and sentenced fifteen of them to six months each. It sentenced Nursi to eleven months imprisonment to be followed by a year's compulsory residence in Kastamonu.

Nursi replied to all the charges with his usual clarity and logic, demonstrating clearly that they were without base or substance. He admitted that he was occupied with "the sciences of belief," which constituted no crime, but denied that these could be exploited for anything but God's pleasure. For thirteen years he had totally withdrawn from public life and politics of all sorts; even rejecting Mustafa Kemal's offers of various posts in 1923. For thirteen years he had not so much as opened a newspaper, "the tongue of politics." No hint of involvement had been found, even when his house was searched. Nursi told the court: "Light has been given me, the club of politics has not been given me."

In answer to the charge of disturbing public order by exciting religious emotions, which was supported by no evidence, Nursi pointed out that: "Religious belief, the source of good characteristics and fine qualities, certainly doesn't disturb public order; it ensures it. It is unbelief that disturbs it, because of its bad character."[72] No *Nur* student had been involved in any disturbance: "Those who receive instruction from the *Risale* certainly do not get involved in any public disturbances, which are the cause of the blood of innocents being spilt and their rights being violated..."[73]

Nursi also denied charges of giving instruction in Sufism, which had been prohibited by law in 1925. There was no one who could claim that he had done so. The *Risale*'s function was to save belief. He said: "There are many who enter Paradise without belonging to a Sufi order, but none who enter it without belief. It is therefore the time to work for belief."[74]

As for setting up a political organization, such an accusation could only have been made with malicious intent. There was no evidence for any such thing; it was also clearly baseless.

---

[72] *Tarihçe*, p. 198.
[73] *Tarihçe*, p. 207.
[74] *Tarihçe*, p. 199.

In reply to the accusation of opposition to secularism and the Republic, in regard to the latter he recalled the famous story of himself and the ants when he was staying in an abandoned cell near Tillo at the age of fifteen or sixteen: he had been "a religious republican" even before most of those present had been born, for at that time he had shared his meagre rations with the ants because he admired their social co-operation and wanted to "reward them for their republicanism."[75] As for the question of secularism, it was imputed opposition to the secularizing reforms that lay at the base of all the charges made against him.

Nursi told the court that as far as he understood it, the secular republic meant the separation of religion from the matters of this world, it did not mean to be totally without religion. He went on to say that just as no nation anywhere could continue its existence without religion, the same was even truer for the Turks, who had always been distinguished by their attachment to Islam.[76] Moreover, by accepting the separation of the matters of this world and religion, the Republican Government had accepted the principle of impartiality. Therefore, just as it did not interfere with those without religion and their irreligion, so it should not interfere with the religiously minded and their religiosity.[77] That is to say, secularism should ensure freedom of conscience. A republican government should not restrict freedom of scholarship. The *Risale* was a scholarly work, and after the author himself, it addressed the philosophers of Europe. The blows it dealt were addressed not at the Government, but at those philosophers and the atheists who worked on their account in Turkey.[78] He attributed the corruption at home to the influence of Europe and materialist and naturalist philosophy. He told the court too that he differentiated between the Government and the members of covert atheistic societies who had infiltrated it and deceived its officials. It was they who tried to smear supporters of religion with accusations of "political reaction" and "exploiting religion for political ends."[79]

On coming to its decision, the court acquitted Nursi on all charges except one related to the infringement of the Civil Code's rulings on inheritance and the veiling of women. He had answered the charges in his defence, pointing out that the pieces in question were scholarly replies to attacks made by European "philosophers" and had been written before the founding of the Republic and adoption of the Civil Code.[80] Nevertheless, it sentenced him arbitrarily to eleven months imprisonment, and fifteen of his students to six months.

---

[75] *Tarihçe*, p. 39; Vahide, *The Author of the Risale-i Nur*, pp. 14 -15.
[76] *Tarihçe*, p. 205.
[77] *Tarihçe*, p. 214.
[78] *Tarihçe*, p. 221.
[79] *Tarihçe*, p. 214.
[80] *Tarihçe*, p. 222.

Kastamonu — March 1936

Nursi's life during the seven and a half years he stayed in Kastamonu was more restricted than in Barla and the conditions, harsher. The first few months he stayed "as a guest" in the police station, until he was moved to a rented house directly opposite it. There, the surveillance under which he was kept was stricter than previously, restricting to a greater degree both his own movements, and those who wished to visit him. Ankara posted governors to this provincial centre whom they knew would give Nursi no respite. Nevertheless, he attracted new students who were to serve him loyally and assist him with the work of the *Risale*. These included Çayci Emin, a fellow-exile from the east, Mehmed Feyzi, a local scholar, and Nazif and Selahaddin Çelebi from Inebolu, which was to become another important centre of *Risale* activity.

Nursi managed to keep in constant touch with his students in the Isparta area, for whom, because of their service to the *Risale*, he had the greatest affection. There was continual correspondence between them.[81] Because of the dangers of using the state postal service, the letters and treatises of the *Risale* were delivered from place to place by "Nur Postmen." In the villages of Isparta Province, and now in Inebolu and Kastamonu, the *Risale* was being written out by hundreds, or even thousands, of pens. Nursi continuously encouraged them in this. His letters were also sources of guidance and spiritual sustenance for them. He directed their work, setting out the principles of the *Risale*'s service, and warned them always to be cautious in the face of their many enemies. Others explain the necessity of avoiding political involvement of any sort, and the need for them to develop complete sincerity in their service. Sincerity was essential, for by virtue of it the *Nur* students could form the collective personality necessary to perform the various functions of the *Risale*. Thus, Nursi and the *Risale* became a source of hope for many people in those dark days of repression, which saved them from idleness and despair, and gave news of the brighter days of the future.

In the four years until 1940 Nursi wrote from the Third to the Ninth Rays. The Seventh Ray, called *The Supreme Sign* (*Âyetü'l-Kübra*), is discussed briefly below. He wrote a concise summary of the Arabic Twenty-Ninth Flash, as a source of reflective thought. He did the final drafts of the First and Second Rays, which he had written in Eskişehir Prison, and probably in 1938, set in order the Fifth Ray, which had been written originally when he was in Istanbul in the years of the Constitutional Revolution.

Nursi continued writing these works, in addition to large numbers of letters and correcting the ever-increasing numbers of the handwritten copies of the treatises of the *Risale-i Nur*, in spite of suffering constant ill-health and the distress of being subject to the continuous harassment of the authorities.

[81] Apart from those included in the other collections of the *Risale* the letters Bediuzzaman wrote his students, and some of those they wrote him, were compiled in three main volumes, one for each of his places of exile: *Barla Lahikası*, *Kastamonu Lahikası*, and *Emirdağ Lahikası*. Bediuzzaman included these in the *Risale* as the Twenty-Seventh Letter.

The Supreme Sign was the most important part of the *Risale* to be written in Kastamonu. Indeed, it is one of the most important parts of the *Risale*. With its original form of learning the testimony to their Creator's existence and unity of all the realms of creation, it represents the final and "permanent" form of the reflective thought on the phenomenal world that Nursi developed throughout the period he was writing the *Risale*.[82]

Nursi's method of reflective thought, which was the way he found through the guidance of the numerous Qur'anic verses calling on man to ponder over the divine works and activity in the universe, is significant in that, by means of it, he was able both to provide convincing proofs of all the truths of belief, and demolish the concepts on which materialist and naturalist philosophy are based. Moreover, he was able to demonstrate that there is no clash or conflict between the physical sciences and religion. For, according to Nursi, when the universe is looked at and pondered over in the Qur'anic manner, for its meaning, the physical sciences and their minute descriptions of the order of beings are transformed in knowledge of God. Essentially, this method demonstrates the complementary nature of the Qur'an, which proceeds from the divine attribute of speech, and "the book of the universe," which proceeds from the attributes of will and power, and consists of expounding the Qur'an of speech by means of the Qur'an of the universe. It was through this original, and genuinely Qur'anic, way that Nursi was successful in developing a new science of *kalam* that addressed the problems posed by the development of materialist science and its attacks on the Qur'an and Islam. Its particular relevance to the situation obtaining in Turkey at that time is also clear.

Among Nursi's visitors in Kastamonu were some schoolboys. Finding him to be kindly and ready to answer their questions, they came to him regularly to hear him speak about the beauties of belief in God and the hereafter. This was in spite of suffering various punishments in school in consequence. One day, they came to him and said: "Tell us about our Creator, our teachers don't speak of God." The answer Nursi gave them he later incorporated in the *Risale* as the Sixth Topic of the Eleventh Ray: "All the sciences you study continuously speak of God and make known the Creator, each with its own particular tongue. Don't listen to your teachers, listen to them!" Then by means of allegorical comparisons, he showed how various sciences make known the Creator together with some of His Names.[83]

After 1940 there were a series of arrests of *Nur* students in the Isparta area, following which they were released. Their houses were frequently raided and searched. Finally a student was informed on and arrested in Denizli. Reports were sent to Ankara, orders were sent from Ankara. Nursi was subject to increased harassment, and his house was searched, finally three times in succession.[84] On all these occasions the authorities were searching for the Fifth Ray. This was a treatise

[82] Nursi, *Kastamonu Lahikası*, p. 228.
[83] See Nursi, *The Rays Collection*, p. 75.
[84] Nursi, *Kastamonu Lahikası*, pp. 266-8.

interpreting Hadiths about the end of time and the fearsome figures, the Antichrists, predicted to appear. Nursi was finally arrested and held for three weeks in the police station. Twenty-two of his students were arrested in Kastamonu. Others were arrested in Isparta, and elsewhere. Again an air of terror was generated. Nursi was sent to Isparta by way of Ankara. Here a number of the students were held for preliminary questioning before being sent to Denizli.

Denizli — October 1943

One hundred and twenty-six *Nur* students were sent to Denizli Prison from all over Turkey.[85] Of them seventy-three entered the prison and the rest were released. With each term of imprisonment, conditions worsened, so that Nursi said of Denizli that a day there was the equivalent of the month in Eskişehir. The concrete building was dark and damp in the extreme and infested with lice and mosquitoes. Nursi was again kept in solitary confinement, this time in a minute airless cell so small a bed could only just fit it in.[86] It had one tiny window overlooking the exercise yard which the prison authorities boarded up when they found him throwing notes out of it to his students. They were forbidden to communicate with him on pain of being beaten. Nursi was again poisoned on several occasions, and two of the *Nur* students died in the prison.

Nevertheless, contrary to all expectations, the imprisonment and trials at Denizli served the cause of the *Risale* positively. The trials received a lot of publicity, and aroused widespread sympathy for Nursi and the *Nur* students. This was reinforced when the favourable report was given by the Experts' Committee in Ankara, and they were unexpectedly acquitted. The trial was also the means of the *Risale* being widely studied in official circles, which Nursi surmised at least ameliorated their opinions of it.[87]

A factor which definitely acted in their favour was the extraordinary way in which the other prisoners reformed under the influence of Nursi and his students, even hardened criminals learning to read the Qur'an and perform the obligatory prayers regularly. They assisted the *Nur* students in writing out the defence speeches, and *The Fruits of Belief*, the Eleventh Ray, which Nursi wrote principally for the prisoners. Initially this was done in the greatest secrecy and with extreme difficulty, for paper was banned in the prison. Then when its generally beneficial results were seen, restrictions were lifted to an extent.[88]

The charges in the Denizli trials were the same as those at the trials in Eskişehir. Only on this occasion, the prosecution put forward the Fifth Ray as its main evidence. Nursi reused his defence from Eskişehir, with additions to answer the new charge. However, on the strength of the Committee of Expert's overwhelmingly favourable report, the court cleared all Nursi's works, acquitted

[85] Şahiner, *Bilinmeyen*, p. 341.
[86] Selahaddin Çelebi, in Şahiner, *Son Şahitler*, i, p. 145.
[87] Nursi, *The Rays Collection*, p. 362.
[88] *Tarihçe*, p. 377.

all the prisoners, and ruled that they be released immediately. The court reached its decision on June 16, 1944. They had spent nine months in the prison.

Emirdağ — August 1944

On the instructions of the Government, Nursi was eventually sent to reside in Emirdağ, a small provincial town situated between Afyon and Eskişehir. He was to remain here until October 1951, with a break of twenty months in Afyon Prison, from January 1948 to October 1949. He and his students and his works had all been acquitted by Denizli Court. Moreover, with increased American influence after the end of the Second World War, single party rule came to an end and there were moves towards a freer society in Turkey. However, Nursi was subject to greater ill-treatment and harassment during these years, rather than less, which culminated in the third mass imprisonment of himself and his students. The reason for this was undoubtedly the fact that their enemies, those opposed to religion and Islam, were both shocked and infuriated by the Denizli acquittals and by the favourable publicity the trials had afforded the movement. Furthermore, it led directly to a considerable expansion in activities related to the *Risale*, outside the two or three areas they had previously been concentrated. The activities were further expanded when *Nur* students bought two of the first duplicating machines to come to Turkey in 1946 or '47, following which they were able to reproduce copies in their thousands. These machines were seized in the prelude to the Afyon arrests.

Another reason for the increase in the entirely illegal ill-treatment Nursi received was his taking advantage of the acquittals and the more positive attitude towards the *Risale* arising from the favourable experts' report, to write a number of petitions and open letters to leading members of the Government and other officials warning them about the trend of events. He informed the high-ranking officials that in his view, Turkey was threatened by two "calamities," which could lead to its destabilization and to anarchy. One of these was communism, which had overrun Russia and eastern Europe, the other was "the severe objections" towards the Turkish people of the Islamic world.[89] In Nursi's view, the efforts to alienate Turkey from its Islamic identity and break it off from the Islamic world had left it without its natural support, weakening it to a degree it would be unable to withstand the destructive plans of the forces of unbelief. In a letter to the Interior Minister, Hilmi Uran, Nursi pointed out that part of the plan of outside forces to divide the Islamic world, was the establishment of "absolute unbelief" in Turkey through "atheistic organizations" inside the country. Their activities, together with those of the other "destructive" current of unbelief, communism, and its sympathizers in the country, were aimed at creating anarchy. Nursi warned that it was only the Qur'an, and the Turkish nation, which was "fused with Islam and was

[89] Nursi, *Emirdağ Lahikası*, i, p. 101.

one with it," that could halt the rushing tide of communism, preventing it from overwhelming the country.[90]

It was also against these "calamities" that Nursi was now directing the increased publication of the *Risale*, part of which was for the first time in the Latin alphabet.

Nursi saw the real dangers as lying in the future. In another letter he called on the judiciary "to protect the *Risale* and its students," rather than working against them. For the moral decline caused by the above currents and by the loosening of the constraints of religion, could result in fifty years time in serious moral degeneration and fearsome social consequences.[91] He insisted that neither the "material penalties" of the law nor politics or diplomacy could halt "the moral and spiritual (*mânevi*)" destruction of these forces; it could be halted and countered only by the Qur'an and belief. Since the *Risale* was "a Qur'anic barrier" before those forces and "a repairer of the power of an atom bomb," the authorities and Government should understand their need of it.

Nursi suggested too that it was these same forces and their representatives who conspired to create disturbances and anarchy, that continually tried to provoke incidents and have himself and his students accused of the same thing. Whereas it had been established in courts of law that the *Risale-i Nur* students were the defenders of public order and security.

Although his movements were much of the time restricted in Emirdağ, as was always his practice, Nursi would go out into the surrounding country with his books to correct or to contemplate "the book of the universe." He became loved by the children of the area, and the reformatory effects on the local society of his advice and guidance have been noted by many.[92]

In reply to criticisms of the Qur'an related to the repetitions it contains, the first piece Nursi wrote in Emirdağ was the Tenth Topic of *The Fruits of Belief.* This was followed by the Eleventh Topic, about the angels. With the exception of *El-Hüccetü'z-Zehra* (The Shining Proof), written in Afyon Prison, and one or two small pieces, these were the final parts of the *Risale* to be written. Nursi put together the treatises in collections and it was thus that they were now mostly published. These included *Asâ-yı Musa* (The Staff of Moses), *Zülfikar*, *Siracünnur* (The Illuminating Lamp), *Sikke-i Tasdik i Gaybi* (The Ratifying Stamp of the Unseen), and *A Guide For Youth*, made up of pieces originally written for the schoolboys in Kastamonu.

The *Risale* and the activities associated with it now began to attract numbers of young people. Its method and refutation of materialitst philosophy were found effective by teachers, university students and lecturers, and others who had been through the new educational system. It also began to spread in the Islamic world at this time. When in 1947 it was again permitted to make the Hajj,

---

[90] Nursi, *Emirdağ Lahikası*, i, pp. 214-15.

[91] Nursi, *Emirdağ Lahikası*, i, pp. 20-1.

[92] See *Tarihçe*, pp. 403-6; Şahiner, *Bilinmeyen*, p. 356.

students took copies to Mecca and Medina, where they distributed them among Muslims from different countries.[93]

Following the usual pattern, before the arrests started, the authorities stepped up their pressure on Nursi and the *Risale* students and carried out raids and assaults. Nursi had his house searched five times by the governor and police chief. He was finally arrested and taken to Afyon, where he was joined by students from Isparta, Denizli, Kastamonu, and other places. They were officially charged and put inside the prison on January 23, 1948.

Afyon Prison — January 1948 - October 1949

In the harshness of its conditions, Afyon Prison far exceeded the previous terms of imprisonment Nursi and his students had endured. Their conviction was apparently a foregone conclusion, for the charges made against them were the same as in the previous two trials. They had anyway been acquitted of them in the last trial, the *Risale* cleared, and all the confiscated copies of it returned. As Nursi pointed out in his defense, it "trampled the honor of three high courts and cast aspersions of their justice" to bring up the same questions again.[94]

A total of fifty-four students were originally arrested and brought to Afyon.[95] Some were released. Those who stayed in the prison had to survive the overcrowded, filthy conditions of the wards. They were severely beaten if they attempted to visit Nursi, who was put alone in a huge empty ward, most of the windows of which had no panes of glass. Most of the accounts of life in Afyon Prison speak of the bitter cold. Nursi suffered several bouts of severe illness, some the result of poison. For much of the time he had no form of heating.[96] He was now over seventy years of age. Yet once again he triumphed over the adverse conditions. For despite everything, he wrote his defence and presented it, wrote large numbers of letters and notes to his students, directed the publicizing of the defence speeches, and wrote *The Shining Proof* for the prisoners, a treatise explaining and proving the truths of belief. And he did, all of this when scraps of paper even were practically unobtainable. Most of all, he never slackened in his prayer and worship.

When it came to the trial, since the matters were the same as previously, Nursi reused his defence with small alterations. Evidence of the pressure brought to bear on the court was that he was denied many legal rights, and was even hindered in the preparation and delivery of his defence. Moreover, the indictments were full of falsehoods; Nursi made out a table showing no less than ninety errors.[97] It was a number of criticisms included in the report of the new experts' committee set up in Ankara to rescrutinize the *Risale* that provided the prosecution

[93] Nursi, *Emirdağ Lahikası*, i, p. 269, pp. 234-6.
[94] Nursi, *The Rays Collection*, p. 370.
[95] Şahiner, *Bilinmeyen*, pp. 364-5.
[96] Şahiner, *Bilinmeyen*, pp. 368-70.
[97] Nursi, *Şuâlar*, pp. 405-27.

with what they considered to be sufficient evidence for a conviction. Nursi, however, replied to these, demonstrating them to be in error.[98] As always his defence was primarily a defense of the *Risale*, and in the face of the blatant abuses in the execution of justice, he arranged for his defence and those of his students, as well as the table of the ninety errors and their corrections, to be duplicated and sent to Ankara and other centres in order to publicize the reality of the case.

Nursi was finally found guilty and sentenced to two years' hard labour, which was reduced to twenty months due to his age. Twenty of his students were sentenced to six months. The case was immediately sent to the Appeal Court, which quashed Afyon Court's decision. However, due to the deliberate delays and postponements, Nursi was made to serve the full term. He was finally released on September 20, 1949.

The Third Said — 1950-1960

The last ten years of Nursi's life, which coincided with Democrat Party [henceforth, DP] rule and an easing in conditions, saw both an expansion in the publication and dissemination of the *Risale* and a growth in the *Nur* movement. Despite the severity of the twenty months in Afyon Prison, which had taken its toll on his health, and his advancing years, Nursi continued his struggle right up till his last moments. These years saw the emergence of a new generation of young students, who organized the printing and publishing activities in Ankara, Istanbul, and other centres. Some of these had served terms in Afyon, and it was they whom Nursi mostly kept with him to assist him. They were to form the nucleus of the *Nur* movement in the future.

This period of Nursi's life is usually associated with his greater concern with social and political matters. For 1950 saw the defeat of the RPP and overwhelming victory of the Democrat Party under Adnan Menderes. Because Nursi saw the Democrats as a means of preventing the return to power of the RPP, and also as "assisting" the *Nur* students in combatting atheistic currents and repairing the moral and spiritual (*mânevî*) damage they caused, he gave them his support. But this was limited to offering them advice and guidance, and urging them to take measures that would strengthen religion and to renew relations with the Islamic world. Despite his support and his considering Menderes to be "a hero of Islam,"[99] he still looked on the Democrats as "the lesser of two evils."[100]

Besides raising the ban on the Arabic call to prayer, one of the first acts of the Democrat Government was to issue a general amnesty. Nursi was now theoretically free to move around as he wished. However, because the governing structure of the country could not be easily changed, and many RPP supporters remained in positions of power, Nursi and his students continued to be subject to pressure and had to act circumspectly as before. Arrests and court cases continued

[98] Nursi, *The Rays Collection*, pp. 510-11.
[99] *Emirdağ Lahikasi*, ii, 142; Giyaseddin Emre, in *Son Şahitler*, ii, p. 56.
[100] *Emirdağ Lahikasi*, ii, p. 217.

throughout the 1950s. Nursi attended the hearing of a case in Istanbul in 1952 that had been brought against him in connection with the printing of *A Guide For Youth* by one of his students, a university student.[101] The charges were approximately the same, and included contravening the principle of secularism by making religious propaganda. He was again acquitted. The trial was followed with great interest and enthusiasm by thousands of young supporters of Nursi. It was the first time he had returned to Istanbul since he had passed through on his way to exile, twenty-seven years before. Large numbers of old friends and the young people flocked to see him. He also took the opportunity of making trips round the city and surrounding areas to visit the places of his youth. He visited Istanbul again the following year in connection with another case.[102]

Nursi rented a house in Isparta, and he divided his time between there, Eskişehir and Emirdağ. In 1954 he returned to Barla. It was the first time he had returned to the first "*Nur* Medrese" since he had been taken from here in 1934. He wept to see it again. The following year, his students clubbed together and brought him a 1953 model Chevrolet. With his advancing years, he was finding it increasingly difficult to get about.

Nursi gave great importance to re-establishing and strengthening relations with the Islamic world in this period, particularly through the *Risale*, "which serves the unfolding of the brotherhood of belief."[103] In connection with this, Nursi applauded the Democrat Government's decision to sign the Baghdad Pact in 1955, and sent a letter of support to the President and Prime Minister.[104] In the letter, as two means to assist their moves through the Pact towards peace and reconciliation between the peoples of Islam, he mentioned the Medresetü'z-Zehrâ, his Eastern university, and the *Risale*. Just as the *Risale* had defeated atheism and served to strengthen brotherhood through strengthening belief; so the Medresetü'z-Zehrâ would serve the brotherhood of the Muslim peoples so that they should not be corrupted by racialism. He had previously congratulated the President, Celal Bayar, for his decision in 1951 to build a university in eastern Turkey, equating it with his project of fifty-five years. Here, he stressed the unifying role of such a university, both culturally and academically. However, he emphasized, since the area's problems stemmed from the "destruction" of outside forces and were of a moral and spiritual nature, religion should be made its basis; the destruction could be halted only by powerful moral and spiritual forces.

It was only in June 1956, being unable to further prolong proceedings, that Afyon Court finally cleared the *Risale* and returned the confiscated copies. The following year for the first time, *Nur* students in Ankara and Istanbul started to have it printed on modern presses in the Latin alphabet.[105] Thus began a new era in

[101] *Tarihçe*, pp. 570-83.

[102] Nursi, *Emirdağ Lahikası*, ii, pp. 135-7; Vahide, *The Author of the Risale-i Nur*, pp. 344-7.

[103] Nursi, *Emirdağ Lahikası*, ii, p. 195.

[104] Nursi, *Emirdağ Lahikası*, ii, pp. 194-7.

[105] M. Emin Birinci, in Sahiner, *Son Şahitler*, i, p. 266.

the publication of the *Risale*. Up to this time its reproduction on duplicating machines and by hand had continued unabated. But now its publication was on a much larger scale and it became accessible to all sections of the population. This was truly a great victory for Nursi, and the fruit of his long years of patient struggle in exile and captivity. He called it "the *Risale-i Nur*'s festival."[106] The greatly increased availability of the *Risale* together with the greater freedom led to a considerable growth in the numbers of *Risale-i Nur* students, and the consolidation of the movement. 'Dershanes' or '*Nur* study-centres' were opened all over the country.

It was to visit the 'dershanes' and his students that Nursi made a series of trips at the end of 1959 and beginning of 1960. These visits also had the character of farewell visits. For after remaining two months in Isparta, Nursi set out by car with three of his students on his last journey, to Urfa in south-eastern Turkey. He was very ill, and there he died peacefully in his sleep on March 23, 1960, which was 25 Ramadan 1379.

Conclusion

In this brief account of Bediuzzaman Said Nursi's life and his exertions in the cause of Islam, an attempt has been made to trace the course of his scholarly life, and some main aspects of his thought, which yielded the fruit of the *Risale-i Nur*. In the first period of his life, that of the Old Said, his endeavours to diagnose the sicknesses afflicting the Islamic world and Ottoman Empire and offer "prescriptions" for them involved him to an extent in social and political life, and preoccupation with science and philosophy. However, as the New Said, having taken the Qur'an as his "sole guide," by means of the original method of expounding the Qur'anic truths of belief, in part described above, he put forward numerous convincing proofs of those truths which at the same time refuted the principles of materialist philosophy. In this way, he found both a direct way to reality which addressed all classes of people by which they could gain firm belief, and a way to offer "the healing remedies of the Qur'an" to those wounded by the misguidance of science and materialist philosophy. In his view, the harm caused by materialist philosophy was so widespread and pervasive at that time that the struggle with the proofs of the *Risale* he called "mânevî cihad," and the "positive action" of its students in society, which "repaired" the moral and spiritual depradations of materialism, had greater importance than any other form of struggle in the name of religion. It was these points that he emphasized above all others the last time he addressed his students before his death.[107]

---

[106] Bayram Yüksel, in Sahiner, *Son Şahitler*, i, pp. 405-7.
[107] Nursi, *Emirdağ Lahikası*, ii, pp. 213-19.

Chapter 2

The Ethics of Pardon and Peace: A Dialogue of Ideas between the Thought of Pope John Paul II and the *Risale-i-Nur*

Thomas Michel, S.J.

At international congresses around the world, there are always many papers and speeches about peace. We hear the speakers of each religious group profess that their religion wants peace, teaches peace, builds peace. The leaders of various nations say how they are committed to peace among nations, peace in their regions, civil peace within their societies. There is a human paradox here that we must face. It seems like everyone is in favor of peace, no one ever admits to being against peace, and yet there is very little peace in the world. The problem, I believe, lies in the fact that we are all in favor of peace *in the abstract*, but without saying in what peace consists, and without examining what is involved in building peace.

Of those religious thinkers of modern times who have attempted to study the concept of peace to explore what is involved in establishing and maintaining peace, I want to compare the thought of two persons who have made an remarkable contribution to the topic. One is a Christian, Pope John Paul II, leader of the Catholic Church, and the other a Muslim, Bediuzzaman Said Nursi, the author of the *Risale-i-Nur*. In this paper I hope to bring together the thinking of these two scholars and religious teachers into a kind of dialogue on the theme: "the ethics of peace." I will do this by summarizing the position of the Pope as the basis or point of view from which I will then read and explain the views of Said Nursi as found in the *Risale-i-Nur*.

1. John Paul II: Peace rests on Two Pillars: Justice and Forgiveness

As he does every year on January 1, in 2002 Pope John Paul II sent a message for the World Day of Peace at the beginning of the New Year. In this message, the Pope proposes that true peace must rest on two pillars: *justice* and *forgiveness*. Without these, you cannot have real peace. Both justice and pardon are necessary. One element without the other is not enough.

The Pope's reasoning is like this. Any real peace, if it is to be more than simply a "cease-fire" or temporary cessation of hostilities, has to get to the heart of the conflict and try to heal the breach in human relations, which was ruptured. When peoples are at war, when individuals are estranged and alienated from one another, they are angry, suspicious, and resentful of one another. They see the other as an enemy to be overcome, defeated, the object of retaliation, rather than a fellow-human with whom one ought to be reconciled. Thus, no talk about peace cannot proceed effectively without addressing the issue of broken relationships and without taking positive steps to repair those relations.

If one group or individual is being oppressed or treated unjustly by another, one cannot hope for peace between the two until there is justice. The Pope sees justice in two ways: firstly, as a "moral virtue," that is, as a human quality which a person can acquire and develop with God's powerful assistance (which Christians call *grace*), and secondly as a "legal guarantee," that is, part of the functioning of the national and international rule of law.[1] The aim of justice, both as a personal quality and as an element of the international system of relations among peoples, is to insure "full respect for rights and responsibilities" and to carry out a "just distribution of benefits and burdens."

Justice is thus a first, indispensable condition for peace. Unless one person treats another justly, that is, with respect for the other's rights and duties and by giving them their proper share of what is due to them, there will be no peace between them. The same holds true between social groups, ethnic groups, peoples and nations. Where there is aggression, oppression, occupation, transgression, there can be no peace. First, justice has to be established, then peace can be built.

All of this the Pope has said before. However, in his Day of Prayer for Peace message, he adds another element that he sees as intrinsic to the peace-making process. This is *forgiveness*, which goes beyond strict justice to strive to heal the historical burdens brought about by one individual's or one group's injustice and wrongdoing towards another.

Every nation, every religious or ethnic group, can draw up a long list of grievances that we have against each other, of wrongs that our group has suffered at the hands of the others. This is the human burden of past misdeeds experienced that we bring into our relations with others, that complicate the way we relate to individual members of the other group, that can poison all efforts at cooperation and reconciliation, and that can flare up into violence the slightest provocation.

Justice alone is not sufficient to heal these wounds; we need to exercise forgiveness. Forgiveness is, as the Pope states, "a personal choice, a decision to go against the natural instinct to pay back evil with evil." In doing so, it always involves an *apparent* short-term loss, but brings about the possibility of achieving a *real* long-term gain. "Violence," the Pope notes, works exactly the opposite:

[1] John Paul II, "No Peace Without, No Justices without Forgiveness," *Message of His Holiness Pope John Paul II for the World Day of Peace*, January 1, 2002, p. 5.

"opting for an apparent short-term gain, but involving a real and permanent loss."[2] "Forgiveness," the Pope notes, "may seem like weakness, but it demands great spiritual strength and moral courage."

It should not be surprising to discover that both Christianity and Islam lay great importance on the notions of justice and forgiveness, if these are to be the indispensable pre-conditions of peace. In the Gospel, Jesus taught his disciples: "You have heard it said, 'Love your neighbor and hate your enemy,' but I say to you 'Love your enemies and pray for those who persecute you.'" In a similar vein, the Qur'an permits vengeance up to the limits of strict justice but no farther, and then always adds: "But it is better to forgive."

2. Social Ethics in the *Risale-i Nur*

When we turn to the *Risale-i Nur*, we find that for Said Nursi, as for Pope John Paul II, ethics, as the study of what is good and bad, is primarily oriented toward the social sphere. In the thought of both men, a religiously based ethical system above all must treat questions of right and wrong in society, and only secondarily regards the goodness or evil of acts of private morality. Moreover, both root this primacy of social ethics in the Scriptural teaching of their respective faiths. For Said Nursi, ethical systems drawn up by philosophers and put into practice by public and private welfare associations fail to reach the levels of social commitment demanded by the teaching of the Qur'an. He states: "Together with all its associations for good works, all its establishments for the teaching of ethics, all its severe discipline and regulations, [society] has not been able to reconcile these two classes of mankind [the rich and the poor], nor heal the two fearsome wounds in human life."

The evils of which he is speaking here are *social complacency* on the part of the wealthy who feel no responsibility to share what they have with the poor and needy, and *class struggle* on the part of the poor who seek to take by force from the rich what they will not give freely. "The Qur'an, however," Said Nursi continues, "eradicates the first [social irresponsibility] with its injunction to pay *zakat*, and heals it, and uproots the second [class struggle] by prohibiting usury and interest, and cures that. Indeed, the Qur'an stands at the door of the world and declares usury and interest to be forbidden. It reads out its decree to mankind, saying: 'In order to close the door of strife, close the door of usury and interest!' and forbids its students to enter it."[3]

Instead of the ethics of the jungle where the rich and powerful take what they can and defend what they have by use of force, and that of class struggle in which the poor and oppressed seek to obtain their rights by force, Said Nursi sees the Divinely-guided ethic proposed by Islam as one in which truth, justice and harmony are paramount. "The civilization the *shari'a* of Muhammad (PBUH)

---

[2]Ibid. p. 12.

[3]*The Words*, Twenty-fifth Word, First Light, Third Ray, p. 422.

comprises and commands is this: its point of support is truth instead of force, the marks of which are justice and harmony. Its goal is virtue in place of [selfish] benefit, and its characteristic marks are love and attraction. Its means of unity are the ties of religion, country, and class, in place of racialism and nationalism, and the mark of these are sincere brotherhood, peace, and only defense against external aggression. In life is the principle of mutual assistance instead of the principle of conflict, the mark of which is accord and solidarity."[4]

Said Nursi holds that philosophically-based ethical systems fail to reach the heights of moral teaching proclaimed by the Qur'an because they fail to take into account an essential element of the human reality, that is, human weakness. If an ethical system presumes that people know what they want and will always work to achieve their desired goal, it will miss the point, for in fact people often act against their best interests out of anger, timidity etc., and for reasons of selfishness, laziness, ignorance, and the like fail to achieve what they desire.

However, a religious outlook, exemplified in Qur'anic teaching, takes into consideration and allows for the reality of human failure by urging believers to return to God in repentance, seeking forgiveness, and starting over. Thus, he calls on believers to be shaped by a "God-given ethics," which he holds to be an essential element in the message of all the prophets. "Be distinguished by *God-given morals* and turn towards God Almighty with humility, recognizing your impotence, poverty, and defectiveness, and so be a slave in His presence." Philosophically-based ethical systems, he holds, tend to ignore this element of human nature and selfishly aim at perfection through human efforts alone.

This Nursi sees as basically self-deception. "The essence of humanity," he states, has been kneaded with infinite impotence, weakness, poverty, and need, while the essence of the Necessarily Existent One is infinitely omnipotent, powerful, self-sufficient, and without need."[5] He concludes: "The aim of humanity and duty of human beings is to be molded by God-given ethics and good character, and, by knowing their [own] impotence to seek refuge with Divine power, by seeing their weakness to rely on Divine strength, by realizing their poverty to trust in Divine mercy, by perceiving their need to seek help from Divine riches, by seeing their faults to ask for pardon through Divine forgiveness, and by realizing their deficiency to be glorifiers of Divine perfection."[6] Thus, if they are to act in an ethical way people need to be informed and guided by God's revelation and to be supported by God's strength or grace. These two elements (Divine guidance and Divine strength) are often ignored in philosophically based ethical systems that do not take into account elements of God's revealed word.

---

[4] *The Damascus Sermon*, Seeds of Reality, p. 106.
[5] *The Words*, Thirtieth Word, First Aim, p. 564.
[6] *The Words*, Thirtieth Word, First Aim, p. 564.

3. Inner Peace

a. How does the concept of peace fit into Said Nursi's ethical thought? In the *Risale-i Nur*, he treats various aspects and elements of peace, not from a theoretical perspective, but as a practical guide for those who seek to pursue peace. In the first place, he treats of peace in the *eschatological* sense, as the ultimate goal of human life, almost synonymous with salvation. Specifically, it is the final destination of the collective personality of those who study the *Risale-i Nur*. He sees the *Risale-i Nur* students, through their efforts carried out in solidarity and sincerity, as contributing in their diverse activities to the building of an eternal realm of peace and happiness. "O *Risale-i Nur* students and servants of the Qur'an! You and I are members of a collective personality...like the components of a factory's machinery which produces eternal happiness within eternal life. We are hands working on a dominical boat which will disembark the community of Muhammad (PBUH) at the Realm of Peace, the shore of salvation. So we are surely in need of solidarity and true union, obtained through gaining sincerity."[7]

This concept not only gives meaning and direction to individual acts, but in this way the believer also achieves a kind of conquest over death. "Through the mystery of true brotherhood on the way of Divine pleasure...there are spirits to the number of brothers. If one of them dies, he meets death happily, saying: 'My other spirits remain alive, for they in effect make life continue for me by constantly gaining reward for me, so I am not dying. By means of their spirits, I live in respect of merit; I am only dying in respect of sin.' And he lays down in peace."[8]

b. A second way in which the Risale-i Nur looks at peace might be called the psychological sense, as tranquility and peace of mind, an inner confidence born of faith that enables the religious believer to face adversity without anxiety or despair. Particularly when one is facing the approach of death, the believer can attain a peace of mind which will enable the person to overcome spiritual turmoil and fear.[9] Reflecting on the long periods of his incarceration, he notes that his close companions, students of the *Risale-i Nur*, who were imprisoned with him did not waste their time or give in to selfish expressions of worry, complaint, or pride, or try to change what cannot be altered, but they achieved a peace of mind and steadfastness that bore witness to the spiritual values and dignity that they had achieved.[10]

This interior peace, not only of individuals but of whole societies, he sees as one of the marks of Islamic civilization. Along with justice, harmony, brotherhood, solidarity, human progress and spiritual advancement, peace should characterize the Islamic community.[11] It is peace as the basis of societal relations which should be the force that attracts others to Islam.

---

[7] *The Flashes*, Twenty-First Flash, On Sincerity, p. 214.
[8] *The Flashes*, Twenty-First Flash, On Sincerity, p. 215.
[9] *The Rays*, Ninth Ray, p. 203.
[10] *The Rays*, Thirteenth Ray, p. 343.
[11] *Letters*, Seeds of Reality, p. 548; *The Damascus Sermon*, p. 106.

c. A third aspect of peace studied by Said Nursi is universal peace. Particularly in his rewriting of the Damascus Sermon in the years immediately following the Second World War, he reflects the widespread conviction of the time that humankind can sink no lower in criminality towards its own kind[12] and expresses the longing for a time of peace and prosperity for all.[13] This Said Nursi sees as the specific mission of Islam, that "God willing, through the strength of Islam in the future, the virtues of civilization will prevail, the face of the earth cleaned of filth, and universal peace be secured."[14] He is optimistic that this hope for peace through Islam is no vain desire, but that people may confidently "expect from Divine mercy to see true civilization with universal peace brought about through the sun of the truth of Islam."[15]

It is in his analysis of peace, based on truth, as the only viable alternative to the use of brute force that the thought of Said Nursi prefigures that of Pope John Paul II. Said Nursi notes that wars and violence can never resolve ethical conflicts concerning who is in the right. All that wars and violent actions can accomplish is to show which party has access to reserves of force which it can use to coerce others to obey and to punish the recalcitrant.[16] Truth, on the other hand, is characterized by justice and harmony and seeks goodness and virtue instead of selfish gain.[17]

He sees a tendency in modern governments and rulers, which is relevant for the discussion of globalization as a theme of this symposium. He criticizes modern governments for fomenting a kind of false nationalism, which in reality amounts to a type of racism, by picturing those of another nationality or religion as the enemy against whom war must be waged. Meanwhile, the governments concentrate on providing amusements to gratify the senses and favor consumerist policies to "create needs." The result, he states, is "a sort of superficial happiness for about 20% of mankind and cast 80% into distress and poverty."[18] By contrast, the Qur'an, he states, takes truth rather than force as its starting point. Hence the Qur'an proposes an alternative to the use of force in resolving conflicts, that of negotiation, compromise and uprightness, rather than the employment of brute force with the very limited aim of "winning."

Said Nursi's opposition to war as an inhumane and ultimately useless endeavor was highly controversial in his time, for in any nation all citizens are expected to support whatever wars are decided and carried out by their governments, and anyone opposing war is accused of being disloyal. In fact, ruling parties and cliques have been known to *foment* conflict and war in an

---

[12] *The Damascus Sermon*, p. 29.

[13] *The Damascus Sermon*, p. 43.

[14] *The Damascus Sermon*, p. 38.

[15] *The Damascus Sermon*, p. 39.

[16] *The Words*, Twenty-Fifth Word, First Light, Third Ray, p. 422.

[17] *Letters*, Seeds of Reality, p. 548.

[18] *The Words*, Twenty-Fifth Word, First Light, Third Ray, p. 422.

attempt to increase their popularity and rally support for unpopular or incompetent government. In *The Flashes Collection*, Said Nursi notes that he was often challenged because of his commitment to peace. Critics claimed that war against British and Italian incursions provided an opportunity to revive Islamic zeal and to assert the moral strength of the nation. They charged Said Nursi, who proposed prayers for peace and negotiated settlement as indirectly supporting the invaders' aims.[19]

In response, Said Nursi held that he wanted release from the attacks of aggressors, but not by using the same methods, which the attackers were employing. In other words, he rejected the practice of opposing force by force. Religion teaches people to seek truth and uprightness, not to try to achieve their aims by use of force. In consequence, he felt that the students of the *Risale-i Nur* could better use their time studying the Qur'an than by engaging in military service. Later in his life he was asked whether freely relinquishing one's rights for the sake of peace could not be considered a form of compromise with wrongdoing. Again reflecting on his prison experiences, he responded, "A person who is in the right, is fair. He will sacrifice his one *dirhem*'s worth of right for the general peace, which is worth a hundred."[20]

In the long run, he concludes, the preoccupation with current events and international crises is of secondary importance to seeking the personal, interior transformation of peace that comes through the study of Scripture. Said Nursi carried this principal to an extreme degree, as he recounts: "For a full two years in Kastamonu and seven years in other places I knew nothing of the conflicts and wars in the world, and whether or not peace had been declared, or who else was involved in the fighting. I was not curious about it and did not ask, and for nearly three years did not listen to the radio that was playing close by me. But with the *Risale-i Nur* I triumphantly confronted absolute unbelief, which destroys eternal life, and transforms the life of this world even into compounded pain and suffering."[21]

This attitude, which places a higher value on interior peace, which is based on the study of God's Word than on current events, presents a challenge to modern people for whom the daily newspapers and evening news on television are fixed appointments in their daily schedules. However, when one reflects on the degree to which the news media is slanted by the prejudices, policies and propaganda, not only of individual journalists but also of those who own and direct the communications industry, one can see in Said Nursi's practice the freedom of the honest individual who renounces an obsession with transitory events which will be forgotten in a few years in favor of the search for eternal, unchangeable truth presented in the Word of God.

The irony here is that Said Nursi was often accused of being a troublemaker guilty of disturbing the peace and inciting his followers to revolt. He

---

[19]*The Flashes*, Sixteenth Flash, p. 144.
[20]*The Rays*, Thirteenth Ray, p. 345; *The Flashes*, Twenty-Eighth Flash, p. 362.
[21]*The Rays*, Fourteenth Ray, p. 373.

was accused of "working secretly in Emirdag. He poisoned the minds of some people giving them the idea of disturbing the peace."[22] In defending himself against false accusations of fomenting public disorder, he also defends the students of the Risale-i Nur against similar charges. "In twenty years, six courts of law and the police of ten provinces...have not recorded any incident involving the disturbance of public order and breaching of security in connection with the 20,000 or perhaps 100,000 people who enthusiastically read copies of the *Risale-i Nur*.

He asserts that this reputation of being a troublemaker and rabble-rouser is based on fear of non-religious people for those who take religious faith seriously. "'The worldly' are exceptionally and excessively suspicious of me. Quite simply, they are frightened of me, imagining non-existent things in me, which even if they existed would not constitute a political crime and could not be the basis of accusation, like being a shaykh, or of significant rank or family, or being a tribal leader, and influential, and having numerous followers, or meeting with people from my native region, or being connected with the affairs of the world, or even entering politics, or even the opposition. Imagining these things in me, they have been carried away by groundless fears."[23]

He makes it clear that his silence must not be interpreted as agreement with all decisions made by public officials, but should be understood rather in terms of passive resistance. He states: "I support neither intellectually nor on scholarly grounds the arbitrary commands, called laws, of a commander, which have made Aya Sophia into a house of idols and the Shaykh al-Islam's Office into a girls' high school. And for myself I do not act in accordance with them. But although for twenty years I have been severely oppressed during my tortuous captivity, I have not become involved in politics, nor provoked the authorities, nor disturbed public order. And although I have hundreds of thousands of *Risale-i Nur* friends, not a single incident has been recorded involving the disturbance of the peace."[24] Along with Gandhi and Martin Luther King, Said Nursi must be seen as one of the Twentieth Century's great exponents of non-violent resistance.

4. Peace and Forgiveness

When we turn to the question of the relationship between peace and forgiveness, the similarity of thought between Said Nursi and the later views of Pope John Paul becomes even more striking. He analyzes the nature of wrongdoing. In the case of a crime such as murder, the killer might derive a momentary satisfaction by having taken revenge on his enemy, but he pays for it over and over by suffering the consequences, not only of imprisonment, but of fear of retaliation by the relatives of the murdered person. The result is fear, anger, and anxiety. "There is only one solution for this," states Said Nursi, "and that is reconciliation, which the Qur'an

---

[22] *The Rays*, Fourteenth Ray, p. 447.

[23] *Letters*, Addendum to the Sixteenth Letter, p. 96.

[24] *The Rays*, Fourteenth Ray, p. 417.

commands, and which truth, reality, benefit, humanity, and Islam require and encourage."[25] He notes that Islam commands that "one believer should not be vexed with another believer for more than three days," and that so long as there is no reconciliation, both sides perpetually suffer the torments of fear and revenge." His conclusion is that "it is essential to make peace quickly."

Often a person's unwillingness to forgive arises, according to Said Nursi, from a lack of self-knowledge, a resistance to finding in oneself many of the same qualities that one condemns in the other. If someone is unwilling to confront the defects in ones own attitudes and actions, it is much easier to demonize the other and regard them as an enemy. Said Nursi's advice is to "Look at the defect in your own soul that you do not see or do not wish to see. Deduct a share for that too. As for the small share which then remains, if you respond with forgiveness, pardon, and magnanimity, in such a way as to conquer your enemy swiftly and safely, then you will have escaped all sin and harm."[26] Thus, self-awareness should lead to repentance, repentance to forgiveness, forgiveness to reconciliation and the seeds for a lasting peace are laid.

So long as no reconciliation takes place, the wounds to the human relations fester and grow and turn into resentment. Discord produces more discord, violence engenders even greater violence, and the state of conflict is perpetuated. The only way out of a spiraling succession of violent reactions and counter-reactions is for one party to take the initiative to reconcile. Reconciliation heals what force can never heal, the suspicion and resentment caused by wrongdoing one against another. As Said Nursi puts it, "A minor disaster becomes a large one, and continues. But if they make peace, and the murderer repents and prays continuously for the man he killed, then both sides will gain much and become like brothers. In place of one departed brother, he will gain several religious brothers."

Said Nursi's analysis of peace and reconciliation is very similar to the words of the Pope with which I began this talk: "Forgiveness is a personal choice, a decision to go against the natural instinct to pay back evil with evil. In doing so, it always involves an *apparent* short-term loss, but brings about the possibility of achieving a *real* long-term gain. Violence works exactly the opposite: opting for an apparent short-term gain, but involving a real and permanent loss. Forgiveness may seem like weakness, but it demands great spiritual strength and moral courage." Here we find a strong convergence between these two great religious teachers.

So important is the element of forgiveness in human relations that Said Nursi commands the students of the *Risale-i Nur* to pardon each other's faults speedily. In fact, mutual forgiveness should be a characteristic mark that identifies students of the *Risale-i Nur*. "It is absolutely essential," he states, "that you completely forgive each other. You are brothers closer to each other than the most

[25] *The Rays*, Fourteenth Ray, p. 484.
[26] Letters, Twenty-Second Letter, First Topic, p. 316.

devoted blood brother, and a brother conceals his brother's faults, and forgives and forgets. I do not attribute your uncustomary differences and egotism here to your evil-commanding souls, and I cannot reconcile it with the *Risale-i Nur* students. I rather consider it to be a sort of temporary egotism found even in saints who have given up their souls. So on your part, do not spoil my good opinion through obstinacy, and make peace with each other."[27]

Since the study of the *Risale-i Nur* creates a relationship even closer than that of blood brothers, there is no offence so serious that it should go unforgiven among its students. Said Nursi goes so far as to state, "I swear that if one of you were to insult me most terribly and entirely trample my honor but not give up serving the Qur'an, belief, and the *Risale-i Nur*, I would forgive him and make peace with him and try not to be offended."[28]

Said Nursi sees a relationship between God's abundant forgiveness of the faults of humans and the need for believers to forgive one another. Just as God is generous in forgiving any one who repents, so Said Nursi encourages the students of the *Risale-i Nur* to imitate these Divine qualities by acting with love and forgiveness toward those who wronged them. "Your sincerity, loyalty, and steadfastness are sufficient reason to disregard one another's faults...For the powerful brotherhood within the *Risale-i Nur* is such a good thing it causes one to forgive a thousand evils. Since at the Last Judgement when good deeds will preponderate over evils, Divine justice will forgive, you too, seeing that good deeds preponderate, should act with love and forgiveness."[29]

One must even forgive one's enemies and those who have done them wrong. Said Nursi repeatedly expressed his forgiveness for his prison wardens,[30] judges,[31] government officials,[32] law officers,[33] and civil authorities,[34] who had treated him unjustly during his period of courtroom trials and subsequent imprisonments. His point in forgiving others is that the relationship of enmity created by the wrong done by one person to another can only be overcome and superceded by forgiveness. Otherwise, one becomes a prisoner of circumstances, events, and the deeds of others, and history becomes a string of injustices and retaliations. This chain of evil and violence can only be broken by one who is willing to take the initiative to forgive.

In conclusion, I might mention that according to Said Nursi forgiveness and peace-making should not be limited only to students of the *Risale-i Nur* or, more generally, to fellow Muslims. He argues that members of the People of the Book, Jews and Christians, if they want to make peace, should be allowed to do so.

---

[27] *The Rays*, Thirteenth Ray, p. 369.
[28] *The Rays*, Fourteenth Ray, p. 510.
[29] *The Rays*, Thirteenth Ray, p. 355.
[30] *The Rays*, Fourteenth Ray, p. 487.
[31] *The Rays*, Fourteenth Ray, p. 416.
[32] *The Rays*, Fourteenth Ray, p. 460.
[33] *The Rays*, Fourteenth Ray, p. 416.
[34] *The Rays*, Fourteenth Ray, p. 395.

"A Christian may," he states, "accept some sacred matters and may believe in some of the prophets, and may assent to Almighty God in some respects."[35]

5. A Convergence of Ideas

When I examine the thought of Pope John Paul and that of Said Nursi, I am stuck by the many similarities. Both understand peace to be not only a universal human longing, but also a cornerstone of the Message, which God has revealed to humans. It is not only that humans long for peace, but God desires and intends that men live in peace. Both are convinced that the use of violence and force can never be the truth path to peace. Both hold that societies can succeed only if they are founded on the principles of justice and harmony. Both agree that the cycle of injury and revenge, wrongdoing and retaliation, violence and counter-violence can be broken when people take recourse to forgiveness and pardon. This act, which seems to be a sign of weakness and to result in a short-term loss, is in fact a courageous effort to move beyond past conflicts and establish reconciliation. Both agree that true forgiveness is beyond humankind's unaided resources and is possible only by the guidance and strength that come from God. The human race would certainly be facing a better future if people would heed the advice of these two great moral teachers.

[35]*Letters*, Twenty-Ninth Letter, Seventh Section, p. 512; *The Flashes*, Seventeenth Flash, Seventh Note, p. 168.

Chapter 3

Renewal and Reformation in the Mid-Twentieth Century: Bediuzzaman Said Nursi and Religion in the 1950s*

John Obert Voll

The great changes and transformations of the modern era affect all aspects of human life. In the past two centuries, the experiences of modernity have had an impact on religious faiths and traditions, and religion played and plays an important role in shaping the modern experiences of all peoples. One of the most interesting and crucial times of interactions between religion and modernity is the middle of the twentieth century.

The decade of the 1950s can be viewed as being both a time of the culmination and climax of many "modern" developments and also a time when the first significant signs of the "post-modern" world were beginning to be visible. Some of the major debates involved in modernity were not being resolved so much as they were being transformed into new issues and tensions. In the arena of religious faith and tradition, this tension took many different forms. Some have called this era a time of religious resurgence. This was not, however, an old-fashioned religious revival familiar to Christians in the West in the form of the eighteeth century Great Awakening led by Jonathan Edwards in the English colonies in North America or to Muslims in the form of the eighteenth century movement of Muhammad ibn 'Abd al-Wahhab in the Arabian Peninsula, although there are continuities and similarities. Neither did this mid-century resurgence take the form of the militant and violent revolutionary movements and cults of the late twentieth century, like the Branch Davidians in the U.S. or some of the jihad movements in the Muslim world.

The mid-century resurgence, in contrast, concerned itself more with the issues of faith and social order that were raised intellectually and morally by modern experiences. The resurgence of the 1950s, for example, laid the theological and intellectual foundations in the Christian world for the Second Vatican Ecumenical Council of the Roman Catholic Church, held in the early 1960s, and liberation theology. Although masked by the concurrent rise of nationalist and radical Marxist movements, new intellectual and organizational foundations were being laid in the Islamic, Hindu, and Buddhist traditions for the later transcending of the debates and tensions of modernity.

Many scholars resist the term "post-modern" because of its narrow identification with a particular school of literary criticism and philosophy. However, it is possibly the most helpful term for describing the transformations in the "established modernity" of assembly-line industrialized society and popular Newtonian scientific views of the universe. Major "post-modern" trends have important roots in the developments of the 1950s, and it may be helpful to think of the religious movements of that decade as being a combination of modern and early post-modern in terms of the issues they faced and the solutions they proposed.

Within the Muslim world, the decade of the 1950s was a time of major changes. In many areas, countries were achieving political independence with startling rapidity. The context of the struggle for indendence shaped the nature of religious developments in those states and there was a relatively close identification between religious activism and nationalism. However, some major Muslim states had been independent for longer periods of time and in these states, the most important of which were Turkey, Iran, and Egypt, religious developments tended to take different forms. It is in these societies that the mixture of the modern and post-modern elements is most tangible. Basic issues involved the relationships between the existing "modern" political and intellectual establishments and the emerging Muslim responses to "established" modernity. In Egypt this is most visible in the suppression of the "modernist" Muslim Brotherhood and the beginning of the articulation of a revolutionary new Muslim Brotherhood ideology in the context of Nasser's articulation of a radical Arab socialism. In Iran, developments were tied to the Westernizing reform programs of the ruling monarchy and the increasing identification of that monarchy with the United States as an interfering foreign power. The "modernization establishment" began to be challenged by an increasingly Islamically-oriented opposition after the more secular nationalism of Mosaddeq failed.

Turkey was seen by many observers as experiencing some kind of a religious resurgence during the 1950s.[1] Much of this activity was discussed in terms of the political developments of the time. Following World War II, Turkey had become a multi-party parliamentary republic and religious issues naturally became a more prominent part of the public debates than had been the case previously. The victory of the Democrat Party in the elections of 1950 opened the way for some changes in policies regarding religion. For example, the traditional call to prayer in Arabic (rather than Turkish) was allowed and there was some

---

* Original English text.

[1] Some of the most helpful of the many articles that appeared at the time are Bernard Lewis, "Islamic Revival in Turkey," *International Affairs* 28 (1952), pp. 38-48; Lewis V. Thomas, "Recent Developments in Turkish Islam," *Middle East Journal* 6 (1952), pp. 22-40, Howard A. Reed, "Revival of Islam in Secular Turkey," *Middle East Journal* 8 (1954), pp. 227-282.

expansion of religious education. However there were broader intellectual trends at the time which were not specifically related to partisan politics. A number of Turkish thinkers and spiritual leaders were engaged in the more long-term activities of explaining and rearticulating Islamic principles in the context of the modern, and emerging post-modern, world. Bediuzzaman Said Nursi is one of the important figures in these developments, althoungh he is not very well known outside of Turkey,[2] and the 1950s was the final decade of his life.

Bediuzzaman Said Nursi's life spans much of the history of modern Turkey. He was born in 1877 in eastern Turkey during the last decades of the Ottoman Empire and served in the Ottoman military. Following World War I, "the nationalistic brochures he wrote at the time put him in the good graces of the nationalist government in Ankara. But this prestige dissolved when he reminded the assembly of the nationalist government that their success was not due simply to their own work but was the result of divine intervention."[3] Later, his position as a popular religious teacher made the new reformist government of Mustafa Kemal Atatürk suspicious, and Nursi spent much of his subsequent life in prison or exiled to remote places in Turkey.[4]

Nursi himself divided his life into three periods. In the first phase of his life, he was "the Old Said." He was an active soldier in the Ottoman army as well as an activist student involved in a number of conservative Islamic causes. Describing his intellectual position in that era, Nursi later stated,

> The Old Said together with a group of thinkers accepted in part the principles of human philosophy as opposed to revealed knowledge and European science, and fought them with their own weapons; they admitted to them to a degree. They accepted unshakeably some of their principles in the form of the positive sciences, and thus could not demonstrate the true value of Islam.[5]

The "New Said" emerged at the end of World War I, following his return to Istanbul from Russia, where he had been a prisoner-of-war for a time. He experienced a spiritual awakening in which he recognized the weakness of human philosophies and the need to overcome his own pride and then the challenge to "take the Qur'an as his sole master."[6] As a result he withdew from active involvement in social and political affairs and undertook a project which filled the rest of his life, the writing of the various parts of "the Message of Light" (*Risale-i Nur*). This is a multi-volume life work that combines Qur'anic commentary with

---

[2] A useful analysis of Nursi's life and significance, which has made him better known outside of Turkey, is Serif Mardin, *Religion and Social Change in Modern Turkey* (Albany: State University Press of New York, 1989).

[3] Serif Mardin, "The Nakshibendi Order of Turkey," *Fundamentalisms and the State*, ed. Martin E. Marty, R. Scott Appleby (Chicago: University of Chicago Press, 1993), p. 218.

[4] A detailed account of his life is presented in Sükran Vahide, *Bediuzzaman Said Nursi* (Istanbul: Sözler, 1992).

[5] Quoted in Vahide, pp. 164-165.

[6] Vahide, p. 167.

instruction to his students and followers, whose number grew over the years, despite his imprisonments and exiles.
During the 1950s, Said Nursi entered the time of "The Third Said." The new political context in Turkey during the 1950s made the publication of the *Risale-i Nur* possible and the readers and students of the *Risale-i Nur* became a more cohesive movement. "The main apparent change in Bediuzzaman due to which this period of his life is known as that of the Third Said was a closer involvement with social and political life."[7] This does not mean that Nursi organized a political party or even that his movement, Nurculuk, took on the formal organizational stuctures of a Sufi order. Instead it is "better seen as a faith movement"[8] involving publishing organizations and a variety of groups of people inspired by Nursi's writings.

In the observed religious resurgence of the 1950s, Third Said made important contributions. His ideas had effective appeal to a wide variety of people and dealt with issues that were not simply distinctively Turkish in their implications. An examination of all of the writings of Said Nursi in terms of their coverage of some of the major issues of the transformation of modernity taking place in the 1950s would involve a long and extensive study. However, concentrating on one set of writings, "*The Flashes Collection*," can provide a starting point for such an analysis.[9]

Modernity, Science, and Reason

Thinkers in all of the major world religious traditions faced important challenges and tasks in presenting the truths of their traditions in ways that were effective and persuasive in the modern era. By the late nineteenth century some of the major issues in "coping with modernity" had begun to be clearly defined and aroused major controversies. Probably the most contentious of all of these issues was the definition of the relationship between religious faith and scientific reason. Faith and Reason were often viewed as being in conflict, especially in the philosophical traditions that had emerged as a result of the period known as "The Enlightenment" in Europe. Religious faith was seen by many espousing the "modern" perspective as being an artifact from premodern times. The medieval era was often described as an "age of faith" while the modern era, building on eighteenth century philosophy, was thought of the "age of reason."

---

[7] Vahide, p. 330.

[8] Serif Mardin, "Nurculuk," *The Oxford Eneylopedia of the Modern Islamic World,* ed. John L. Esposito (New York: Oxford University Press, 1995) 3: 256.

[9] For this paper, the following edition of "*The Flashes Collection*" has been used: Bediuzzaman Said Nursi, *The Flashes Collection*, translated by Sükran Vahide (From the *Risale-i Nur* Collection 3; Istanbul: Sözler, 1995). Subsequent references to this work will be cited as *The Flashes Collection*.

The clash between reason and revelation was an important part of the modern awareness of the 1950s. It was clearly presented in an influential book published in 1950 called *The Shaping of Modern Mind* by Crane Brinton.[10] Brinton argued that "much of what men and women of the eighteenth and later centuries believed was incompatible with some very important parts of traditional Christian belief," and that this involved a new cosmology, "the belief that all human beings can attain here on this earth a state of perfection hitherto in the West thought possible only for Christians in a state of grace, and for them only after death."[11] The cornerstone of this new cosmology was a combination of rationalism and modern science. The rationalist, in this context,

> ...not merely banished the supernatural from his universe; he was prepared to place man himself wholly within the framework of nature or 'the material universe' ... Rationalism... owed much of its slowly growing prestige to the achievements of natural science. Finally, when with Newton science succeeded in attaining to a marvelously complete scheme of the universe, one that could be tested mathematically and that worked in a sense that it enabled successful prediction, the stage was set for the new rationalist worldview.[12]

It was this "modern mind" that had come to dominate much of the world by the middle of the twentieth century and it was this "scientific rationalism" which all religious thinkers encountered. The great debates of religious modernism dealt with whether or not a revealed religion could also accept modern rationalism and Newtonian science. Two basic positions developed: Atheistic rationalists and literalist fundamentalists agreed that faith and reason, modern science and "true religion" were not compatible, while all major world religions developed "modernist" schools of thought which sought to show that the religions could be understood in modern terms. The modernists adopted what was basically an apologist position in which they accepted the validity of modernity and then worked to show how their region was in accord with modernity. In the Muslim world, the modernist tradition is strong with the works of intellectuals like Muhammad Abduh in the late nineteenth century.

By the 1950s, the basic issues involved in the "religion versus science" debate had begun to change as the implications of important developments in scientific theory began to filter into the popular mind and the discussions of intellectuals. Werner Heisenberg, one of the most important physicists of the twentieth century, described the evolution of the debate between science and religion in his book *Physics and Philosophy*. He stated that,

> ...the nineteenth century developed an extremely rigid frame for natural science which formed not only science but also the general outlook of the great masses of

---

[10] Crane Brinton, *The Shaping of the Modern Mind* (New York: Mentor Books, 1950).

[11] Brinton, pp. 107-113.

[12] Brinton, pp. 110-111.

> people, ... This frame was so narrow and rigid that it was difficult to find a place in it for many concepts of our language that had always belonged to its very substance, for instance, the concepts of mind, of the human soul or of life. ... [A]n open hostility of science toward religion developed... Confidence in the scientific method and in rational thinking replaced all other safeguards of the human mind.[13]

Heisenberg noted that "the scientific language of Newtonian mechanics... had erroneously been accepted as final" but the old rigid framework was beginning to dissolve in the twentieth century as a result of the impact of the theory of relativity and quantum mechanics.[14] Heisenberg's conclusions were not to insist on a new rigid framework, but to note that while modern science might be disruptive of old cultural patterns as civilizations around the world engage in this new activity, "the openness of modern physics may help to some extent to reconcile the older traditions with the new trends of thought."[15] Although the spread of modern technology may damage old cultural traditions, "since this whole development has for a long time passed far beyond any control by human forces, we have to accept it as one of the most essential features of our time and *must try to connect it as much as possible with the human values that have been the aim of the older cultural and religious traditions*."[16]

This endeavor described by Heisenberg represents the new tone of the debates of the 1950s and provides a dimension for understanding the impact of Said Nursi. The old "modern" debates involved trying to show whether or not science "disproved" religion, where as the new (early "post-modern") effort involved working to see connections between science and religion, and viewing "science" and "religion" both as parts of our natural language. Nursi's biographer tells of an incident which reflects the different modes of debate. In the mid-1950s, an "English orientalist" came to Istanbul and gave a lecture in which he said that the Qur'anic verses which speak of the "seven heavens" show that the Qur'an is contrary to science because modern astronomy shows that there are not seven heavens in space. Two students of Nursi were in the audience and they asked their teacher about this. Nursi wrote a letter based on selections from the *Risale-i Nur*, which his students duplicated and distributed the next day at the orientalist's lecture. According to the biography, the letter "was read to the orientalist, who as a result cut short his lecture that day and abandoned his remaining ones."[17]

This incident is interesting for many reasons, not the least of which was the nature of the debate. The "English orientalist" was clearly debating in the old mode of "modern" disputation, using modern science to "refute" the clams of a revealed scripture. In this kind of debate, the so-called scientist and the old-

[13] Werner Heisenberg, *Physics and Philosophy: The Revolution in Modern Science* (New York: Harper & Row, 1958), pp. 197-198.
[14] Heisenberg, pp. 198-199.
[15] Heisenberg, p. 202.
[16] Heisenberg, pp. 202-203 (Emphasis added).
[17] Vahide, p. 346.

fashioned fundamentalist agree on the need for a literalist interpretation of the scripture. Bediuzzaman's response was not in this old format. The letter he gave to his students probably included material in "*The Flashes Collection*," dealing with specifically the question of how to understand the meaning of the seven heavens. Put succinctly, Bediuzzaman begins his analysis by stating, "since the sciences of geography and astronomy have been unable to ascend to the heavens of the Qur'an with their abbreviated laws and narrow principles and tiny scales, and since they have been unable to discover the seven levels of meanings in the stars of its verses, they have criticized the verse, and foolishly even tried to deny it."[18] Nursi put the debate into terms of trying to understand "levels of meaning" rather than "proving" specifics literally. In his explanation, he emphasizes this, noting that "the verse's meaning is one thing and the parts of the meaning and points confirming it, another," and speaks of "the universal meaning concerning the seven levels of the heavens."[19]

Bediuzzaman further structured his explanation in terms of a theme that appears regularly in his teaching, utilizing a "middle way." In this case, he explained,

> Former philosophy conceived of the heavens as nine: accepting in the *tongue of the Sharia* Throne of God and Seat of God together with the seven heavens, they depicted the heavens in a strange manner. The glittering terms of the brilliant philosophers of that time held mankind under their sway for many centuries... As for the new philosophy, called modern philosophy, in the face of the excesses of ancient philosophy about the heavens, it went to the other extreme and quite simply denied the existence of the heavens... As for the sacred wisdom of the All-Wise Qur'an, it left aside such excess and negligence, and choosing the middle way said that the All-Glorious Maker created the seven levels of the heavens.[20]

Bediuzzaman then went on to say that put this way, different people can understand the verses in ways that are appropriate to their levels of understanding.

> Yes, the breadth of *the Qur'anic address* and the comprehensiveness of its meanings and indications and its conforming to and flattering all the degrees of understanding from the most uneducated common people to the highest of the elite shows that all its verses have an aspect which looks to each class. Thus, as a consequence of this mystery, as an example, seven classes of men understand of follows the meaning of seven various levels from the universal meaning of 'seven heavens.[21]

Nursi then discussed different ways that "seven heavens" can be understood, and concluded that a "particular event which is not literally true but is commonly

---

[18] *The Flashes Collection*, p. 97.

[19] *The Flashes Collection*, p. 97.

[20] *The Flashes Collection*, p. 99 (Emphasis added).

[21] *The Flashes Collection*, p. 101 (Emphasis added).

accepted may be included in the universal meaning in order to conform to the generally held ideas."[22]

This example provides an illustration of Nursi's effort to synthesize science and religion. During the 1950s, he wrote a group of letters which were the last pieces to be added to the *Risale-i Nur* collection. These letters, as his biography states, "illustrate further one of the most important aspects of the *Risale-i Nur*, its relating science to the truths of belief... and its showing that rather than their conflicting in any way, if considered in the light of the Qur'an science may broaden and strengthen belief."[23] However, as the discussion of the "seven heavens" verses shows, the relationship between science and religion is not viewed in the terms of the "modern" controversies and debates, where rationalist literalism argued with fundamentalist literalism. Instead, Bediuzzaman spoke in terms of the "breadth of the Qur'anic address" and the "tongue of the *Sharia*," as well as different understandings depending upon time, place, and social location. While this was not specifically presented in terms of a hermeneutic analysis, it is clearly part of the powerful post-modern mode that was emerging in the 1950s rather than being a repetition of the old arguments framed in terms of the "modern" discourse of the battle between science and religion.

Moderation and the Middle Way

In the middle of the twentieth century, many of the most visible aspects of society and world affairs involved competing polarities, with two clearly opposing positions in conflict. On the global level, the Cold War competition between the United States and the Soviet Union, West against East, Capitalism against Communism, set the frame of reference for many dimensions of life. The decade of the 1950s witnessed the emergence to major prominence of the wars of national liberation and social revolution. A prominent political scientist, Harold Lasswell, wrote at that time, "That our epoch is a time of revolutionary change on a global scale is no longer in dispute. We disagree only when the issue is the specific nature of the revolution."[24] It was, to use the words of a widely-read book of the time, the era of "the True Believer." Eric Hoffer wrote in 1951, "It is necessary for most of us these days to have some insight into the motives and responses of the true believer. For though ours is a godless age, it is the very opposite of irreligious. The true believer is everywhere on the march, and both by converting and antagonizing he is shaping the world in his own image."[25] In this analysis, the "true believer"

---

[22] *The Flashes Collection*, p. 102.

[23] Vahide, p. 336.

[24] Harold D. Lasswell, "The World Revolution of Our Time," (Essay originally published in 1951 by Stanford University Press) *in World Revolutionary Elites: Studies in Coercive Ideological Movements*, ed. Harold D. Lasswell and Daniel Lerner (Cambridge: The M.I.T. Press, 1965), p. 29.

[25] Eric Hoffer, *The True Believer: Thoughts on the Nature of Mass Movements* (Perennial Library Edition, 1966; New York: Harper Brothers, 1951), p. 10.

was the absolutist fanatic who was viewed as the necessary key for a successful mass movement. "Those who would transform a nation or the world cannot do so by... demonstrating the reasonableness and desirability of the intended changes or by coercing people into a new way of life. They must know how to kindle and fan an extravagant hope."[26]

The great revolutions of the time emphasized the importance of separate and competing groups and peoples. Even when major revolutions based themselves on ideologies of the rising of "global" groups, as seen in the Marxist revolutionary ideologies based on "the uniquely universalist role of the proletariat," it has been observed that "all revolutions which succeed in the twentieth century succeed by establishing a government of a nation state in a world of other nation states."[27] In many ways, the revolutionary conflicts of the twentieth century, as reflected in the wars at mid-century, were a climax of the modern. The nation state was and is the manifestation of political modernity. In the middle of the twentieth century, the processes of "modernization" were frequently associated conceptually with "nation-building." While nation states could work together, the nationalist and revolutionary "true believers" were a prominent part of states and societies around the world. The decade of the 1950s was a time of highly visible extremism. Nationalism and revolution, exclusivism and modern warfare, were (and are) manifestations of the processes of global modernization during the twentieth century. At the same time, there were profound movements that were also visible, which went beyond these. Just as in the natural sciences, where Einstein and Heisenberg transcended Newtonian physics, in politics and religion there were similar important changes. F.S.C. Northrop noted at the time that the "twentieth century opened with Einstein's and Planck's surprising reconstructions of man's conceptions of nature. It reached its midpoint with a similar reformation in both domestic and international politics. Less publicized, but equally significant, are comparable changes in religion."[28] In terms of religious development, Northrop noted that "comparative religion and mutual respect among the world's religions born of sympathetic understanding from within, rather than missionary zeal from without, have become of the essence. It is not an accident, therefore, that the most novel religious characteristic at mid-century is its ecumenical mentality."[29] In many ways, this perspective was a move away from the militancy of literalist fundamentalism in favor of moderation and a middle way, combining conviction with toleration. This reflects the beginnings of the post-modern awareness of the importance of accepting pluralism and rejecting militant exclusivism.

---

26 Hoffer, p. 18.

27 John Dunn, *Modern Revolutions* (2nd ed.; Cambridge: Cambridge University Press, 1989) p. xii.

28 F.S.C. Northrop, "The World's Religions at Mid-century: An Introductory Essay," in *Religions and the Promise of the Twentieth Century*, ed. Guy S. Metraux and Francois Crouzet (New York: New American library, 1965), p. xiv.

29 Northrop, p. xv.

In this world, Said Nursi was not a "true believer" in Hoffer's sense of the word. He was, instead, a committed believer in Islam as the "middle way." Bediuzzaman's approach to bringing together science and religion rather than viewing them as competing opposites was characteristic of his broader approach to issues of faith and practice in the modern context. In his writings and teachings there is a repetition of the theme that Islam is a middle way, a path of moderation rather than extremism. This represented an important expression of the theme in world religions at mid-century discussed by Northrop.

Nursi frequently would discuss two opposing positions and then define the truly Islamic way as the middle way between the two. Even in the contentious issues involving Sunni and Shi'i Islamic traditions this was his approach. In his discussion of Sunni and Shi'i differences, he concludes:

> Too much or too little of anything is not good. Moderation is the middle way... O Sunnis, who are the People of Truth, and 'Alawis, whose way is love of the Prophet's family! Quickly put an end to this meaningless, disloyal, unjust, and harmful dispute between you... Since you are believers in Divine Unity, it is essential to leave aside unimportant matters which necessitate division while there are a hundred fundamental sacred bonds between you which command brotherhood and unity.[30]

Similarly, Nursi did not fit into the "modern" pattern of a leader of a revolutionary mass movement as defined either by Hoffer or Laswell. He emphasized the reasonableness of Islam's message and spoke in many different contexts about moderation as a major expectation of Islam. In a discussion of the Prophet Muhammad as a model for behavior, for example, he wrote,

> Since the Noble Prophet (Upon whom be blessings and peace) was created with a most moderate character and in the most perfect form, his actions and rest all proceeded on moderation and equanimity... In all his Practices, daily conduct, and injunctions of his *Sharia*, he chose the way of moderation and avoided excess and negligence.[31]

Nursi's approach also reflects the emerging post-modern ecumenical mood described by Northrop in terms of an openness to diversity and some pluralism. Nursi was not frequently in a position to engage in interfaith relations with non-Muslims and this was not a highly visible part of his vision or mission. He was, however, aware of the importance of developing ecumenical relations and visited the Greek Orthodox Patriarch in Istanbul in 1953. In broader terms, "although Bediuzzaman always upheld and struggled for the independence of the Islamic world against the West and the maintenance of its cultural integrity, he foresaw the co-operation of Islam and sincere Christians in the face of aggressive

---

[30] *The Flashes Collection*, p. 43.
[31] *The Flashes Collection*, pp. 92-93.

atheism."[32] In this context, discussing a major political policy, he wrote a letter of strong support for Turkish involvement in the Baghdad Pact, which allied Turkey with other Muslim countries and major Chiristian states against the Communist bloc.[33]

The concept of alliance with Christians to fight atheism is in many ways a continuation of older attitudes and is not a major manifestation of acceptance of pluralism. However, Bediuzzaman was relatively pluralistic in terms of methods and approaches to interpretation. Post-modern thought is frequently accused of being relativistic and accepting the conclusion that there is no truth. While that is true of some post-modern thinkers, an acceptance of the reality and legitimacy of pluralism and diversity of opinion is not relativism. The modern conviction of the possibility of discovering and proving an absolute scientific truth is in contrast to extreme post-modern relativism. However, there are "middle ways" between these extremes, and Said Nursi provides an example of one of these ways.

In terms of Qur'anic commentary, Said Nursi argues that the verses of the Qur'an reflect the vastness of God's message and depths of meanings.

> As the Qur'an of Miraculous Exposition expresses truths through its explicit, clear meanings and senses, so it expresses many allusive meanings through its styles and forms. Each of its verses contains numerous levels of meanings. Since the Qur'an proceeds from all-encompassing knowledge, all its meanings may be intended. It cannot be restricted to one or two meanings like man's speech, the product of his limited mind and individual will. It is because of this that innumerable truths contained in the Qur'an's verses have been expounded by Qur'anic commentators, and there are many more which have not been expounded by them.[34]

This openness to many different levels of understanding reflects a pluralism that is not a relativist position, but rather emphasizes the importance of the role of the individual in the interpretation. The carefully balanced, pluralistic affirmation of truth is clearly presented by Bediuzzaman in a discussion on sincerity:

> [I]f Obstinacy and egoism are present one will imagine himself to be right and the other to be wrong; discord and rivalry take the place of concord and love... Now the only remedy for the critical consequences of this awesome state consists of Nine Commands: ... 3. To adopt the just rule of conduct that the follower of any right outlook has the right to say, 'My outlook is true, or the best,' but not that 'My outlook alone is true,' or that 'My outlook alone is good,' thus implying the falsity or repugnance of all other outlooks.[35]

---

[32] Vahide, p. 344.
[33] Vahide, pp. 353-354.
[34] *The Flashes Collection*, p. 51.
[35] *The Flashes Collection*, p. 203.

This position reflects a middle way that is neither relativist nor absolutist in its approach to the diversity of the ways that people can comprehend truth. In this perspective, God's revelation presents truth to all people, but, because of their different capacities, times, and contexts, they will understand that truth in different ways. The "Qur'an contains allegories and comparisons, and by means of them teaches most profound matters to the ordinary people."[36] However, on "comparisons and metaphors passing from the elite to the common people, that is on their falling from the hands of learning to those of ignorance, with the passage of time they are imagined to be literally true."[37] Bediuzzaman gave as an example the older popular belief that the earth rests on a bull and a fish, while modern astronomy teaches that it hangs in space. The fact that the bull and fish imagery are part of an important metaphor rather than being understood as literally existing, in no way shows that the Qur'an or Hadith are somehow in error; it simply emphasizes the variety of ways that the truth can be envisioned.[38]

With this type of approach, Bediuzzaman might be seen as reflecting an early style of "post-modern" religious thinking which responds to the "anti-metaphysical propensities within modernist thought and culture" but in a manner that is more in the mode of what has been called the "metaphoric post-modern" rather than the "analytic post-modern."[39] Like most of the religious thinkers of the 1950s who were beginning the process of going beyond the constraints of "modern" thought Bediuzzaman was not a fully "post-modern" or pluralist thinker. He clearly viewed the world and worldviews through an explicitly Islamic perspective, in much the same way that the pluralism of the Roman Catholic scholar Karl Rahner viewed religious pluralism through the conceptual framework of "anonymous Christianity." However, in both cases, this was a significant step beyond the exclusivist categories of the modern fundamentalist and missionary visions, and was firmly presented in terms of moderation and Islam as the middle way.

The Turkish Context of the 1950s

Turkey, like many other parts of the world, was experiencing significant transition in the 1950s. This was particularly so in the fields of economics, international affairs, and politics, with the successful emergence of multi-party politics by the 1950 election. Most observers also indentified religion as a major area of development and transition. The decade from 1950 to 1960 was, in political terms, the period of government control by the Democratic Party, and evaluations of this

---

[36] *The Flashes Collection*, p. 129.

[37] *The Flashes Collection*, p. 128.

[38] This issue is fully discussed in "The Fourteenth Flash," *The Flashes Collection*, pp. 127-132.

[39] Carl Raschke, "Fire and roses, or the problem of postmodern religious thinking," in *Shadow of Spirit: Postmodernism and Religion*, ed. Philippa Berry and Andrew Wernick (London: Routledge, 1992) pp. 101-102.

era saw religious issues as crucial in the history of the time. One study of the revolution of 1960, which brought an end to the Democratic Party rule, for example, affirmed,

> There will be arguments in Turkey for many years about whether the Democratic party period was one of the betrayal of secularism, the exploitation of religion, the restoration of freedom of worship, or the beginning of a new period of 'modernized Islam'.[40]

In the late 1950s, Wilfred Cantwell Smith wrote an influential study of the Islamic experience in the modern era. He described the Turkish experience as being the most successful in the Muslim world in adapting to modernity. The "Turks are the only Muslim people in the modern world who know what they want. Theirs is the only Muslim nation that has evolved intellectual and social foundations that in the main they can and do regard as substantially adequate to modernity."[41] This Turkish experience was seen by Smith, and many others, in the context of the contrasting but complementary efforts of "renascence" and "reformation." The contrast is between "the reviving of an ancient reality that has lapsed (renascence), and the modifying of an existing one that has gone wrong (reformation)."[42] Observers at the time spoke frequently of the Turkish "reformation," involving both the affirmation of liberal secularism and the visible reaffirmation of Islamic identity visible in the 1950s. This issue in the minds of many was whether or not the primary religious developments would be in the direction of increased efforts to revive an older orthodoxy or in the direction of defining an Islamic reformation involving a new and Turkish version of Islamic modernism.[43] The basic context was seen by most people as being a stage in the process of, as well as response to, modernization.

There were, however, indications that some more profound transformations were taking place. Some of the conflicts in the 1950s between the government and Muslim "revivalist" groups could clearly be viewed in terms of the old context of modernization and reactionary, old-fashioned responses. This was the case, for example, with incidents involving the Tijaniyyah order.[44] However it was also possible to begin to see developments that transcended the old tensions between modernity and reaction. The older generations of conservative Muslim leaders in the provincial towns and rural areas were dying off and the products of the new schools that had been established to train mosque leaders were

---

[40] Walter F. Weiker, *The Turkish Revolution, 1960-1961* (Washington: The Brookings Institution, 1963), p. 9.
[41] Wilfred Cantwell Smith, *Islam in Modern History* (Princeton: Princeton University Press, 1957), p. 163.
[42] Smith, *Islam*, p. 170.
[43] Smith, *Islam*, pp. 189-190.
[44] See for example, the discussion in Lewis Thomas, "Recent Developments," pp. 22-23.

beginning to have an impact on local religious life. The force of reactionary Muslim revivalism was significantly weakened.

Richard Robinson, a well-informed observer of the time, defined the emerging religious mood, contrasting it with the older, revivalist Muslim mood:

> By 1960, despite a religiously conservative element of politically significant size, it no longer endangered the secular republican state. Islam itself had been undergoing a subtle transformation even on the village level. Economic incentive, material well-being, innovation, the machine, commerce, and social change no longer appeared as challenges to religion. A village in the process of building a 100,000 lira mosque was, I found, likewise proud of its neat, well-attended secular school... The new mosque did not, in this community, at least, represent religious reaction, for the villagers talked incessantly of the material improvements in their lives and of those soon to come. And yet the casual observer might have seen only the new mosque and automatically equated this with renewed interest in traditional folk Islam. But he would have been wrong. An accommodation between folk Islam and modern life was in fact taking place.[45]

Bediuzzaman was part of this society in a distinctive and important way. He was not part of the reactionary rearguard who continued to be opposed to modernization. Neither was he a part of the reformist intellectual elite identified by W.C. Smith as being "liberal modernists." Like the villagers described by Robinson, Bediuzzaman was neither, in Smith's terms, striving for a revivalist "renascence" nor for a modernist "reformation." A new "middle way" was emerging which was not so much mired in the old arguments of the advocates and opponents of "modernization" as it was intent on building on existing foundations and then going beyond them to what might later be thought of as a "post-modern" future. The terms "renascence" and "reformation" both reflect movements that took place within the broader context of "the modern," while the 1950s saw the inception of movements that transcend the modern. In much of what Bediuzzaman wrote, one can see his articulation of such a post-modern "middle way" for the Islamic faith.

In global terms, Bediuzzaman was part of long term transformations which were visible in the middle of the twentieth century. This transformation involved the movement from "modern" to "post-modern," with the latter, even by the end of the century still representing only an unclearly defined transitional phase. In discussions of religious transition, it is useful to note how one scholar distinguishes between "religion" and "paradigm." A paradigm is a "total constellation of conscious-unconscious convictions, values, and patterns of behavior," and religion "is not only a conscious-unconscious basic model of the world, society, religion, and the Church; it is in the context of such models, a

---

[45] Richard D. Robinson, *The First Turkish Republic: A Case Study in National Development* (Cambridge: Harvard University Press, 1963), p. 205.

consciously believing view of life."[46] Seen in this perspective, the middle of the twentieth century was a time of transition from the paradigm that had developed as the "Modern Enlightenment" paradigm to an emerging "post-modern" paradigm defined by a more pluralist perspective and a hermeneutical approach to issues of theology. Bediuzzaman's "middle way" is in some important ways a reflection of this transition. It is not so much a part of the debates *within* the older "Modern Enlightenment" paradigm between the secularists and reactionary traditionalists as it is the beginning of the definition of a new, post-modern Islamic paradigm.

---

[46] Hans Küng, *Theology for the Third Millennium*, Trans. Peter Heinegg (New York: Doubleday, 1988), pp. 211-212.

PART II
ETHICS AND DIALOGUE

Chapter 4

Secular or Religious Foundations for Ethics: A Case Study of Bediuzzaman Said Nursi

Ian S. Markham

For many in the West, it is just 'obvious' that a secular basis for ethics is preferential to a religious one. Precisely because the secular does not assume a religious vantage point, many argue, it is the only basis that can accommodate pluralism effectively. Although it is true that an adequate ethic must safeguard pluralism, there are increasing numbers of theologians and scholars who believe that it is not best done in a non-religious (or secular) way. One illustration is Bediuzzaman Said Nursi (1876-1960), the Turkish Islamic thinker, who offers a deeply religious ethic, which is committed to pluralism and conversation.

In this chapter, we shall start by identifying the key aspects of the secular basis for ethics. We then shall contrast this with the ethic found in the writings of Beduizzaman Said Nursi. The ethical system of Nursi will be explored under six headings. These aspects are (a) source, (b) method, (c) approach to disagreement and pluralism, (d) personal ethics, (e) social ethics, and (f) factors that can corrupt a moral disposition. I shall demonstrate that there are problems with a secular foundation for ethics, which include the fact that most deeply committed religious people will not be able to accept the secular assumptions. So instead of requiring all religious people to become semi-secular in outlook, we should instead strive for a 'tradition-constituted' justification for ethics. In other words, we need deeply committed, orthodox, exponents of each tradition to outline an ethical system that is both true to the beliefs and practices of that tradition and, at the same time, affirming of pluralism and diversity. In my view, for Islam, Said Nursi provides the perfect example of this.

The Secular Basis for Ethics

The word 'secular' has different meanings in different contexts. For many in Islamic countries, it means 'non-observant' or 'non-practicing'. These secular Muslims often do believe in God and accept the authority of the Qur'an, but they are not participating in daily prayers or perhaps observing the food laws. This is not the meaning in this chapter. Here it describes the philosophical traditions that emerged from the Enlightenment and gave birth to a certain set of ethical distinctions that have proved important for the ordering of society in many European countries and in the United States. Due to the complexity of these post-Enlightenment traditions, it is difficult to describe briefly those traditions. So while recognizing that much more could be said, for the purposes of this chapter, I shall concentrate on three post-Enlightenment traditions.

The first tradition is the claim that there are adequate non-religious alternative foundations for ethics. This is what Alasdair MacIntyre called the 'Enlightenment project'.[1] With the rejection of religious authority, the Enlightenment started to search for an alternative foundation. Kant argued for reason, while Hume suggested the passions. Whether or not these philosophers were successful, they did feed a widespread secular assumption that morality does not need religion. Indeed building on the commitment of the Renaissance to humanism, some secular theorists have argued that religion can obscure the necessary ethical priority that should be placed on human well-being.[2]

The second tradition is the tendency of much post-Enlightenment thought toward epistemological agnosticism.[3] By epistemological agnosticism, I mean the view that states that there is no way of knowing the truth about metaphysics. Descartes is normally given the credit for making the issue of epistemology central for the Enlightenment, while Hume, it is claimed, showed the problem of epistemology was irresolvable. Kant followed Hume by trying to distinguish between 'scientific' knowledge (about which we can have confidence) and metaphysics (about which we have to acknowledge the almost insurmountable difficulties). For many who are shaped by the western liberal tradition of John Locke and John Stuart Mill, the main argument for toleration and pluralism is this epistemological agnosticism or metaphysical uncertainty.[4] So in Mill one finds the implication that given we are no longer sure about our religious truths, it is absurd to insist on imposing our views on others.[5] The outcome of all this is that the secular starts from a presumption that any certainty in religion is impossible. No one can know, the argument goes, whether there is an ultimate reality – let alone the nature of that reality.

For the secularist, if we cannot be sure about religion, then the presumption becomes that religion should matter less. Furthermore there is no

---

[1] See Alasdair MacIntyre, *After Virtue* Second Edition (London: Duckworth 1985).

[2] For a good example of this, see Bertrand Russell, *Mysticism and Logic* (London: Longman 1919).

[3] The term 'epistemological agnosticism' was used by John Hick in *Faith and Knowledge* (London: Fount 1957) to describe Pascal's starting point for his Wager.

[4] It is important to stress that I am talking about the liberal tradition as it *evolved* from Locke. There is in Locke a strong commitment to theism. For more on this see my *Plurality and Christian Ethics*, (Cambridge: Cambridge University Press 1994).

[5] See John Stuart Mill, *On Liberty* (Harmondsworth: Penguin 1974).

entitlement to impose your uncertain beliefs on someone else. So epistemological agnosticism is a key aspect for the secular foundation for ethics.

The third tradition is the distinction made between the public and private realms. It was John Locke who perhaps was the clearest proponent of this distinction. In his *Letter Concerning Toleration*, published in 1689, and his *Two Treatise of Government*, Locke explained that it is possible for the State to tolerate the private beliefs and practices of groups that do not affect public policy. For Locke, dissenters (i.e. Baptists and the like) could be tolerated, but not Roman Catholics or atheists. The Baptists were not a threat to the state – letting them meet in their own churches would not undermine society. The latter was a problem because Roman Catholics acknowledged the sovereignty of a foreign power and atheists cannot be trusted. Now granted, outlawing atheists does not sound secular, but Locke is secular when suggesting that the State should only worry about the public realm. In the private lives of its citizens, the beliefs and practices should not be controlled. But the public square, to use the famous phrase of Richard John Neuhaus, the space should be neutral and value free. No one should be allowed to give expression to particular beliefs in the public square because those that disagree would want to do the same and public disorder would ensue.

Now as already noted at the start of this chapter, these three traditions that underpin secularism have been widely attacked by theologians and philosophers in the west. Probably Alasdair MacIntyre's classic *After Virtue* did the most damage. He undermined very effectively the first two arguments of the Enlightenment secularists. The thesis of the book was simple: moral discourse emerged in an age when faith made sense. Without this framework of tradition, and in particular the tradition of the virtues, the language of morality makes no sense. He starts his book with a famous thought exercise, where he imagines a reaction against science that leads to the destruction of all scientific discourse (books are burnt and laboratories are destroyed). He then further imagines centuries later scientific language is still being used but instead of describing the way things are, the words are used to describe attitudes. This is what western culture did to moral discourse. MacIntyre completely rejects the claim of post-Enlightenment thinkers to find an alternative secular foundation for ethics. Hume, Kant, and Kierkegaard, explains MacIntyre, all tried to find an alternative foundation for ethics and all failed. Hume suggested the passions; Kant suggested reason; and Kierkegaard suggested criterionless fundamental choice. Each author, in order to sustain his case, had to provide negative arguments against the others. The result, explained MacIntyre, is as follows:

> The project of providing a rational vindication of morality had decisively failed; and from henceforward the morality of our predecessor culture – and subsequently of our own – lacked any public, shared rationale or justification. In a world of secular rationality religion could no longer provide such a shared background and foundation for moral discourse and action; and the failure of philosophy to provide what religion could no longer furnish was an important cause of

> philosophy losing its central cultural role and becoming a marginal, narrowly academic subject.[6]

MacIntyre believes that all we now possess 'are the fragments of a conceptual scheme, parts which now lack those contexts from which their significance derived.'[7] We are still using moral words, but they no longer make any sense for us. We have lost the framework that makes them intelligible.

For the West, the task for MacIntyre is to rediscover Aristotle. It is, says MacIntyre, a straight choice between Aristotle of Nietzsche. Aristotle would be the decision to locate our moral assertions in an intelligible framework that makes sense of moral discourse. Nietzsche would be the recognition that a secular framework for morality has failed and therefore moral terminology – as traditionally understood – is no longer binding on us. This is the choice for the West.

MacIntyre's sequel *Whose Justice? Which Rationality?* attacked the epistemological agnosticism of the Enlightenment. It was, he explained, built on an absurdity that no other age or tradition required. The absurdity was the expectation that all knowledge must be derived from an unquestionable certainty. To set this as the benchmark for knowledge makes knowledge impossible to obtain. Disregarding metaphysics for a moment, the sciences cannot meet this expectation. We can always find reasons to question our senses – we might be dreaming or we may be in a middle of the film *The Matrix*. We can never be sure therefore, according to Enlightenment expectations for knowledge, we do not have any knowledge. The mistake, MacIntyre explains, is to set this absurd expectation for knowledge. Instead of requiring conceptual certainty, we need to recognize the tradition-constituted nature of all knowledge. The purpose of the traditions that we all occupy (be it secular, Catholic, Protestant, Sunni or whatever) is to make sense of the complexity of the world. And we compare different traditions by learning to live inside two simultaneously and comparing the result in terms of explanatory power and coherence. As we do so, we can then decide between traditions. MacIntyre has very effectively exposed the problems with the Enlightenment's commitment to epistemological agnosticism and the quest for a post-Enlightenment alternative to a religious basis for ethics.

On the back of MacIntyre others have joined the fray. Richard John Neuhaus exposed the problems with the public/private distinction. This is, he explains, tantamount to a naked public square.[8] The agnostics triumph by default. All the people of faith are prohibited from making moral arguments for positions. It is undemocratic because the majority of people might want a moral dimension to their public life. And it is dangerous because moral factors should (and in practice – do) shape our public life. The basic commitment to decency in our public discourse is a moral judgment that the public square needs.

---

[6] Alasdair MacIntyre, *After Virtue* Second Edition (London: Duckworth 1985), p. 50.
[7] Ibid. p. 2.
[8] See Richard John Neuhaus, *The Naked Public Square* (Grand Rapids: Eerdmans 1984).

So it is clear that a secular justification for ethics is in trouble. It is not just in trouble conceptually but sociologically. As Grace Davie, the sociologist of religion, has shown religion is as strong as ever.[9]

However, the secular concern that any alternative must accommodate pluralism effectively is a legitimate one. So as we turn to the Said Nursi case study, we shall now examine his ethical approach and see to what extent he can safeguard pluralism.

Said Nursi is, in my view, one of the most interesting and innovative Islamic thinkers of the 20th century. During his lifetime, he saw the demise of the Ottoman Empire and the emergence of an aggressive secularism in Turkey. As such, he reflected in a very creative way on how best to interpret Islam in this secular setting. It is for this reason he is the perfect case study for this chapter.

The Ethical System of the *Risale-i Nur*

As already noted, my description of his ethical system is organized under six headings. These are (a) source, (b) method, (c) approach to disagreement and pluralism, (d) personal ethics, (e) social ethics, and (f) factors that can corrupt a moral disposition.

Source

Unlike the secular approach to ethics, which wants to reduce the significance of religion, Nursi insists that a religious foundation is essential. For Nursi, the ultimate source of all ethical reflection is the Qur'an. Nursi believes that the ethical teaching of the Qur'an – its plain commonsense and wisdom – is one of the primary evidence for its value and truth. So Nursi writes, 'Indeed, since the Qur'an's principles and laws have from pre-eternity, they shall go to post-eternity. They are not condemned to grow old and die like civilization's laws.'[10] We can have confidence in the wisdom of the Qur'an because of its timeless quality. Indeed the impact of the Qur'an is so great, that he uses a *reductio ad absurdum* argument to defend its divine origin. After noting how the 'common people' cannot help but admit that the Qur'an is totally different from any other book, he explains:

> The Qur'an, then, is of a degree either above all of them or below all of them. To be below them is impossible, and no enemy nor the Devil even could accept it. In which case, the Qur'an is above all other books, and is therefore a miracle. Therefore, the Qur'an is the Word of the Creator of the universe. Because there is no point between the two; it is impossible and precluded that there should be.[11]

---

[9] See Grace Davie, *Europe: The Exceptional Case* (London: Darton, Longman, and Todd 2002).

[10] Said Nursi, "Twenty-Fifth Word" in *The Words*. From vol. 1 of the *Risale-I- Nur* Collection, p. 421.

[11] Ibid, 'The Addendum to the Fifteenth Word', p. 204.

The second source for Nursi's ethics is the life of the prophet Muhammad. When identifying the seven reasons why Muhammad ascends into heaven, the fifth explains that:

> Anyone who considers the facts and is fair and just cannot hesitate to agree that, as is unanimously agreed by friend and foe alike, good moral qualities were to be found at the highest degree in his personality, and that, in accordance with the testimony of all his dealings and actions, attributes and character of the greatest excellence were apparent in the way he performed his duties and proclaimed Islam, and, in accordance with the fine qualities and conduct enjoined by the religion of Islam, laudable virtues of the highest order were to be found in the law he brought.[12]

For Nursi, these sources, of which, of course, the Qur'an is primary, provide a means by which we can know what the Creator is requiring of us.

So unlike the secularist, Nursi is a moral realist (i.e. there are moral truths that we can discover). He would not have any sympathy with a 'cultural relativist' or a 'subjectivist', who believes that the ethical is a matter of invention or cultural evolution. For Nursi, it is a duty of all humanity to seek the truth in ethics. In addition, he believed that there are strong arguments for the Qur'an as the primary source and the life of Muhammad as a shining example of a life lived obedient to the will of God. He is uncompromising in this. In this respect any traditional Muslim should be able to identify with the starting point of his ethical system.

Method

Nursi's basic ethical methodology is simple. To discover the truth in ethics (i.e. what the creator intended for us) we should study the Qur'an and apply its moral insights to our situation. Frequently in the *Risale-i-Nur*, Nursi takes a verse of the Qur'an and explores its ethical implications. The 'Twenty-Fourth Flash', for example, takes Sura 33 verse 59: 'O Prophet! Tell your wives and daughters, and the believing women, that they should cast their outer garments over their persons.' He then identifies four reasons why the veil is a wise ethical injunction. First, Nursi explains, the veil protects the feelings of those who are less attractive than others. The second is that the veil ensures that the marriage (an eternal institution) is the place where beauty is shared and celebrated. Third, the veil reduces the male propensity to lust and therefore reduces the chances of infidelity. And the last reason, which is linked to the third, is that the veil encourages sexual expectations that are appropriate to martial commitment and childrearing because immodest attire does not provoke excessive sexual appetite.[13]

---

[12] Ibid. p. 603.

[13] See 'The Twenty-Fourth Flash' in *The Flashes Collection*. From vol. 3 of the *Risale-i-Nur* Collection, pp. 255-59. Perhaps in the notes, I might be permitted to observe that I do not agree with Nursi statistics that 'seven out of ten women are either old or ugly' (p. 256).

It is not my purpose at this stage to evaluate Nursi's arguments for the veil; instead, I wish to simply note his method. For Nursi, the revealed injunction is compatible with rational reflection on the right and good. In this respect, one recognizes a form of 'Natural Law'. Granted it does not involve the Aristotelian expectation that the right is the natural purpose of any given activity, but there is this sense that Nursi does recognize that the ethical conclusions reached using reason are compatible with the wisdom of God's commands. Now this is important. As with all 'natural law' systems, Nursi is presuming that the basic moral intuitions of non-Muslims can and often will coincide with the expectations of the Qur'an.

Presumably Nursi would insist that one should still be 'obedient' to the Qur'an even if one cannot see its wisdom. However, his assumption is that given God desires the best for us all, then one can expect to find rational justifications for the Qur'anic injunction. In terms of methodology, reason meets revelation and together they can discover the truth. This is encouraging. He is assuming the importance of rational justification and presuming that there is a value in conversation with the moral intuitions of non-Muslims.

Approach to Disagreement and Pluralism

Now we turn to the crucial question: what is Nursi's attitude to disagreement and pluralism. It must be admitted that all religious traditions have found disagreement difficult to handle. Given we all believe that we are discovering the truth of what God requires of us all, to permit others who are teaching heresy or falsehood seems very misguided. In the history of religions, many traditions only discover the arguments for pluralism and toleration when they are a minority. In situations of power, these arguments seem to disappear and very often a tradition uses 'violence' to undermine those that disagree.

The secular solution handled disagreement by assuming epistemological agnosticism. For secularists, the claims of religion are very difficult to justify, therefore there is no reason for alternative metaphysical viewpoints to be excluded. Granted for those who are inclined to agnosticism, this is a good argument for toleration and pluralism. However, the problem is that the majority of people in the world are not so inclined. A justification for pluralism needs to be grounded in something other than agnosticism.

Said Nursi is especially interesting in this area. He condemns those who would resort to violence as a form of weakness. It demonstrates a lack of confidence in Islam. For Islam is sufficiently strong that good arguments can bring about victory. Sükran Vahide in her biography of Nursi explains his position thus:

> [T]he way of the Risale-i Nur was peaceful *jihad* or '*jihad* of the word' (*mânevî jihad*) in the struggle against aggressive atheism and irreligion. By working solely

---

Old age in both men and women is often accompanied with a beauty that only maturity can bring.

> for the spread and strengthening of belief, it was to work also for the preservation of internal order and peace and stability in society in the face of the moral and spiritual destruction of communism and the forces of irreligion which aimed to destabilize society and create anarchy, and to form "a barrier" against them.[14]

In other words, Nursi is committed to handling disagreement with peaceful means not because he shares a western skepticism about the truth of religion, but because of the truth of religion. Nursi wants an Islamic renewal; he wants Muslims to realize the power of their tradition. And in so doing, he believes that the power of argument and reason is sufficient to hold those who already belong and attract others who are seeking God. He calls this a *mânevî jihad*, which is a 'jihad of the word' or a 'non-physical jihad'. One of the reasons why the jihad can be non-physical is because he is confident that God will bring about the necessary victory through such a peaceful witness that uses arguments rather than violence. The God Said Nursi believes in can work wonders with the sincere effort of faithful Muslims.

So when it comes to secularist and followers of other traditions, Nursi calls for non-violent witness to the beauty and coherence of Islam. Within Islam, Nursi insists that it is an obligation on all faithful Muslims to stand united. So he writes:

> Practice the brotherhood, love and cooperation insistently enjoined by hundreds of Qur'anic verses and traditions of the Prophet! Establish with all of you powers a union with your fellows and brothers in religion that is stronger than the union of the worldly! ...Do not say to yourself, "Instead of spending my valuable time on such petty matters, let me spend it on more valuable things such as the invocation of God and meditation." For precisely what you imagine to be a matter of slight importance in this moral jihad may in fact be very great.[15]

Once again there is an interesting argument embedded in this text. However tempting it might be to evade disagreements and squabbles in the Islamic community by an act of piety, Nursi insists that it would be wrong to do so. Living in amongst these arguments is the religious duty. For we do not know what the implications of the disagreement are for the sake of the 'moral jihad'.

Nursi accepts the reality of pluralism (i.e. that there are many religious traditions) and the inevitability of disagreement both within and outside the Islamic community. However, his response is not to call for a 'recognition that Islam is just one truth amongst many' (the popular strategy of many western theologians,

---

[14] Sükran *Vahide, The Biography of Bediuzzaman Said Nursi: The Author of the* Risale-i Nur, *Part three.*

[15] Said Nursi, 'On Sincerity' in 'The Twentieth Flash'. From vol. 3 of the *Risale-i Nur*, p. 208.

for example John Hick),[16] but to call for a deeper faith more committed to its distinctive claims and beliefs. For Nursi, part of the renewal he wants amongst Muslims is a greater self-confidence in the arguments for the Islamic faith that enables Muslims to enjoy the pluralist world. Like a much-loved child at home, one can venture into the world unafraid of difference and diversity because one is secure in one's own identity.

Linked to the idea that a committed Muslim is one that can enjoy engaging with other traditions because of the power of their arguments, one final comment should be added under this heading. Nursi had plenty of secular critics who were ready to argue that committed Muslims made bad citizens. Again Nursi turns this argument around: instead of sharing the secular assumption that citizenship requires uncommitted religious people, he insists that properly committed Muslims will make model citizens. They are not a threat to the political order; they need not be committed to overthrow of the government. So in the Damascus Sermon he explains:

> What we want now is the awakening and attention of believers, for the effect of public attention is undeniable. The aim of the Union and its purpose is to uphold the Word of God, and its way is to wage the 'greater *jihad*' with one's own soul, and to guide others. Ninety-nine per cent of the endeavors of this blessed society are not political. They are rather turned towards good morals and moderation, which are the opposite of politics, and other lawful aims.[17]

At every point, Nursi handles the challenge of diversity and disagreement not by resorting to the epistemological uncertainty that has shaped many western apologetics for pluralism, but by insisting on a deeper love of God and a greater understanding of the Qur'an. For Nursi, a faith commitment is the best way of handling diversity not semi-agnosticism.

Personal Ethics

Thus far we have seen how Nursi's ethics take the wisdom of the Qur'an and expound on its significance. Given this is a renewal movement for Muslims; it is not surprising that much of the *Risale-i Nur* calls for a deeper personal morality. We find repeatedly a call for righteous living and virtuous habits. Two illustrations of this will suffice.

The first is found in his critique of 'greed'. His discussion is provoked by the Qur'anic injunction that one should 'eat and drink, but waste not by excess' (Qur'an, 7: 31). He then develops seven points, of which the last stresses the tragic

---

[16] John Hick is an advocate of 'pluralism' in the Christian Theology of Other Religions debate. Pluralism entails that each religion should see itself as a way to the Cosmic real, not the way. For Hick, see *An Interpretation of Religion* (Basingstoke: Macmillan 1989).

[17] Said Nursi, *The Damascus Sermon*, First Addendum, Third Part, p. 84.

consequences of 'greed'. Greed, explains Nursi, leads to dissatisfaction, disappointment and loss, and a lack of religious faithfulness. He concludes:

> Excess and wastefulness lead to lack of contentment. And lack of contentment destroys enthusiasm for work; it causes laziness, opens the door to complaining about life, and makes the dissatisfied person complain continuously. Also it destroys sincerity, and opens the door to hypocrisy. And it destroys self-respect, and points the way to begging.[18]

Gregg Easterbrook in his recent study of wealth and unhappiness called *The Progress Paradox* confirms Nursi's analysis almost exactly. Easterbrook finds it very odd that the wealthiest nations of the world seem to be also the unhappiest and depressed. And in amongst his explanations for this he identifies two features of human behavior: 'complaint proficiency' and 'complaint yearning'. Complaint proficiency is simply the human capacity to moan about everything. So Easterbrook writes, 'We complain to our parents for bringing us into the world; complain to our teachers for educating us; complain to our bosses for employing us; complain to the merchants who feed and clothe us; complain to the lovers and spouses who embrace us; complain to the children we summon to join us; complain to the Maker for starting the world in which all this happens.'[19] And complaint yearning is when we desire a situation where we can complain because it removes the responsibility of serving others. Easterbrook writes, 'When you're feeling sorry for yourself, you don't expect to help others or show them kindness, or to do important things, or even stop and smell the flowers. When you've got a grievance against the world, all the pressure is off.'[20] Nursi's emphasis on 'complaining' seems entirely justified.

A second illustration is found in his reflections on sickness. The first illustration is ethical reasoning that focuses on certain actions; this second illustration locates the problem of sickness firmly in the context of worship and faith. Through the eyes of faith, one must turn the adversity into an act of worship. So Nursi explains:

> O ill person who lacks patience! Be patient, indeed, offer thanks! Your illness may transform each of the minutes of your life into the equivalent of an hour's worship. For worship is of two kinds. One is positive like the well-known worship of supplications and the five daily prayers. The other are negative forms of worship like illness and calamities. By means of these, those afflicted realize their impotence and weakness; they beseech their All-Compassionate Creator and

[18] Said Nursi, 'On Frugality' – 'The Nineteenth Flash'. From vol. 3 of the *Risale-i Nur*, p. 197.

[19] Gregg Easterbrook, *The Progress Paradox* (New York: Random House 2003), p. 118.

[20] Ibid. p. 120.

> take refuge in Him; they manifest worship which is sincere and without hypocrisy.[21]

Nursi is requiring that we appreciate the religious value of pain and suffering. At moments like this we recognize our vulnerability and dependence upon God. And in so doing our worship can be so much more authentic and deep.

Both illustrations capture a personal ethic that calls for an underlying disposition of gratitude and acceptance. The gratitude should be to God for the many good things that we receive. The acceptance is for that which will come to past.

Social Ethics

One problem for the secularist is the social agenda of the religious person. Nursi is deeply committed to the social witness of Islam. Although the 'new Said' (as opposed the earlier and older Said) is eager to show how Muslims can be Muslims in a secular state, he does call on Muslims to witness to the wisdom in the Qur'an.

Although I have discussed Said Nursi's social ethics elsewhere,[22] it is necessary to introduce one illustration here. At the end of volume two of the *Risale-i Nur,* 111 aphorisms are published under the heading 'Seeds of reality'. Number 42 is a good summary of his social teaching, it reads:

> The origin of all revolutions and corruptions, and the spur and source of all base morals are just two sayings:
>
> The First Saying: "So long as I'm full, what is it to me if others die of hunger?" The Second Saying: "You suffer hardship so that I can live in ease; you work so that I can eat." There is only one remedy for extirpating the First Saying, and that is the obligatory payment of *zakat.* While the remedy for the Second is the prohibition of usury and interest. Qur'anic justice stands at the door of the world and says to usury and interest: "No entry! It is forbidden! You don't have the right to enter here!" Mankind did not heed the command, and received a severe blow. So it must heed it before it receives one even more severe![23]

This is an excellent summary of Nursi's social teaching for several reasons. First, the social teaching extends to the entire structure of society. He makes the claim that all 'revolutions and corruptions' are rooted in certain dispositions. For Nursi, the explicit task of renewal, which is the focus of his teaching, does not preclude the social dimensions of Islam. Muslims are required to offer a critique of society and warn those in power that society must be rightly ordered. Second, the two corrupting dispositions are 'selfishness' and 'exploitation'. Although many of us

---

[21] Said Nursi, 'For the Sick' – The Twenty-Fifth Flash. From vol. 3 of the *Risale-i Nur*, p. 267.

[22] See Chapter 13 in this book.

[23] 'Seeds of Reality' in *Letters*. From vol. 2 of the *Risale-i Nur*, p. 546.

might want to complicate this picture (revolutionary moments are often shaped by many factors), as a summary of the two key underlying problems it is helpful. Third, his solution to the problem of selfishness is compulsory social redistribution (by means of *zakat*); and to the problem of exploitation, he wants the prohibition of usury and interest. On the former, Nursi suggestion is helpful. On the latter, Nursi is less convincing. Although the Christian tradition did share some of the Islamic objections to usury (Roman Catholics up until 1830), treating purchasing power as a commodity, especially when the purchasing power is used for investment rather than consumption, is not considered problematic any longer. Nevertheless Nursi is right to stress that exploitation is wrong; and he is also right to identify 'access to capital' as a key difficulty.

Now a secularist is completely at liberty to disagree with Nursi. However, accommodating a real pluralism in society must entail that Nursi should be allowed to set forth his vision of the common good. And a pluralist society should welcome his participation. Let the Christian, Muslim, and secularist all bring their respective visions of the common good to the conversation. We should have nothing to fear in this. It is perfectly possible that a consensus might emerge around say Nursi's commitments to greater equality in society and redistribution from those who have to those who have not.

Corrupting Factors

The last aspect to Nursi's ethics is his sensitivity to the factors that can corrupt a virtuous person. His major concern is secularism. For a culture to lose its sense of God is a very serious matter. An atheist civilization is for Nursi a contradiction: civilization depends on the recognition of transcendence. Although he celebrates the technical achievements of modernity, he fears the philosophical skepticism. So for example, he writes:

> O miserable pseudo-patriot who fervently encourages Muslims to embrace the world and forcibly drives them to European industry and progress! Beware, do not let the bonds with which certain members of this nation are tied to religion be broken.[24]

To be driven to celebrate modernity at the price of the faith of a people is a recipe for a degenerate civilization and a people that will be impossible to govern. He explains:

> You should be certain that if your intention in forcibly driving the people of belief to degenerate civilization in this way is the country's order and security and easy administration, you are mistaken and you are driving them down the wrong way. For it is more difficult to govern a hundred degenerates whose belief is shaken and

[24] 'Seventh Note' in *The Flashes*. From vol. 3 of the *Risale-i Nur*, p. 168.

> moral corrupted, and to maintain public security among them, than to govern thousands of the righteous.[25]

For Nursi, faith is a prerequisite for social harmony and order. Without this, a culture is in trouble. In this respect, Nursi would agree with Alasdair MacIntyre that an irreligious culture finds it very difficult to sustain virtue.

For Said Nursi, the task is for Muslims to recommit themselves to Islam and not imitate western philosophical enthusiasms for moral relativism and subjectivism. *After Virtue* concludes by making a link between the crisis facing modernity and the crisis facing the Roman Empire. MacIntyre writes:

> It is always dangerous to draw too precise parallels between one historical period and another; and among the most misleading of such parallels are those which have been drawn between our own age in Europe and North America and the epoch in which the Roman empire declined into the Dark Ages. Nonetheless certain parallels there are. ... What matters at this stage is the construction of local forms of community within which civility and the intellectual and moral life can be sustained through the new dark ages which are already upon us. And if the traditions of the virtues was able to survive the horrors of the last dark ages, we are not entirely without grounds for hope. This time however the barbarians are not waiting beyond the frontiers; they have already been governing us for quite some time. And it is our lack of consciousness of this that constitutes part of our predicament. We are waiting not for a Godot, but for another – doubtless very different – St. Benedict.[26]

In my view Said Nursi would recognize MacIntyre's critique of the west. He would share MacIntyre's view that the liberal secular tradition is undermining the foundations of morality. In addition, Nursi would have understood MacIntyre's call to create communities that can sustain the virtues, while those with power are opting to surrender to the barbarians. Indeed the case could be made that Nursi is an Islamic St. Benedict. Benedict of the Italian town of Nursia (480-547) was the founder of monastic life, who, as MacIntyre alludes, did indeed provide the safe space for the Christian tradition of the virtues to survive. Nursi saw his task as doing the same: he needed to speak to a situation where the Ottoman empire was disintegrating; the barbarians are already in control in the West and eager to import its values to the Islamic world; and Muslims need to rediscover the coherence and beauty of Islam. The *Risale-i Nur* is the elegant response. And the communities that are needed to sustain the virtues are the thousands of members in Turkey that for decades circulated hand-written copies of the *Risale*.

---

[25] Ibid. p. 169.

[26] Alasdair MacIntyre, *After Virtue*, p. 263.

Conclusion

The argument of this chapter is that we need a foundation for ethics (that incorporates a commitment to pluralism) that is grounded on the truths of the faith traditions and not on the doubt and skepticism of the Enlightenment. Each tradition will do this in a different way. What we find in Said Nursi is an outstanding account that is clearly grounded in the Islamic tradition, yet, simultaneously, committed to pluralism.

It is important therefore that both Muslims and non-Muslims engage with the thought of Said Nursi. In a variety of different ways, he is able to challenge conventional ways of thinking of about the relationship between faith and morals. Nursi is a 'both/and' thinker rather than an 'either/or' one. So his ethic is both firmly rooted in the Qur'an, and yet discernable to anyone willing to reason properly about the world. He accepts both the reality of pluralism, and insists on the truth of Islam. He has both a demanding renewal ethic for individual Muslims to cultivate, and continues to call for an appropriate transformation of society. He both celebrates the achievements of modernity and yet is not afraid to question its coherence. It is not surprising that Said Nursi will continue to attract more and more attention and become a key conversation partner both within Islam and beyond.

Chapter 5

"Patience is Beautiful:" Qur'anic Ethics in Said Nursi's *Risale-i Nur*

Asma Afsaruddin

Patience (*sabr*) is a predominant virtue in the Qur'an. The word *sabr* itself is repeated many times in the Qur'an in different chapters and it is a virtue whose cultivation is strongly recommended for the believers. *Sabr*, from the Qur'anic viewpoint, is an essential component of *Iman* or faith itself. In Surat al-Baqara, verses 156 - 157, God declares to the believers: We shall test you with a bit of fear and hunger, plus a shortage of wealth and souls and produce. Announce to patient people who say, whenever some misfortune strikes them: "We belong to God, and are returning to Him;" that they will have their prayers accepted by their Lord, and granted mercy. These are the guided ones." An earlier verse from the same chapter counsels Muslims, "O those who believe, seek help through patience and prayer; for God is with those who are patient" (2:153). The patient are moreover assured of God's love and support; Surat Al 'Imran, verse 146 says, "God loves the patient;" while Surat al-Anfal, verse 46 assures the believers that "God is with the patient." God promises the patient boundless reward; Surat al-Zumar, verse 10 states, "Indeed the patient are given their recompense without measure." Patience, furthermore, is beautiful, according to the Qur'an (Surat Yusuf, 18, 73), and the faithful urge one another to be patient (Surat al-'Asr, 3). Without this constant enjoining of one another, the Qur 'an warns, humans tend to be impatient (in Arabic, "*halu'an*;" Surat Mi'raġ, 19), a trait that is disagreeable in a Muslim.

The hadith literature is also full of references to patience and its many beneficial consequences. Once again, patience is described as a basic hallmark of the true believer. One well-known hadith quotes the Prophet as saying, "Strange is the affair of the believer (*al-mu'min*); indeed all his affairs are good for him. If something pleasing befalls him he thanks God and it becomes better for him. And if something harmful befalls him he is patient (*sabr*) and it becomes better for him. And this is only for the true believers (*al-mu'minin*)." A hadith related by Abu Sa'id al-Khudri states that the Prophet said, "Whoever is patient, God will grant him patience. No one has been given anything better nor more bountiful *(awsa')* than patience."[1]

In another hadith, the Prophet says, "When God brings together the people [sc. on the last day], a herald will call out, "Where are the people of patience?" These people will rise up and they are few in number, and they will speed off to heaven. The angels will meet them and say, "Indeed we see you rushing off to heaven; so who are you?" They reply, "We are the people of patience." And they ask, " And what did your patience consist of?" They say, "We were patient in obedience to God and we were patient in averting ourselves from disobedience to God." Then it was said to them, "Enter heaven! Great is the reward of those who do [good]."[2]

The Views of Some Muslim Thinkers on Patience

Many scholars and other luminaries of Islam have extolled the virtues of patience. For example, 'Ali b. Abi Talib, is quoted as saying, "Does not patience in relation to faith have the position of the head to the body, so that if the head is severed, the body perishes?" Then he raised his voice and proclaimed, "Is it not so that whoever does not have patience, does not have faith?"[3] The famous Basran *tabi'i* al-Hasan al-Basri (d. 728), "Patience is a treasure-trove among the treasure-troves of goodness; He does not grant it to any except a worshipper to whom He is generous." The Umayyad caliph 'Umar b. 'Abd al-'Aziz (d.720) is said to have declared during a sermon, "Whenever God confers on a worshiper a blessing, then withdraws it from him, and substitutes patience for what He withdrew, then that which He substituted is far better than what was withdrawn." Then 'Umar recited, "Indeed God grants the patient their recompense without measure."[4]

Said Nursi's Views

In his inspirational work, *Risale-i Nur*, Bediuzzaman Said Nursi rebukes the human carnal soul (*nafs* or more completely *nafs ammara*) for its inclination toward impatience, among other negative traits. Without refining and restraining the carnal soul, humans are inevitably led down the path of physical indulgence and spiritual ruination. In a striking passage, Said Nursi addresses the erring soul:

> And so, my impatient soul! You are charged with being patient in three respects. One is patience in worship. Another is patience in refraining from sin. And a third is patience in the face of disaster. If you are intelligent, take as your guide

---

[1] Found in Sahih al-Bukhari, Kitab al-zakat, bab al-isti'faf 'an al-mas'ala, ed. Qasim al-Shamma'i al-Rafa'i (Beirut, 1987), vol. 2, p. 621.

[2] See Ibn, Abi'-l-Dunya , *Al-Sabr wa-'l-thawab 'alayhi* (Beirut, 1418/1997), p. 23.

[3] Ibn, Abi'-l-Dunya, *Sabr*, p. 24.

[4] Ibn Abi'-l-Dunya, *Sabr*, p. 30.

> the truth apparent in the comparison in this Third Warning. Say in manly fashion: "O Most Patient One!" and shoulder the three sorts of patience. If you do not squander on the wrong way the forces of patience Almighty God has given you, they should be enough for every difficulty and disaster. So hold out with those forces![5]

Bediuzzaman's moving address to his soul incorporates many of the major themes of Qur'anic and hadith discourse on the desirability of cultivating patience for the believer. The three major aspects of patience delineated by our author : 1) patience in worship; 2) patience in refraining from sin; and 3) patience in the face of disaster, are particularly reminiscent of a well-known hadith related by 'Ali b. Abi Talib. In this report, 'Ali says,

> The Messenger of God, peace and blessings be upon him, said, 'Patience is of three kinds: patience during tribulations; patience in obedience to God, and patience in avoiding sin. Whoever has patience during a tribulation until he averts it by the seemliness of his forbearance, God will ordain for him three hundred levels [of recompense]; the distance between each level would equal that between the sky and the earth. And whoever has patience in obedience to God, God writes down for him six hundred levels; the distance between each level would equal that between the boundaries of the earth till the edge of the divine throne. And whoever has patience in avoiding sin, God prescribes for him nine hundred levels; the distance between each level is twice the distance between the boundaries of the earth up to the edge of the divine throne.[6]

As is implicit in Said Nursi's supplication and made clear in this hadith narrated by 'Ali, these three types of patience stand the believer in good stead and cover the full gamut of life's experiences that requires patience. In this typology of patience, avoidance of sin and God's displeasure earns the highest merit for the believer, for that is clearly the most difficult goal to strive for.

Humility

Closely related to patience is humility, another cardinal Islamic virtue. Among the frequent adjectives the Qur'an uses to describe those believers who approach their Lord with humble penitence are: *khashi'un*, *munibun*, and *muttaqun*. These adjectives point to composite characteristics of those possessed of true humility. In general, "*khashi'un*" refers to the God-fearing, who abase themselves in awe before God's majesty and are constantly mindful that they are accountable to Him for their actions. For example, the Qur'an (23:2) refers to the believers as "those who are humble (*khashi'una*) in their prayers," and also advises the believers (Qur'an 2:45) to "seek help in patience and prayer, for indeed it is hard except for

---

[5] *The Words: On the Nature and Purposes of Man, Life, and All Things*, translated by Sükran Vahide (Istanbul, 1992), vol. 1, p. 278.

[6] Ibn Abi '-l-Dunya, *Sabr*, p. 31.

the humble-minded (*al-khashi'in*)." Furthermore, "... men who are humble (*al-khashi'in*) and women who are humble (*al-khashi'at*)" are promised God's forgiveness and a generous recompense (Qur'an 23:35).

The *munibun* are those who constantly turn toward God, seeking His forgiveness for and repenting of their voluntary and involuntary misdeeds. God promises them His reward, which is reserved "for every penitent and heedful one, who fears the Beneficent in secret and comes with a contrite heart (*qalb munib*)" (Qur'an 50:33). The great patriarch of monotheism, Abraham, is described in the Qur'an (11:75) as "gracious, tender-hearted, and penitent (*munib*)." The believers are commanded to "turn to Him (*munibin ilayhi*) and to be mindful of Him, perform the prayer and be not of those who ascribe partners [to Him]" (Qur'an 30:33).

The *muttaqun*, "the pious and righteous believers," are so termed because they possess *taqwa*, which Fazlur Rahman has glossed as an "inner torch"[7] possessed by those who are always conscious of God. They are the truly humble because the term *muttaqun* subsumes the complementary and overlapping characteristics of the *khashi'un* and the *munibun*, and they earn this term because their mind-set and their conduct testify to the centrality of God's presence in their lives and their dynamic relationship with him. It is the *muttaqun* who are promised success in the Qur'an; as one verse (3:200) counsels: "Believers, be patient and forebear. Stand firm in your faith, and fear and obey God (*ittaqu*), in order that you may succeed (*tuflihuna*)." Another such verse (Qur'an 24:52) promises that "he who obeys God and His messenger, and fears God (*wa-yakhsha Allah*) and is mindful of his duty to Him (*wa-yattaqih*): such indeed are the victorious (*al-fa'izun*)." Patience and God-consciousness are a particularly meritorious combination in the Qur'anic constellation of virtues; verse 90 of the 12th chapter Yusuf , "[As for] one who is mindful of God and patient *(man yattaqi wa-yasbir)*, indeed God will not forfeit the recompense due to those who do good."

The opposite of the humble believer is the individual who is disdainful (*yastaknif*) and haughty (*yastakbir*), refusing to acknowledge his or her servitude to God; the Qur'an warns of the severe retribution that awaits such a one.

> The Messiah will never disdain to be a servant of God, nor will the favored angels. Whoever disdains to worship Him and is proud, all of them He will assemble unto Him. Then as for those who believed and did good works, He will give them their wages in full, adding more to them of His bounty. And as for those who were scornful and proud, He will punish them with a severe punishment. And they will not find for themselves against God any protector or helper. (Qur'an 4:172-73).

Several other verses in the Qur'an point to the terrible consequences of human pride and ingratitude towards God. In Islamic ethics, humility thus leads to true success (*al-falaah*), which is largely defined as earning God's approval and avoiding His displeasure. In a well-known hadith, the Prophet Muhammad said,

---

[7] See his *Major Themes of the Qur'an* (Minneapolis, 1994), p. 9.

"Whoever is humble, God raises him up, and whoever is arrogant, God will bring him down low."[8] In another hadith, the angel Gabriel is said to have addressed the Prophet thus, "O Messenger of God, God greets you and asks, 'Do you wish to be a prophet-king or a prophet-servant?' Gabriel counseled, "O Muhammad, be humble towards your Lord!" And the Prophet answered that he wished to be a prophet-servant. For a Muslim following the sunna of the Prophet, service to God must, therefore, be the ultimate objective of his or her life. To this end, in addition to patience, the believer must also cultivate humility, on which characteristic we will now dwell in further detail.

Humility in Said Nursi's Thought

In his *Risale-i Nur*, Said Nursi emphasizes that without God's help and magnanimity, humans are incapable of achieving anything. Whatever they have received – whether that is intelligence, beauty, knowledge, or strength – all emanates from the same divine source. Thus humans should not boast of their individual qualities as if only they were responsible for them without mention of their Creator who has bestowed these qualities on them and mandated their proper use. Said Nursi points to the Qur'anic example of Qarun, who had been given much riches by God; but who, instead of expressing his gratitude to his divine benefactor, boasted "I have been given it on account of the knowledge I have." (Qur'an 28:78). The divine retribution that was consequently visited on him was on account of his unseemly arrogance and ingratitude. Said Nursi therefore warns humankind, "O man! Since the reality of the matter is thus, give up egotism and arrogance. With the tongue of seeking help proclaim your impotence and weakness at the Divine Court, and with the tongue of entreaty and supplication, your poverty and need. Show that you are His slave. Say: 'God is enough for us, for He is the Best Disposer of Affairs, [Qur'an 13:173] and rise in degree."[9]

Indeed, one of the best and commonest epithets of the Muslim which he wears proudly is *'abd Allah*, "the servant or slave of God;" for a woman, we have the term *amat Allah*, "the handmaid of God." Willing and grateful servitude to one's Creator fundamentally defines the true believer in Islam, who humbly acknowledges the debt he or she owes to the Divine Being. Said Nursi articulates this joyous servitude to God on the part of the believer in an arresting supplication:

> O God! You are our Sustainer, for we are mere slaves; we are powerless to sustain and raise ourselves. That is to say, the One Who sustains us is You! And it is You Who is the Creator, for we are creatures, we are being made! And it is You Who is the Provider, for we are in need of provision, we have no power! That is to say, the One Who creates us and bestows on us our provisions is You! And it is You Who is the Owner, because we are totally owned property; someone other

---

[8] Hindi, *Kanz al-'ummal*, vol. 3, p.113; Haythami, vol. 10, p. 325.

[9] *The Words*, Vol. 1, p. 337.

> than us has power of disposal over us. That is to say, it is You Who is our Owner! And You, You are Mighty! You possess grandeur and sublimity! As for us we look to our baseness and see that there are manisfestations of a mightiness on us. That is to say, we are mirrors to Your mightiness! And it is You Who is the Possessor of Absolute Riches, because we are utterly wanting, and riches are bestowed on us that our indigent hands could not obtain. That is to say, it is You Who is rich, the One Who gives is You! And You, You are the Ever-living, Ever-Enduring One, because we, we are dying, and in our dying and in our being resurrected we see the manifestation of a perpetual giver of life! And You, You are Ever-Enduring, because we see Your continuation and perpetualness in our demise and transience! And the One Who responds to us and answers us, the Granter of Gifts is You. For all of us beings, we are ever crying out and requesting, entreating, imploring by tongue and by state. And our desires are brought about, our aims are achieved. In other words, the One Who answers us is You! [10]

This supplication is an eloquent testimony to the majesty and transcendence of God and the total dependence of human beings on Him. Constant remembrance of God and His bounties toward mankind fosters this kind of exemplary humility and awe in the worshipper. As is well-known, the individual who denies the fundamental gratitude and obedience that he or she owes to the Creator is called a *kafir*; which means an ingrate or an ungrateful person. *Kufr al-ni'ma*, "the denial of God's bounties" is the ultimate act of baseness for a human, for such a denial makes a him or her an unbeliever in the existence of God Himself. The reverse *shukr al-ni'ma*, "gratitude for God's bounties" is the ultimate affirmation of the basic compact that exists between the Supreme Being and His creation.

If we look at this supplication closely, we can distinguish several elements in it that are worthy of further commentary. According to Said Nursi, humans need to be particularly humble before God because, first, He is their Sustainer or Guardian while they are His mere servants or slaves. Second, He is the Supreme Creator who gives and takes life while humans are only created beings who can neither give nor take life. Third, it is God alone Who provides for His creation; humans, like all other created beings, are dependent on Him for their nourishment and livelihood. Fourth, God is the complete owner or master of humankind; humans are beholden to their Lord and Master for everything they own and do on material earth and ultimately accountable to Him on the last judgement. Fifth, He is the possessor of unequalled majesty and splendor; none can rival Him in His sublimeness. Before Him, humans are aware of their lowly state and, yet, at the same time, as Said Nursi points out, they are able to discover in themselves some reflection of that divine might and glory. And the implication is, that by cultivating this paltry human reflection of that awesome, divine majesty, humans can attain to a loftier state of being and thinking denied to those who do not make this effort. Sixth, God's attribute as the supreme and sole Bestower of benefits

---

[10] *The Words*, Vol. 1, p. 682.

and bounties on humankind is emphasized. He is the possessor of limitless riches and abundance while we are destitute and wanting, in dire need of His generosity and grace. Seventh, God is the only Eternal Being, the one who endures through time while humans are mortal and finite beings. Mindfulness of our own perishability before the infiniteness of God again points to our extremely humble status before Him. And finally, Said Nursi points out in this supplication, it is only the Almighty Who listens and responds to our entreaties and can grant our wishes; without His will, we can accomplish and attain to nothing. Enumeration of these divine traits rehearses in the worshipper's mind a fraction of the reasons why he or she must be completely aware of one's abject humility and lowliness before God.

It is clear from the preceding discussion that Bediuzzaman is referring to many of the 99 attributes or the most beautiful names (*al-asma' al-husna*) of God in this supplication. The Sustainer or Guardian (*al-Wali*), the Creator (*al-Khaliq/al-Bari'*), the Provider (*al-Razzaq*), the Owner (*Malik al-mulk*), the Mighty (*al-'Aziz/al-Jabbar*), the Possessor of Absolute Riches (*al-Ghani*), the Ever-Living (*al-Qayyum, al-Samad, al-Baqi*), the Granter of Gifts (*al-Wahhab*), and the One Who Answers (*al-Mujib*) are nine of the essential attributes of God. In a very insightful manner, he has offered us through his selection and explanation of these apposite divine names a clear sense of the fundamental and intimate nature of the relationship that exists between humans and their Creator. One may say that humility on the part of the Muslim is already implied in the name "Muslim" and is the *sine qua non* of his or her identity: one who submits to the Creator must a priori admit one's abnegation before Him. This brief exposition by Said Nursi reminds us of the brilliant treatise by al-Ghazali (d. 1111) on the divine attributes known as *al-Maqsad al-asna*. Said Nursi, therefore, continues this honored tradition of praising the Almighty's myriad exquisite names and extrapolating from them the deep-seated meanings that illuminate our relationship with the Almighty.

Relevance of These Two Virtues in the Age of Globalization

At first blush, it may appear that patience and humility are not terribly relevant in our rapidly globalizing, materialistic world in which speed, self-assurance, and self-reliance are in greater demand. Patience may indeed appear to some as lack of energy and resolve; humility might imply an embarrassing lack of confidence in oneself. And yet globalization which has brought economic well-being for some have come under criticism from other quarters for showing a disregard for universal ethical and moral values. The phenomenon of economic globalization is attributed by its detractors to motives of greed and commercial profiteering which has fueled a callous disregard for general ethical concerns and a disdain for specific cultural values of traditional societies in less economically privileged parts of the world. Many of these critics often say that economic profit in itself has not brought happiness or emotional well-being to the industrialized nations either; if anything they are more than ever afflicted by alienation, emotional instability, and spiritual malaise. Therefore, the time has come to vigorously push for the adoption or re-adoption of ethical principles such as patience and humility, not only in our interpersonal relationships but also in transnational contacts among individuals, governments, and by multinational corporations in the competitive world of business.

Recent religious resurgent movements throughout the world speak to a desire on the part of increasingly vocal groups clamoring to infuse the world of politics and business corporations with religiously inspired ethical values. Some sociologists, like Jose Casanova, have observed that this may increasingly lead to a deprivatization of religion in industrialized countries or, at least, increasing demands for such an action. He sees this as a healthy development regardless of whether revitalized religion can regain its role, at least in the West, "of systemic normative integration" of all sectors of society. The reason for this is, as he suggests, is that by crossing boundaries, by raising questions publicly about the autonomous pretensions of the differentiated spheres to function without regard to moral norms or human considerations, they may help to mobilize people against such pretensions, they may contribute to a redrawing of the boundaries, or, at the very least, they may force or contribute to a public debate about such issues. Irrespective of the outcome or the historical impact of such a debate, religions will have played an important public role."[11]

Casanova's opinion flies in the face of much received wisdom concerning the modern Western civil society which, in general, tends to relegate, if not altogether banish as in some European contexts, religion to the private and largely domestic sphere. Religiously-inspired ethical values are suspect in the public sphere and generally regarded by government policy-makers and corporate board officials as largely irrelevant and sometimes even subversive. And yet the rebellion of considerable segments of the citizenry of various polities today have brought this tension between the "amoral public" and "moral private" spheres, characteristic of secular modernity, to the fore. There appears to be a burgeoning desire to resacralize public life and to find a congruence between the values one subscribes to in one's personal and family life and in one's professional life, at least on the part of more reflective and religiously committed people. For example, in a recent publication issued by the Templeton Foundation Press, the author John Templeton, formerly a financial moghul on Wall Street, emphasizes the key role humility has to play in a re-spiritualized world order.[12]

It is commonplace to assert that Islam recognizes no such dichotomy between the public and private spheres[13] but posits instead the holistic unity of the two, both sacred and equally moral. The Qur'an and the sunna together provide extensive moral directives for the individual's domestic and non-domestic lives.

---

[11] See Jose Casanova, "Private and Public Religions," in *Social Research* , 1992, vol. 59, Issue 1.

[12] See his Possibilities for Over One Hundredfold More Spiritual Information (Philadelphia, 2000).

[13] This Hegelian notion of a strict division between the public and private spheres has been criticized as largely artificial in many quarters.

The traditional division between *'ibadat* (worship) and *mu'amalat* (deeds), while recognizing a bifurcation of functions – the first intensely personal and the second mainly social – recognizes no parting of the ways with regard to the applicability of religio-ethical norms. One is reminded of the elaborate medieval manuals with its clear, Qur'anically derived prescriptions for principled and moral conduct in the marketplace, among other places of work. Furthermore, the principle of *hisba* which requires able Muslims "to command right and forbid wrong" recognizes no spatial boundaries in which this principle would not be incumbent. The conscientious Muslim would thus be morally bound to register disapproval of ecologically unsound practices and demonstrably exploitative practices, for example, of a company in which he or she was employed.

This general Islamic attitude is reflected in Bediuzzaman's *Risale-i Nur.* Righteous action, committed with true intent and spirit, is a continuation of faith and enables both the individual and the society to grow. This is the true meaning of progress, which is gauged not in terms of material prosperity but in terms of the moral elevation of the human soul and temperament and the spread of commonweal among mankind. Said Nursi compares the human being to a seed in which there is much potential; whether this seed grows into a thriving, fruit-bearing tree from which much benefit may be derived depends on how this seed is nurtured. He points out that should man waste his potential in satisfying the desires of his carnal soul and in the pursuit of worldly pleasures, "he will decay and decompose in the midst of difficulties in a brief life in a constricted place like the rotted seed ... .[14] Bediuzzaman continues, "If, however, he nurtures the seed of his abilities with the water of Islam and light of belief under the soil of worship and servitude to God, conforms to the commands of the Qur'an, and turns his faculties towards their true aims, they will produce branches and buds in the World of Similitudes and the intermediate realm; he will be a seed of great value and shining machine containing the members of an everlasting tree and permanent truth which will be the means to innumerable perfections and bounties in Paradise. And he will be a blessed and luminous fruit of the tree of the universe."[15]

Such growth and true progress of course do not occur overnight; it is through patient cultivation of one's soul and by acknowledging one's gratitude to God that one is able to realize one's true potential, and it is through individual growth that one ultimately also effects true social progress. Thus we see a genuine reflection of classical Islamic ethics in Said Nursi's *Risale-i Nur.* His work offers an insightful explication of the bedrock moral values and principles that the Muslim individual and the community have tried to subscribe to in the past and to which they must still subscribe, if they are to realize the objective of establishing a just and ethical social and world order. We have further indicated that a significant cross-section of people maintain that these values and principles are of continuing relevance in a globalizing world. Works like the *Risale-i Nur* ensure that these

[14] *The Words*, Vol. 1, p. 331.
[15] *The Words*, Vol. 1, p. 331.

crucial ethical values remain a part of the transnational discourse on globalization and its impact.

Chapter 6

The Ethics of Bediuzzaman Said Nursi's Dialogue with the West in Light of His Concept of 'Europe'

Patrice C. Brodeur

Introduction

As a Turkish Muslim, Bediuzzaman Said Nursi lived a rich life in constant relationship with the West, especially ideationally. Throughout his life, his involvement at different levels of Ottoman and Turkish political and educational institutions brought him in contact with ideas from and about the West as well as with people sharing different degrees of attraction and repulsion to European things and ideas. Nursi's limited travels to different parts of Europe, mostly during the First World War, raise two complementary questions: How much were his perceptions of Europe shaped by those experiences? And how much were these perceptions the result of pre-existing notions among Ottoman religious intellectuals? In addition, a number of ethical lessons ensue from Nursi's dialogue and resistance to Western imperialism in an early age of globalization. Exploring these topics provides insights into inter-civilizational interactions that reveal both useful and unhelpful models of dialogue when facing today's globalization challenges.

In this chapter, I examine the ethics of Bediuzzaman Said Nursi's dialogue with the West primarily through his use of the topos 'Europe' in the *Risale-i Nur* Collection. To achieve this end, I intertwine the critical methodogies of two academic disciplines: history and literature. First, I sketch the historical context of Nursi's travels to Europe. This biographical reconstruction is indispensable for the second task: deconstructing the literary usage he makes of the concept 'Europe'. The combination of such historical and literary approaches is necessary to achieve the aim of this paper: increase our understanding of Said Nursi's ethics of dialogue with the West.

1. Nursi's Travels to Europe

The contemporary usage of the word 'Europe' today refers both to a geographical entity and to a cultural construct or 'topos'. The former, the subject of this first section, implies boundaries coextensive with the continent of Europe, which includes several areas of Southeast Europe (the Balkans, Rumelia, etc.) which were part of the Ottoman empire at some point during the earlier part of Said Nursi's life. The latter, the subject of the next section, refers to a cultural construct shaped by the overlapping ideologies of nationalism, liberalism, constitutionalism, etc. associated to the Western European nation-states of France and England in particular, as well as fledgling others such as Germany and Italy and emerging others such as Russia, Poland, Bulgaria, Greece, Albania, etc. All of those constructs changed radically during the course of Nursi's long life, making it difficult to be precise in such a brief overview. Nevertheless, such distinction is crucial to avoid confusion between these two different yet often ambiguously overlapping definitions of 'Europe'.

Nursi's travels to Europe can be divided into two parts: first, his travels within European areas of the Ottoman Empire; second, his travels beyond those fluctuating boundaries, especially towards the end of the First World War. The former travels included visits to Salonica in 1909 (Vahide, 53-56), Macedonia and Albania as part of the entourage of Sutan Mehmed Resad's Rumelia journey in the summer of 1911 (Vahide, 107) and, in June 1918, a brief stopover in Sophia on his way back from his two-year captivity in Russia. These travels seem to reveal little contact with non-Muslim Ottoman subjects.

The latter 'travels' comprised a forced captivity as a prisoner-of-war to the Russians in the Northern province of Kostorma on the Volga river between the early fall of 1916 and the spring of 1918 followed by an escape route that included Warsaw, Berlin, Austria, and Bulgaria, with a brief side trip to Switzerland from Berlin. Nursi's official biography reveals very little of his escape following the Bolshevik revolution and his three-month journey back home to Istanbul in the spring and early summer of 1918. It is clear that he did not learn Russian during his captivity nor could he easily communicate with Germans when he spent two months in Berlin, staying at the Adlon Hotel, from where he seemingly traveled to Switzerland for three days to study its successful integration of various linguistic and confessional identities. Through indirect sources, enough pieces of that period of traveling through central Europe have emerged to elucidate Nursi's itinerary, but little to divulge how he spent his time and what kind of first-hand interaction he had with local Europeans (Vahide, 137-141).

This brief overview reveals the paucity of information we have to understand with any amount of certainty the impact of Nursi's travels to continental Europe on his usage of the topos 'Europe'. Only two points can be surmised: his time in Russia must have led him to discussing the radical changes in Russian politics and his two-month stay in Berlin must have shaped his understanding of the German nation-state building process and its various underpinning Enlightenment philosophies. The only useful second-hand information comes from our learning about Nursi's aim in visiting briefly Switzerland (Vahide, 140). In brief, such conjecture remains weak, thus the need to turn to a literary analysis of Said Nursi's use of the topos 'Europe'.

2. The Topos of 'Europe'

In literary theory, the Greek word 'topos' is defined not only in terms of a geographical 'place' (i.e. as in 'topography') but also in terms of a symbolic dimension attached to a place or concept. A 'topos' is more than a 'topic' by virtue of its symbolic dimension. Therefore, 'Europe' in the writings of Said Nursi refers to more than a geographical place; it conveys a powerful symbolic construction that greatly enhances and complicates the strictly geographical dimensions normally associated to the word 'Europe'. As mentioned above, while there is definitely an overlap between the geographical and symbolic meanings of 'Europe', the use of 'Europe' as a topos reflects the fluidity of its meanings for people who self-identify with this concept as much as for people who reject it, as Said Nursi mostly did. The only way to make sense of that fluidity of meanings in Nursi's use of 'Europe' is to take every single appearance of the word in the *Risale-i Nur* Collection and compare their meanings within their respective literary contexts.

The word 'Europe' appears forty-seven times in the *Risale-i Nur* Collection, not counting another eight occurrences of the noun or adjective 'European(s)' and the single appearance of the neologism 'Europeanism'. All of these occurrences can be divided into three broad categories. First, there are the rare strictly geographical references found in a string containing various regions of the world. Second, there are the occasional references to a 'positive' Europe worth emulating. Third, there are the many instances of a 'negative' Europe to be avoided at all cost. I use the adjectives 'positive' and 'negative' to reinforce the dichotomous and often moralistic (i.e. 'good' or 'bad') meanings that implicitly characterize, in my opinion, Nursi's usage of 'Europe'. From the outset, I admit to imposing my own interpretative categorization onto Nursi's writings, in part for heuristic purposes. I will consequently describe each category in turn before elaborating on the latter two whose contradictory usages throw light on a few ambiguous passages that reveal Said Nursi's understanding of the topos 'Europe'.

The first kind of usage of the word 'Europe' – attached to a string of geographical regions – appears once in *The Words* (616), once in the *Letters* (250), and once in *The Flashes* (97). The first two instances are identical: they contrast 'Europe' to "the English, Chinese, Japanese, and Americans", making the place of 'English' in 'Europe' ambiguous. The third instance simply lists 'Europe' as one of the seven well-known continents together with "Africa, Oceania, the two Asias, and the two Americas;" The division of Asia into two parts may have been part of a then commonly shared understanding or else a way to make up the number seven in a passage that is carefully constructed around seven repetitions of the word 'seven'. In addition, there are three unusual passages bereft of the moralistic overtones associated with the use of the word 'Europe' in most other occurrences: the expression 'to go to Europe' (*Words*, 573), which implies a strictly geographical context; "the lands of Europe which are powerfully cold" (*Flashes*, 64), which reduces continental Europe with its wide range of climates to Nursi's own limited experience of Russia and to a lesser degree Germany; and "the momentous events of Europe well-known by all" (*Words*, 422), which refer to the late nineteenth and early twentieth centuries rapid succession of political transformations in Europe, from medieval feudal to modern nation states as well as the rise of communist ideologies. In short, this first category does not reveal any useful insight into Nursi's own understanding of 'Europe'.

The second category, which is in direct opposition to the third, displays a valuable insight despite its rare occurrences. Nursi understood that part of 'Europe' was worth emulating because it was, in a nutshell, a 'positive' Europe. In fact, he even admitted that "The Old Said and certain thinkers in part accepted the principles of human and European philosophy, and contested them with their own weapons; they accepted them to a degree" (*Letters*, 516). But by the time he is writing the *Flashes*, the New Said made it clear in the one instance quoted below that he was concerned only with what he called the 'second' Europe, or what I have called 'negative' Europe.

> It should not be misunderstood; Europe is two. One follows the sciences, which serve justice and right and the industries beneficial for the life of society through the inspiration it has received from true Christianity; this first Europe I am not addressing. I am rather addressing the second corrupt Europe, which, through the darkness of the philosophy of Naturalism, supposing the evils of civilization to be its virtues, has driven mankind to vice and misguidance. As follows: On my journey of the spirit at that time I said to Europe's collective personality, which apart from beneficial science and the virtues of civilization, holds in its hand meaningless, harmful philosophy and noxious, dissolute civilization (*Flashes*, 160).

As a form of effective literary device, this passage continues over the next two pages with the rhythmic appearance of the following synonymous injunctions: "Know this, O second Europe"; "O you unhappy spirit"; "O evil-commanding soul of mankind"; "O Europe corrupted with vice and misguidance and drawn far from the religion of Jesus!"; and "O second corrupted Europe". The only two other passages where a 'positive' meaning of 'Europe' is derived from their literary context occur in the same collection one after the other: "...it becomes necessary for there to be present in every bit of soil as many factories and printing-presses as there are in Europe so that each bit of soil can be the means for the growth and formation of innumerable flowers and fruits..." (*Flashes*, 239) and "...to the number of presses and factories in Europe..." (*Flashes*, 240). Finally, the one indirect use of the expression 'one-eyed genius' that can be linked to a 'positive' meaning of Europe reinforces in fact my dichotomous nomenclature because it is immediately followed by "proceeding from the sick philosophy of Europe" (*Flashes*, 165), thereby bringing us to the third and most fruitful category.

'Negative' Europe is a category that regroups a wide variety of sub-categories through both the words 'Europe' and 'Europeans'. They can be subdivided into five themes: (1) opposition between Europe and Islam, or Europe and Asia; (2) Europe as a source of sickness, manipulation, and untrustworthiness;

(3) Europe as a source of imitation, misguidance and undeserved love; (4) Europe as religiously bigoted or irreligious; (5) Europe as ideologized politics; and (6) European women. Cutting across those themes are recurrent traditional Islamic 'root-paradigms' (Mardin, 3-8) that insert themselves into Nursi's understanding of 'Europe'. Therefore, there are numerous overlaps between these themes and various Islamic root-paradigms, such as the dichotomy between Abode of Peace and the Abode of War. Because of the fluid nature of any concept or genre (Beebee), it is necessary to first distinguish between these various meanings and Islamic root-paradigms before describing how they overlap.

The first sub-category of 'negative' Europe relates to the opposition between Europe and Islam, or Europe and Asia. "Also you do not defend Islam against Europe in the manner of the philosophers and thinkers" (*Letters*, 516). Despite one extreme passage, "Our country cannot be compared with Europe..." (*Flashes*, 259), this opposition takes on different comparative forms. It can be based on generalized differences in climate: "Also the people of Europe are cold and frigid, like the climate. Asia, that is, the lands of Islam, are relatively torrid countries" (*Flashes*, 259). The equation between 'Islam' and 'Asia' recurs frequently, as in: "Exactly like this example, the World of Islam and Asia is a huge mosque, and the people of belief and truth within it are the respected congregation in the mosque" (*Letters*, 484-485). By opposition, "Furthermore, the lands of Europe are the realm of Christendom" (*Letters*, 506). But this equation between Europe and Christianity is not frequent and often ambiguous, as will be elaborated further below. In fact, more often, Europe is not linked to religion at all. "If Europe is a shop, a barracks, Asia is like an arable field and a mosque" (*Letters*, 383). Similarly: "Moreover, the appearance of most of the prophets in Asia, and the emergence of the majority of philosophers in Europe is a sign..." (*Letters*, 383). Such opposition can also take on military imagery:

> In just the same way, at this time of denial and the assault of the customs of Europe and the legion of innovations and the destruction of misguidance, to open up new doors in the citadel of Islam in the name of *ijtihad*, and make openings that will be the means of those bent on destruction scaling the walls and entering it, is a crime against Islam (*Words*, 495).

This imagery feeds the old Islamic Abode of Peace versus Abode of War root-paradigm that dichotomizes the world into two:

> In London, Europeans who have embraced Islam translate many things like the call to prayer and *iqama* into their own languages in their own country. [...] There is such a glaring difference here that no conscious being could make such an analogy and imitate them. For the European lands are called the Abode of War in the terminology of the Shari'a, and there are numerous things which are permissible in the Abode of War which are not lawful in the Abode of Islam (*Letters*, 506).

The second sub-category of 'negative' Europe regroups passages where Europe is perceived as a source of sickness, manipulation, and untrustworthiness, as in the following three quotes: "For years, I have considered negative nationalism and racialism to be a fatal poison, since it is a variety of European disease. And Europe has infected Islam with that disease thinking it would cause division, and Islam would break up and be easily swallowed" (*Letters*, 86). "It is mostly lies and there is the possibility of unknowingly being a tool in the hand of Europe" (Letters, 84). "Now you must refrain from succumbing to the stratagems of Europe and the dissemblers who imitate them…" (*Letters*, 382).

The second part of the above quote overlaps with the next sub-category that focuses on Europe as a source of imitation, misguidance and undeserved love:

> Utter abhorrence and a thousand regrets should be felt for those who take the way of misguidance due to the Europeans' idols and sciences of Naturalism, and for those who follow them and imitate them blindly! O sons of this land! Do not try to imitate Europeans! How can you reasonably trust in and follow the vice and invalid, worthless thought of Europe after the boundless tyranny and enmity it has shown you? No! No! You who imitate them in dissoluteness, you are not following them, but unconsciously joining their ranks and putting to death both yourselves and your brothers. Know that the more you follow them in immorality the more you lie in claiming to be patriots! Because you're following them in this way is to hold your nation in contempt, to hold the nation up to ridicule! *God guides us, and you, to the Straight Path* (*Flashes*, 166; italics in the English translation of *Risale-i Nur*).

Other shorter examples include the following four passages: "Embracing the idea of nationalism, the peoples awakening in Asia are imitating Europe precisely in every respect, and on the way sacrificing many of their sacred matters" (*Letters*, 382). "The recompense for illicit love, like love for Europe, is the cruel enmity of the beloved" (*Letters*, 546). "The one I'm addressing isn't Ziya Pasha, it's those enamoured of Europe" (*Words*, 223). "The dissolute loafers are those villains who follow Europe and have no nation or religion. While the European spectators are the journalists who spread the ideas of the Europeans" (*Letters*, 484-485).

For Said Nursi, 'negative' Europe is both religiously bigoted and irreligious: "…because Europe is bigoted in religion" (Letters, 511). "In fact, there are many like the former American President, Wilson, and the former British Prime Minister, Lloyd George, who were as religious as bigoted priests" (*Letters*, 510-511). Similarly:

> It is a grievous error to compare the religions of Islam and Christianity and to be different towards religion like Europe. Firstly, Europe has its religion. The fact that European leaders like foremost Wilson, Lloyd George, and Venizelos, are bigoted in their religion like priests, testifies that Europe has its religion, and is even bigoted in one respect. Thirdly: To compare Islam with Christianity is a false comparison and wrong. For when it has been bigoted in its religion, Europe has not been civilized; it has become civilized on giving up its bigotry (*Letters*, 383).

The challenge continues in the following passage:

> For through the strength of the All-Wise Qur'an, I challenge all Europe including your irreligious people. [...] If all Europe was to gather, of which your irreligious people are a part, through God's assistance, they could not make me recant a single matter of that way of mine. God willing, they could not defeat me... (*Letters*, 95).

In fact, Nursi not only lumps together philosophy with irreligiousness, but he also implies a close link between irreligious Europe and the Devil: "And as for this, O Devil, neither you nor the philosophers of Europe and hypocrites of Asia on whom you rely..." (*Letters*, 372). This language of the 'devil' (*shaytan*), 'hypocrites' (*munafiqun*), or 'unbelief'(*jahiliya)*, as in the passage "...from unbelief and from Europe" (*Letters*, 504), all point to how Nursi projects Islamic root-paradigms unto how he perceives Europe.

Nursi strongly rejects anything that will threaten any Islamic paradigms and he abhors the use of Islamic means to radically change a long time religious practice for a politics of imitation. In particular, he claims that there was always a seamless overlap between the Turkish 'nation' and Islam, so that no one should fall into the trap of imitating the European ideology of nationalism, 'Europeanism':

> In accordance with which principle is it to propose through a corrupt and innovative *fatwa*, 'performing the *iqama* in Turkish,' in a way completely contrary to Turkish nationalism, which is sincerely religious and sincerely respectful towards religion and has since early times blended and united with Islam, in the name of Turkism, which has the meaning of Europeanism, to those like me who belong to another religion? Yes, although I have friendly and brotherly relations with true Turks, I have in no respect any relation with the Turkism of imitators of Europe like you (*Letters*, 503-504).

This overlap between religion and politics emerges clearly from the following passage too:

> What enabled this Islamic state, while only numbering twenty or thirty million, to preserve its life and existence in the face of all the large states of Europe was the following idea in its army, which arose from the light of the Qur'an: "If I die, I shall be a martyr; and if I kill, I shall be a ghazi." They met death with complete eagerness and longing, laughing in its face. They always made Europe tremble. [...] Whenever the dragons (large states) of Europe have dealt a blow at this Islamic state, [...] (*Letters*, 384-385).

Of course, this paradigm of the ghazi is a central metaphor in Turkish Islam in particular (Mardin, 3-5). It goes hand in hand with its maiden Islamic paradigm of waging battle against the infidel, as in "The rest is either stolen or seized by the European infidel tyrants or the dissemblers of Asia" (*Flashes*, 169).

The same use of a strong Islamic religious language surfaces when Nursi defends Islam against European cultural practices, especially surrounding the theme of women.

> Thinking "My son is going to be a Pasha," she [mothers in general] gives him all her property, takes him from the Qur'an school and sends him to Europe. But it does not occur to her that her child's eternal life has fallen into danger. She tries to save him from prison in this world, and does not take into consideration his being sentenced to the prison of Hell (*Flashes*, 261).

In an apologetic stance reminiscent of what can still be heard today, Nursi argues that:

> We even hear that in Europe, the place of open dress, many women are fed up at being the object of attention, and complain to the police, saying: "These brutes keep staring at us and disturbing us." This means that present-day civilization's unveiling women is contrary to their natures" (*Flashes*, 256).

Rooted in the Europe/Islam dichotomy mentioned in the first sub-category of 'negative' Europe, Nursi uses a then popular argument to try to explain the differences in women dress codes:

> Also the people of Europe are cold and frigid, like the climate. Asia, that is, the lands of Islam, are relatively torrid countries. It is well known that the environment has an effect on people's morality. Perhaps in those cold countries immodest dress does not stimulate the animal appetites and carnal desires of those cold people, and be a means of abuse. But the immodest dress which continually excites the carnal lusts of the easily influenced and sensitive people of hot countries is certainly the cause of much abuse and waste and the weakening of the young generation and a loss of strength (*Flashes*, 259).

This explanation reflects a kind of Orientalism that proves how inter-dependent images of 'self' and 'other' are in the construction of Western-Islamic understanding of one another.

3. Nursi's Ethics of Dialogue

The ethics of Said Nursi is the result of his own unique integration of, on the one hand, his rural Kurdish identity and, on the other, his initially Ottoman and later nationalist Turkish Muslim identity. While he did engage with many ideas that had emerged in Europe, this ideational interaction seems to have been mostly conducted through books, journal and newspaper articles. It is not clear how many in-depth conversations he may have had with non-Muslims in general, and Europeans in particular, according to both official and unofficial biographies. It should therefore not be surprising to find in Nursi's writings many generalizations and stereotypes of Europeans and Europe that reflected a morally judgmental approach to 'Europe'. In all fairness, his construction of the topos 'Europe' reflects no better or worse a projection from his own cultural/religious worldview than the reverse phenomena of Orientalism so prevalent at that time among Europeans. Therefore, in the context of the unequal power dynamic that played out during the course of Nursi's lifetime, it is understandable that an apologetic ethics defending Islam became the corner stone of Nursi's enterprise, thereby shaping his ethics of dialogue.

In fact, Nursi's approach to dialogue is unusual: it was a one-way street where "Here all questions are answered, all problems solved, but no questions are asked" (Vahide, 38). Nursi is said to have posted this famous sign on his hostel door during his second visit to Istanbul in 1907. According to one unofficial biography, this unique behavior was the result of a dream Nursi had in Nurs during the winter of 1890 or 1891, at the age of thirteen or fourteen: "Finally, the Prophet Muhammad (PBUH) came. Said kissed his hands and asked for knowledge from him. The Prophet said: 'Knowledge of the Qur'an will be given you on condition you ask no questions of any of my community.' Upon which Said awoke in a state of great excitement" (Vahide, 8). Said followed the Prophet's suggestion to the letter from that time onwards. Whether or not this behavior came across as arrogant, the fact remains that such a one-way communication could not foster an ethics of equal sharing in dialogue.

This imbalance in communication made Nursi dependent on written material or on his encounter with people who on their own would provide information on a given topic. This serious limitation resulted in his writing many generalizations about Europe and Christianity that reflected his own projections, as mentioned earlier. In particular, his apologetic approach led him to generalize positively about Islam and negatively about Christianity, especially in the realm of history as demonstrated in the following two passages:

> Islamic history is there for all to see. Apart from one or two incidents, no internal wars of religion have occurred. Whereas the Catholic Church caused four hundred years of internal revolutions. Furthermore, Islam has been the stronghold of the common people rather than of the upper class. [...] Also history testifies that whenever the people of Islam have adhered to their religion, they have advanced in relation to the strength of their adherence. And whenever they have become less firm in their religion, they have declined. Whereas with Christianity, it is the opposite. This too arises from an essential difference (*Letters*, 510-511).

> Secondly, the people of innovation obtained the following inauspicious idea from the European reformists; being dissatisfied with the Catholic Church, foremost the revolutionaries, reformists, and philosophers, who were innovators according to the Catholic Church, favored Protestantism, which was considered to [be] Mu'tazilite and taking advantage of the French Revolution they partially destroyed the Catholic Church, and proclaimed Protestantism. Then the pseudo-patriots here, who are accustomed to imitating blindly, say: "A revolution like that came about in the Christian religion. At first the revolutionaries were called apostates, then later they were again accepted as Christians. So why should there not be such a religious revolution in Islam? (*Letters*, 508)

Another characteristic of Said Nursi's ethics of dialogue is his lifelong quest for truth and justice expressed through candid, not to say blunt, discursive language in both writing and speech. The boundaries between the two were sometimes fluid as in the following example: "Let the ears ring of the leaders of Europe, savage beneath their humanitarian masks" (*Letters*, 502). Such honesty reveals both his passion for justice and his subjective quest for truth displayed through a strong critical awareness of Muslim behaviors in his days but a weaker and even at times blind acceptance of key Islamic root-paradigms, as in the following case:

> Also, whenever the people of Islam have adhered in earnest to their religion, they have advanced proportionately, achieving great progress. Witness to this is the greatest master of Europe, the Islamic state of Andalusia. And whenever the Islamic community has been slack in religion, it has sunk into wretchedness, and declined (*Letters*, 383).

This passage represents a classical example of how Qur'anic and Hadith literature on the direct link between true religious practice and the outward success of the Islamic community constitutes another Islamic root-paradigm in Nursi's *Risale-i Nur* collection. It also points to the serious limitation a one-way approach to dialogue can lead to in a serious quest for truth.

In conclusion, I would argue that Said Nursi's ethics of dialogue and construction of the topos 'Europe' not only reflect his own worldview as a Kurdish/Ottoman/Turkish scholar of Islam, an obvious realization; it also attests to a powerful 'middle path' between adopting an ideology of modern nationalism and preserving the sacred dimensions of Islam, both private and public.

> Embracing the idea of nationalism, the peoples awakening in Asia are imitating Europe precisely in every respect, and on the way sacrificing many of their sacred matters. However, every nation requires a dress suitable to its particular stature. Even if the material is the same, the style has to be different (*Letters*, 382).

The pursuit of the suitable 'dress code', of what this careful balance actually means in practice today, continues to be most relevant at the beginning of the twenty-first century of the Common Era.

Chapter 7

Ethics in the Confucian Text: Comparative Study with *Risale-i Nur*

Jemil Hee-Soo Lee

Introduction

This chapter is designed to identify certain common ethical elements that can be found in the Confucian Text and *Risale-i Nur* based on comparative analysis. *Risale-i Nur* is a Qur'anic commentary providing the truths of beliefs by Bediuzzaman Said Nursi. It blends science and the truths of religion and uniquely addressed the mentality of modern men. The principles and ethical teaching of the *Risale-i Nur* in many parts are parallel with the Confucian texts.

In the famous Damascus Sermon (Hutbe-i Samiye), Said Nursi pointed out the importance of truthfulness. He said this is the basis and foundation of Islam. Truthfulness and honesty are the principles of Islam's social life. Hypocrisy, flattery and artifice, duplicity and double-dealing are all forms of lying. Unbelief in all its varieties is lying and falsehood, while belief is truthfulness and honesty. But politics and propaganda have mixed and confused them, and as a result have confused man's achievements. Also salvation, he told them, is only to be found through honesty (Vahide: 102). The keynote of Confucian ethics is jen, variously translated as "love," "goodness," "humanity." Jen is a supreme virtue representing human qualities at their best. In human relations, jen is manifested in chung, or faithfulness to oneself and others, and shu, or altruism, best expressed in the Confucian golden rule, "Do not do to others what you do not want done to yourself." Other important Confucian virtues include righteousness, propriety, integrity, and filial piety.

These basic ethics and guidance can be found in the *Risale-i Nur* to a great extent. It is very clear that the ethics and teaching of a great Ustad, which are based on Qur'an and Islamic principles, are in parallel with an East Asian ethical system, which is much based on Confucian teachings. It is time to rediscover and reinterpret the teachings of the great Ustad Said Nursi, by which we would secure a strong foundation for Islamic upgrading in East Asia and new cooperation with Asian counterparts.

Confucian Conception on Ethics

Ethical goods are goods in relation to persons — goods for persons. There are multiple persons, and these are divided generally into self and others. Ethical goods thus fall into two categories: goods for the self and goods for others. All ethical goods are autonomously defined by selves (i.e. people know what they like), except in relation to morality, which contains absolute ethical goods. The pursuit of goods for the self is self-interest, and in general it is not moral duty, only prudence, to pursue one's own self-interest.

"Their own interests" are self-defined in the areas or matters where, according to the types of interests considered below, we have rights of possession, use, and exchange. It has become common to say that people have rights wherever they have interests, but this principle does not allow for "compossibility," the possibility that the rights can all be exercised at the same time, since many interests overlap and conflict. Such "rights" must necessarily be abridged, a dangerous characteristic, since any rights can then be abridged for any expedient reason. If all interests are not protected by rights, however, then rights can be moral and legal claims that cannot be abridged.

Interests of person and property in general forbid wrongs of commission, i.e. fraudulent or violent damaging acts against persons and property, by others. Moral duty also forbids wrongful acts of omission - or posits duties of commission (or duties to act) — requiring positive actions for the sake of another because of a contract or where fundamental interests, such as life and limb, are endangered. The Gentleman in the Confucianism should keep the most righteous virtue as above mentioned and have the task of guidance for other ordinary people.

Morality in the Risale-i Nur

The one who undertakes the task of guidance should have a better character than everyone else. Universal moral values should irradiate from him, like knowledge, chastity, patience, self-sacrifice, compassion, kindness, and altruism. As far as possible, he should not think unfavorably of others, but should think well of them. He should aim to be affable, pleasantly spoken, mild, ready to uphold right.

Bediuzzaman Said Nursi gathered together in himself all the above-mentioned qualities and this is testified by both his works and his biography. In this sense, Islam very clearly shows that selfishness is harmful to his own community.

Common Background of Civilizations between Islam and East Asia

Civilizations ordinarily affect and transform one another. The give-and-take among civilizations is the norm of history. Islam also played a kind of civilizational bridge between Eastern and Western civilizations. In this sense, the notion of "middleness" is a key concept in the understanding of the civilizational nature and identity of Islam. The idea of Islam as the "middleness" is to be found in Islam's holy book,

Al-Qu'ran (2:143). Under the notion of "middleness", through the 1400 years' Islamic history, Islam clearly showed the wisdom of ethnic and cultural pluralism, inter-cultural cooperation in the pursuit of the common good for all mankind and a common responsibility for the protection of human society. The notion of "middleness" is the basic teaching of Confucianism on which East Asian culture absolutely relies.

Even in an historical sense, cultural contacts between the Islamic world and East Asian countries (China proper - Korea - Japan) have more than 1000 years of long history since the first Hijra century without any antagonism and wars. This peaceful and gradual Islamization gave valuable opportunity for East Asians to become cosmopolitan, open-minded, tolerant and amenable to cultural diversity. So, relations between Muslims and non-Muslim Asians must be governed by moral and ethical considerations.

Therefore, the future of Islam-East Asia relations seems to be very optimistic due to such factors as Islamic and Confucian tolerance toward other's civilizations. Moreover, many aspects of the East Asian Confucian tradition's value system are in agreement with Islamic principles and historically there have existed friendly relations between East Asia and the Islamic world since the first Hijra century.

Common Values Described in the *Risale-i Nur*

Ethical Teachings of Risale-i Nur Comparing to Confucian Ethics

The *Risale-i Nur* is a Qur'anic commentary providing the truths of beliefs by a response developed by Bediuzzaman Said Nursi. It blends science and the truths of religion and uniquely addresses the mentality of modern man. The principles and basic thought of *Risale-i Nur* are in many parts parallel with the Confucian value system. Balanced personality and Confucian middleness is extraordinarily important for both teachings.

Balanced Personality and Confucian Middleness

Power of Animal Appetites
Excess ⇒ profligacy
Deficiency ⇒ apathy
Middleness ⇒ chastity, uprightness

Power of Anger
Excess ⇒ recklessness
Deficiency ⇒ cowardice
Middleness ⇒ courage

Power of Intellect
Excess $\Rightarrow$ perfidious deception
Deficiency $\Rightarrow$ stupidity
Middleness $\Rightarrow$ wisdom

Excess and Wastefulness

These two factors lead to greed, and greed has three serious consequences: Dissatisfaction; disappointment and loss; destroying sincerity. In short, excess and wastefulness lead to lack of contentment. And lack of contentment destroys enthusiasm for work; it causes laziness, opens the door to complaining about life, and makes the dissatisfied person complain continuously. Also, it destroys sincerity, and opens the door to hypocrisy. And it destroys self-respect, and points the way to begging.

In Confucian texts, contentment and frugality are main topic, which are regarded as the most important virtue in the daily life and community.

> Just as lavishness leads easily to presumption, so does frugality to meanness. But meanness is a far less serious fault than presumption.

To the gentleman and leaders, the Confucian analects require frugality as the basic condition. The contentment arising from frugality opens the door of thanks and closes the door of complaint. It means the door of sincerity is opened, the door of hypocrisy closed.

According to the Hadith, "The contented person is respected, and the greedy person despised", a consequence of contentment is self-esteem. Also it encourages effort and work increasing enthusiasm. The famous Muslim physician, Ibn-i Sina also advised with us that the most harmful thing for the body is to eat without having had a break of four to five hours, or to fill the stomach with a variety of foods one on top of the other. These eating habits are completely paralleled with daily life in East Asia, which are based on Confucian teaching.

Sincerity

> O my brothers of the Hereafter! And O my companions in the service of the Qur'an! You should know that in this world sincerity is the most important principle in works pertaining to the Hereafter in particular; it is the greatest strength, and the most acceptable intercessor, and the firmest point of support, and the most wondrous means of achieving one's goal, and the highest quality, and the purest worship. Since in sincerity lies much strength and many lights... (*Flashes*, p. 212).

The noble saying of the Prophet on sincerity is as follow:

> All men will perish, except the scholars, and all scholars will perish except those

> who act in accordance with their knowledge, and all of them will perish except the sincere, and even the sincere are in great danger, (*Flashes*, p. 200).

Said Nursi evaluated the value of sincerity as follows; as conflict and rivalry arise, concord is changed into discord; and agreement into dispute. The cure and remedy for this appalling disease is sincerity. Sincerity may be attained not by one's own soul, but by the worship of God (*Flashes*, p.201-202).

In Confucian culture, sincerity means one's best efforts without any egoism or interfering with other rights. And it teaches us that man should exert all his capability and potentiality under the sincerity spirits, and then wait for response from Heaven.

Self and Other

Confucius is clear that this does not mean complete denial of self. We have seen a hint of this with *Analects* XV:23, which begins with the character for "self and ends with the characters for "others" (or "persons"). If what you don't want for yourself, you shouldn't to do others, then you would like others to do for you what you would indeed like for yourself. We see a similar word structure, and stronger implication, at *Analects* VI:28, "If you desire to establish yourself, also establish others." This sounds "mutual profitableness," but it is clearly essential to Confucius. This can, of course, also be read in Chinese, as shown. It contains different characters for "self" and "other" than Confucius uses, but these could easily be substituted, as can be seen by the animated image displays of the older characters. Helping oneself and others at the same time is characteristic of what we might even call the "worldliness" of Confucianism and Chinese civilization.

Risale-i Nur teaches us "My outlook is true, or the best", but not that "My outlook alone is true and good" Bediuzzaman always advises us to act positively avoiding enmity for other outlooks, not criticizing them, interfering in their beliefs and sciences. Moreover he emphasizes to overlook each other's faults, closing one's eyes to each other's shortcomings and to behave according to the rule of courtesy established by the criteria. The Qur'an also clearly mentioned the remedy for the disease of discord among peoples.

> Do not fall into dispute, lest you lose heart and your power depart. (8:46)
> Work together for the sake of virtue and piety. (5:3)

Fearing God

The Prophet Muhammad (s.a.w) said, "I swear that I fear God more than any of you, but nevertheless some days I fast and some days I don't fast. At night I pray, but I also sleep. I also approach my wives. Whoever turns away from my Sunna, turns away from me". He said too, "Piety in this world is not to consider the licit to be illicit", which is mean, as a warning to those who, unsatisfied with the principles of the Qur'an and Sunna, try to find a way following their own caprice.

For Said Nursi, the enemy of human happiness and ethical uprightness is unbelief and irreligion. It is people deciding to find their own path through life, not seeking Divine Guidance, not caring about God's will or wise design for humankind, not wishing to give up their own pet desires and ideas to submit to God's teaching about human nature and destiny.

He emphasized several times in the Damascus Sermon the essential virtue of ethical uprightness mentioning six dire sicknesses on European development while comparing it to the backwardness of the Islamic world. He pointed out such sickness as the despair, hopelessness, and the death of truthfulness in social political life restricting endeavor to what is personally beneficial. Bediuzzaman had started by quoting the verse, "Do not despair of God's mercy", and the Hadith: "I came to perfect good moral qualities", which provide the theme of the six *Words* of which the Sermon is composed.

Confucian Basic Thought Compared to *Risale-i Nur*

Confucianism, the major system of thought in China, developed from the teachings of Confucius and his disciples, and was concerned with the principles of good conduct, practical wisdom, and proper social relationships. Confucianism has influenced the Chinese attitude toward life, set the patterns of living and standards of social value, and provided the background for Chinese political theories and institutions. It spread from China to Korea, Japan, and Vietnam and has aroused interest among Western scholars.

Although Confucianism became the official ideology of the Chinese state, it has never existed as an established religion with a church and priesthood. Chinese scholars honored Confucius as a great teacher and sage but did not worship him as a personal god. Nor did Confucius himself ever claim divinity.

Unlike Christian churches, the temples built to Confucius were not places in which organized community groups gathered to worship, but public edifices designed for annual ceremonies, especially on the philosopher's birthday. Several attempts to deify Confucius and to proselytize Confucianism failed because of the essentially secular nature of the philosophy.

The keynote of Confucian ethic is jen, "goodness" and "human-heartedness". While the essence of morality is the limitation of self-interest, the core of Confucianism are all attributed to the Master. The range of topics is wide, Ritual and Sacrifice; The Individual Path; Goodness; Aesthetics; Government and A Gentleman's Conduct. A few excerpts and paraphrases follow:

> *Is courage to be prized by a gentleman?* A gentleman gives the first place to Right. If a gentleman has courage but neglects Right, he becomes turbulent. If a small man has courage but neglects Right, he becomes a thief.
>
> *It is Goodness that gives to a neighborhood its beauty. ... Imperturbable, resolute, tree-like, slow to speak - such a one is near to Goodness.* Neither the scholar who has truly the heart of a scholar nor the man of good stock who has the qualities that

belong to good stock, will ever seek life at the expense of Goodness, and it may be that he has to give his life in order to achieve Goodness.

There are three things that a gentleman fears: he fears the will of Heaven, he fears great men, he fears the words of the Divine Sages. The small man does not know the will of Heaven and so does not fear it. He treats great men with contempt, and he scoffs at the words of the Divine Sages.

Wealth and rank are what every man desires, but if they can only be retained to the detriment of the Way he professes, he must relinquish them. Poverty and obscurity are what every man detests, but if they can only be avoided to the detriment of the Way he professes, he must accept them. ... Never for a moment does a gentleman quit the way of Goodness. He is never so harried but that he cleaves to this; never so tottering but that he cleaves to this.

In short, Confucian ethical teachings include the following values:

- Li: includes ritual, propriety, étiquette, etc.
- Hsiao: love within the family: love of parents for their children and of children for their parents
- Yi: righteousness
- Xin: honesty and trustworthiness
- Jen: benevolence, humaneness towards others; the highest Confucian virtue F. Chung: loyalty to the state, etc.

In the practical daily life East Asian people are still under the strong influence of Confucian philosophy and its basic maxims. The essence of relationships is fivefold, and fundamental to social order: ruler and subject; father and son; husband and wife; older brother and younger brother; older friend and younger friend. The ideal of conduct, ordering all human relationships and resulting in an ideal social structure and harmony is li.

Later on his disciples developed ten attitudes that are to govern the five relationships: love of father and filial piety in the son; gentility of the oldest brother and humility and respect of the younger; righteous behavior of the husband and obedience of the wife; humane consideration to elders and deference of juniors; benevolence of rulers and loyalty of subjects.

Conclusion

Through history, Islam played a central mediating role by introducing East Asians to the highest scientific and academic achievements of Muslims. At the same time, East Asian technology and philosophy penetrated into the Muslim world through the Silk Route. Thus Islamic-East Asian interactions were mostly peaceful. For centuries, both worlds interacted with each other in a positive framework as we evaluated the historical mutual relations. This was an essential point for mutual cooperation because of the common cultural values and trade interests.

For all the above, Islam is a religion of tolerance and Islamic civilization usually respects the rights of others and freedom and has a positive attitude toward others. In this concern, it is time to review and reflect on mutual relations and cultural confluence in history between the Islamic world and East Asia. Surely it leads to mutual benefit and world peace.

Surprisingly, this basic Confucian philosophy and guidance and, in particular, the matter of ethics and morality, can be found in the *Risale-i Nur* to a great extent. The *Risale-i Nur* is a most comprehensive source book for East Asia for most desirable direction to new life. The Islamic principles explained by Said Nursi in the *Risale-i Nur* are more attractive than any other traditional ways of Islamic teaching.

It's very clear that the thought and teaching of a great Ustad Bediuzzaman Said Nursi, which are based on the Qur'an and Islamic principles, are in parallel with the East Asian value system and philosophy, which is based on Confucian teachings. The latter is confined to the regional teaching in East Asia, the former, as a universal model text might be adapted to all human beings through reinterpretation. In this sense, *Risale-i Nur* has a great possibility, to disseminate in East Asia by more systemic and comparative academic research in the days to come.

The *Risale-i Nur* is no longer the message for Turkish or certain limited areas and peoples. The *Risale-i Nur* is a universal reinterpretation of the Holy Qur'an and has most effectively appealed to the West and the East as well. It is time to rediscover and reinterpret the teachings of the great Ustad Said Nursi, by which we would secure a strong foundation for Islamic upgrading in the East Asia and new cooperation with Asian counterparts.

Note

1. Confucius was born in 551 BC in China. He lived during the Chou dynasty, an era known for its moral laxity. Later in life, he wandered through many states of China, giving advice to their rulers. He accumulated a small band of students during this time. The last years of his life were spent in Lu. Where he devoted himself to teaching. His writings deal primarily with individual morality and ethics, and the proper exercise of political power by the rulers. In China, and some other areas in Asia, the social ethics and moral teachings of Confucius are blended with the Taoist communion with nature and Buddhist concepts of the afterlife, to form a set of complementary, peacefully co-existent and ecumenical religions. There are approximately 6 million Confucians in the world. About 26,000 live in North America; almost all of the remainder is found throughout China, Korea and the rest of Asia.

Chapter 8

An Outline of Bediuzzaman Said Nursi's Views on Christianity and the West

Sükran Vahide

Introduction

For Bediuzzaman Said Nursi, the West and Christianity were not synonymous; in a work first published in 1922, he wrote that Europe, as representing the West, was "twofold." The first Europe, which he was not opposed to, through the inspiration it had received from "the true religion of Jesus," had contributed positively to social justice and mankind's material progress. The second Europe, however, having grown out of materialist philosophy, had only a corrupt and harmful civilization to offer mankind.[1] This counterposing of divine revelation and "man-made" philosophy underlies virtually all Nursi's mature thought, and it will be useful to bear it in mind while investigating his views on Christianity and the West.

Another point to mention is that since the study of Christianity was not Nursi's prime concern, his works contain little in the way of doctrinal discussion. He did however consider that strands of Christianity were following an evolutionary course towards the acceptance of divine unity (*tawhid*) in the Qur'anic sense,[2] a question linked to the Second Coming of Jesus (PUH), which he did deal with in some detail. Said Nursi's interpretations of Hadiths related to the end of time are both highly original, and foresaw a reconciliation between Islam and Christianity. Also original and far-sighted was his view that Christian victims of wartime atrocities should be considered martyrs along with Muslim victims, and among the saved.

The above are questions Said Nursi dealt with in the second main period of his life, that of the New Said, which commenced after the First World War. A third period, influenced by the wide changes in the balance and configuration of the

---

[1] Bediuzzaman Said Nursi, *The Flashes Collection* [Eng. tr. Sükran Vahide] (Istanbul: Sözler Publications, 2000), p. 160.

[2] Bediuzzaman Said Nursi, *Letters 1928-1932* [Eng. tr. Sükran Vahide] (Istanbul: Sözler Publications, 1997), p. 544; Nursi, *The Words* [Eng. tr. Sükran Vahide] (Istanbul: Sözler Publications, 1998), p. 736.

world powers after the Second World War and the great upheavals in the world of humanity, saw a development in his ideas, and at this time he is seen to actively urge general peace and reconciliation, and to support the political alliance of Turkey and the West against communism and aggressive atheism. The views he evinced at this time have important implications for the future, as will be mentioned.

The Old Said

During the first period of Said Nursi's life, that of the Old Said, Nursi engaged in various activities aimed at reversing the decline of the Ottoman Empire and securing its progress. As far as the West was concerned, he advocated taking only what was beneficial from it, namely science and technology, while in regard to Christianity, references in his works are confined to the question of the Christian minorities of the Empire and their gaining equal rights under the 1908 Constitution, and to relations with People of the Book.[3] Said Nursi's replies to the Kurdish tribesmen, allaying their fears about the equality accorded the Armenians and Greeks, illustrate his fairness and tolerance, as well as the importance he attached to persuasion in these matters and a reasoned approach, and it will be useful to include a few brief quotes from his work *Münâzarat*. His arguments are interesting also because although it was then government policy to unite all the ethnic elements of the Empire (*ittihad-i anasir*), and according to the Shari'a the non-Muslim minorities had always been according full religious rights and freedoms, Said Nursi was justifying their now being granted full civil and political rights with arguments again based on the Shari'a.

> *Question:* There are [now] Christians and Jews in the Chamber of Deputies. What value do their votes have in the Shari'a?
>
> *Answer:* Firstly, in mutual consultation, the decision is the majority's, and the majority are Muslims. ... Secondly, the opinion of an Armenian or Jew is valid in [a craft like] clockmaking or running a machine. Just as the Shari'a does not reject their opinions in these, so it shouldn't reject them in questions of political and economic advantage...[4]
>
> *Question:* All right, we accept that freedom [as opposed to absolutism; that is, constitutionalism] is good, but the freedom of the Greeks and Armenians seems bad to us, and makes us think. What's your opinion?
>
> *Answer:* Firstly, their freedom consists of leaving them in peace and not oppressing them, and this is what the Shari'a enjoins. More than this is their aggression in the face of your bad points and craziness, their benefiting from your ignorance...[5]

---

[3] A Qur'anic term generally agreed to refer to Jews and Christians.

[4] Bediuzzaman Said Nursi, "Münâzarat," in *Asâr-i Bedi'iyye* (n.p., n.d.), p. 417.

[5] Nursi, *Münâzarat* (Istanbul: Sözler Yayinevi, 1977), p. 20.

> *Question:* How can we be equal with non-Muslims?
>
> *Answer:* Equality is ... before the law. A king and a beggar are equal before the law. How could a Shari'a that forbids the deliberate crushing of an ant, or causing it pain, neglect the rights of the sons of Adam? No! We didn't comply with it![6]
>
> *Question:* In the Qur'an, friendship with Jews and Christians is proscribed. .. Why do you say therefore that we should be friends?
>
> *The Answer:* ... For the Qur'anic proscription is not general, it is absolute. If it is absolute, it can be restricted. Time is a great interpreter; if it determines its limits, it cannot be gainsaid [that is, when a matter becomes clear in the course of time, one may not object to it]. ... Besides, a man is loved not for himself, but for his attributes or skills. In which case, just as it is not necessary for every attribute of every Muslim to be Muslim, so it is not necessary for all the attributes and skills of every unbeliever to be unbelieving. Consequently, should it not be permitted to consider good and adopt an attribute or skill which is Muslim? If you have a wife from the People of the Book, of course you should love her![7]

A passage from Said Nuri's Qur'anic commentary, *Isharat al-I'jaz*, begun 1913, although essentially setting out the Qur'anic stand towards the People of the Book, again illustrates his reasoned approach. It is part of his exposition of verse 4 of Sura al-Baqara:

> It is as though the Qur'an is saying: O People of the Book! You should not experience any difficulty in taking this new way [Islam], for you are not casting away your outer shell altogether, but completing your beliefs and building on the fundamentals you already possess. For the Qur'an does not bring any new fundamentals or principal beliefs; it modifies and perfects existent ones; and it combines in itself the virtues of all the previous books and the essentials of all the previous laws. It only establishes new ordinances in secondary matters, which are subject to change due to differences of time and place. For just as with the change of seasons, food and dress and many other things are changed; so too in the stages of a person's life the mode of their education and upbringing changes. Similarly, as is necessitated by wisdom and need, religious ordinances concerning secondary matters change in accordance with the stages of mankind's development. For very many of these are beneficial at one time, yet at another are harmful, and very many medicines were efficacious in mankind's infancy, yet ceased being remedies in its youth. It is why the Qur'an abrogated some of its secondary pronouncements. That is, it decreed that their time had finished, and the turn had come for other decrees.[8]

---

[6] *Münâzarat*, pp. 24-5.

[7] *Münâzarat*, pp. 26-7.

[8] Bediuzzaman Said Nursi, *Signs of Miraclousness: The Inimitability of the Qur'an's Conciseness* [Engl. tr. Sükran Vahide] (Istanbul: Sözler Publications, 2004), p. 57.

The New Said Period

Said Nursi's interior struggles, which were resolved with the emergence of the New Said and were a sort of struggle between reason and revelation, resulted in his finding a way of ascertaining truth through the Qur'an alone and freeing himself from the influences of philosophy. From this time, his works contain numerous comparisons between revelation, usually represented by the Qur'an, which he asserted was the source of all positive progress and "the virtues of civilization," and the philosophy that rejects divine revelation, which he considered to be the source of its evils. Thus, the occasionally unfavourable comments about Western civilization to be found in the *Risale-i Nur* [henceforth, *Risale*], are directed at "the second Europe," mentioned above, which had grown out of materialist philosophy of this sort. It may be said that Nursi's mission with the *Risale*, was besides the renewal of belief, the combatting of materialist philosophy. Thus, according to his ideas, the injustices in the world, which had resulted in the carnage of two world wars, were the direct consequences of materialist philosophy with its rejection of revelational principles.[9]

It is in the light of the above that Nursi's original statement should be seen, that whatever their religion, innocent victims of the wars should be looked on as not only being among the saved, but as having attained the high rank of martyrdom. He expresses this opinion, probably unprecedented among Islamic scholars, in two letters written in Kastamonu around 1941. Parts of them are as follows:

> One time during the First World War, I was extremely grieved at the enemies' slaughter of Muslims, particularly women and children, and their atrocities towards them. Because of the excessive compassion and pity in my nature, the torments I suffered were insupportable. But then suddenly it occurred to me that those slaughtered innocents had become martyrs and saints, their transitory lives had been transformed into immortal life, and their destroyed property become like almsgiving and made into imperishable property. Even if those innocents were unbelievers, in return for the tribulations they suffered due to that worldly disaster, they receive such reward from the treasury of divine mercy that if the veil of the Unseen were to open, a great manifestation of mercy would be apparent on them. I knew they would declare: 'O Lord, we offer You thanks! All praise is God's![10]

The second letter, which Nursi marked "extremely important," mentions each of the groups involved and the recompense they will receive:

> ...While for three or four months I had had no news of the [Second World] War and the world situation, I fell to pitying the families and children in Russia and Europe. ...If those who died and were ruined by that heavenly visitation, which occurred

[9] See, for example, Nursi, *The Words*, pp. 745-8, p. 764; *Emirdağ Lahikasi* (Istanbul: Envar Neşriyat, 1992), ii, p. 98.
[10] Bediuzzaman Said Nursi, *Kastamonu Lahikası* (Istanbul: Sinan Matbaası, 1960), p. 45.

> due to the crimes of tyrants, were fifteen years of age or less, they were martyrs of a sort whatever religion they belonged to. Like Muslims, their great spiritual reward reduces the calamity to nothing. If those who were fifteen and older were innocent and oppressed, their reward is great; indeed, it will save them from Hell. For since in recent times, as though it were a time between prophets (*fetret*), there is a general attitude of indifference towards religion and [towards] the religion of Muhammad (PBUH), and since at the end of time the true religion of Jesus (Peace be upon him) will prevail and will stand shoulder to shoulder with Islam, it may be said with all certainty that the calamity which the oppressed among Christians suffer, those connected to Jesus (UWP), who at present remain in an interregnum-like obscurity, is a sort of martyrdom for them. Especially the old and the afflicted, and the poor and the weak, they suffer adversity under the violence and force of mighty and despotic tyrants...[11]

As is seen in the above letter, during this period Nursi linked the events of the 20th century to the end of time and the second coming of Jesus.[12] These are questions he deals with in some detail, sometimes in response to questions put to him, but chiefly for the purpose of elucidating allegorical Hadiths about the end of time that had been the cause of misunderstanding and therefore of doubts.[13] His interpretations of these Hadiths are of considerable interest in that they not only relate the rise of atheistic philosophy to the antichrist, but also foresee the emergence of "true" Christianity and its joining with Islam in a triumphant struggle against those atheistic currents of thought.

Nursi interprets the vast stature and colossal power ascribed to the antichrist in these Hadiths as a "collective personality," an idea unfamiliar to the people of earlier times, which led to the misunderstanding of the Hadiths.[14] The collective personality of materialism and irreligion will become so powerful, it will only be the collective personality of Jesus, that is, true, revealed religion, that will be able to defeat it. He writes, "At that point when the current appears to be very strong, the religion of true Christianity, which comprises the collective personality of Jesus (UWP), will emerge. That is, it will descend from the skies of divine mercy."[15] For, according to the Nursi, "It will be the truly pious followers of Jesus who will kill the gigantic collective personality of materialism and irreligion that the Dajjal (antichrist) will form — for the Dajjal will be killed by Jesus' (PUH) sword — and destroy his ideas and disbelief, which are atheistic. Those truly pious Christians [or clergy — *Isevî ruhaniler*] will blend the essence of the religion of Jesus with the essence of Islam and rout the Dajjal with their combined strength, in

---

[11] Nursi, *Kastamonu Lahikasi*, p. 75.

[12] See also, Nursi, *The Words*, p. 736 fn 12.

[13] See Nursi, *Kastamonu Lahikasi*, 49; Nursi, *The Rays Collection* [Eng. tr. Sükran Vahide] (Istanbul: Sözler Publications, 1988), pp. 97-102. The latter is the explanatory introduction to the Fifth Ray, about allegorical Hadiths and their interpretation.

[14] Nursi, *The Rays Collection*, p. 101.

[15] Nursi, *Letters*, p. 78.

effect killing him."[16] Present-day Christianity will thus be "purified" and following the Qur'an, will be transformed into "a sort of Islam." This union will signal the descent of Jesus from the heavens, who will come to lead the now mighty force of true religion.[17] In another place, he describes Jesus' pious followers as:

> [A] zealous and self-sacrificing community known as a Christian community but worthy of being called 'Muslim Christians,' [who] will work to unite the true religion of Jesus with the reality of Islam, and will kill and rout that society of the antichrist, thus saving humanity from atheism.[18]

It may also be mentioned that in one place Said Nursi relates Hadiths of this sort, again for the purpose of correcting misunderstandings, to current events, that is, countries which, at that time during the Second World War, either defended Christianity or furthered the cause of irreligion.[19]

The Communist Threat and the Post-World War Two Period

The Second World War brought about great changes in the balance of world powers, with their eventual realignment into the western bloc, in which the United States was the dominant power, and the communist bloc under the leadership of Soviet Russia. Having overrun eastern Europe, and with its aggressive demands over the Bosphorus at the end of the war, communist Russia's overwhelming presence to the north drove Turkey to turn to the western bloc. Communist influence had also been felt increasingly within Turkey in the 1940s.[20] Moreover, a number of Muslim countries entered the Soviet sphere of influence in this period. It is against this background that what appear to be the changes in Nursi's stand towards the West should be seen, and his calls for peace and reconciliation. However, a closer examination of his letters and writings in these last ten years of his life shows that these changes are in fact a development of the ideas he had first formulated after the First World War.

In a piece written during the Second War, Nursi described communism as "an alarming current of irreligion [that] has embarked on a mighty struggle with the revealed religions." But he intimated that "the two great religions," by which he presumably meant Christianity and Islam, were making moves towards "peace and reconciliation."[21] It is not clear precisely what he is referring to here, but it was also around this time that rather than the theoretical union previously mentioned, in

---

[16] Nursi, *The Rays Collection*, p. 108.

[17] Nursi, *Letters*, p. 78.

[18] Nursi, *Letters*, p. 515.

[19] See Nursi, *Kastamonu Lahikası*, pp. 49-50.

[20] Şükran Vahide, *The Author of the Risale-i Nur, Bediuzzaman Said Nursi* (Istanbul: Sözler Publications, 2000), pp. 301-2.

[21] Bediuzzaman Said Nursi, *A Guide For Youth* [Eng. trans.] (Istanbul: Sözler Publications, 1991), p. 33.

one or two places he urges active union and co-operation between Muslims and Christians. He wrote: "At this time too [Muslims] need to unite sincerely not only with their own brothers and fellow-believers, but also with the truly pious Christians (or clergy — *ruhanîler*), temporarily refraining from the discussion and debate of points of difference, in order to combat their joint enemy — aggressive atheism."[22] He also warned that those attempting such an alliance should act with great caution, since "the current from the north" would try to break it.[23]

After the Democrat Party came to power in 1950 and it became possible for him to do so, Nursi himself made moves towards establishing relations with the Christian world. This took the form of his having one of his students send a copy of *Zülfikâr*, a work containing the Twenty-Fifth Word about the Qur'an's miraculousness, and the Nineteenth Letter, about the miracles of Muhammad to the Pope in Rome. He received a gracious letter of thanks, dated February 22, 1951.[24] Also, during his three-month visit to Istanbul in the spring of 1953, he made the move, unprecedented among Islamic scholars—certainly under the Republic, of visiting the Greek Orthodox Patriarch, Patriarch Athenagoras. Most of what passed between them on this courtesy visit has not been recorded, only that in the course of it Nursi said: "If you accept that the Qur'an is God's Word and Muhammad is His prophet, and you act in accordance with true Christianity, you will be among the saved." The Patriarch replied that he did accept this. But when Nursi asked whether the other religious leaders accepted it, he replied in the negative. Nursi related also how well he had been received.[25]

When the Democrat government demonstrated its intention to allow greater religious freedom and combat communism, it won Nursi's support not only in its internal policies, but also in its pro-Western foreign policy. In this post-war period, Nursi looked to the United States in particular as a country that understood the necessity and value of religion, and as such encouraged the Democrat Party to cultivate friendly relations with it.[26] He supported Turkey's participation in the Korean War as part of the struggle against atheism;[27] and according to his student who fought there with his blessing, at that time (1952) supported NATO.[28] He also applauded Turkey's signing of the Baghdad Pact, writing letter of congratulation to the President and Prime Minister,[29] not only because the Pact was a means of re-establishing relations with the Islamic world, but also because he saw it as an

[22] Nursi, *The Flashes Collection*, pp. 203-4 fn 8. See also, Nursi, *Emirdag Lahikasi*, i, p. 206.
[23] Nursi, *Emirdag Lahikasi*, i, p. 159.
[24] Necmeddin Sahiner, *Bilinmeyen Taraflariyla Bediüzzaman Said Nursi* (Istanbul: Nesil Basim Yayin, 13th edn. 1998), p. 384.
[25] Mehmed Firinci, in Sahiner, *Son Sahitler Said Nursi'yi Anlatiyor* (Istanbul: Nesil Basim Yayin, 1999), iv, p. 358.
[26] Nursi, *Emirdag Lahikasi*, ii, p. 25; ii, p. 209.
[27] Vahide, *The Author of the Risale-i Nur*, p. 336.
[28] Bayram Yüksel, in Sahiner, *Son Sahitler*, iii, p. 36.
[29] Nursi, *Emirdag Lahikasi*, ii, pp. 222-5.

important step towards general peace and reconciliation, of which "800 million Christians and members of other religions" were "in severe need." It would win their friendship for Turkey, as well as that of "400 million brother Muslims."[30] Nursi also commented in one of his letters that because of the rise of atheism, irreligion, and anarchy, the gravest dangers facing mankind, America and Europe should no longer be opposed to Islamic unity.[31]

Another dimension of reconciliation, central to the Baghdad Pact letter, was that which would be achieved by the university that for more than fifty years Nursi had striven to found in eastern Anatolia, and was now planned by the government. Nursi urged the President and Prime Minister to give it the form he proposed whereby, by making the religious sciences the basis of it, it would be a means of rapprochement both between the peoples of the region and the eastern Islamic world, and between the inmates of the modern secular schools and the religious schools. It would also bring together the modern sciences and traditional religious sciences, as well as achieving "a full reconciliation between European civilization and the truths of Islam." This last phrase appears nowhere else in his works, and it is not immediately clear what is intended. However, since one of the the main purposes of Nuri's works was to prove the falsity of the materialist philosophies out of which had sprung the civilization of "the second Europe", mentioned at the beginning of this chapter, it sems fair to say that what he is referring to here is a full reconcilation with "the first Europe", which inspired by "the true religion of Jesus," had contributed positively to human progress.

From one or two letters it seems clear that Nursi hoped that the Risale itself would be a means of solidarity and reconciliation between Muslims and Christians, as it was among Musilms. He pointed out that it was now being read by Christians in Europe,[32] and just as it was gathering into its fold Muslims of all shades, so there were signs some Christians missionaries and truly pious followers of Jesus would enter it. For this reason he wanted everyone to perceived the need for reconcilation, and to avoid raising contentious issues.[33]

Finally, a matter that implicitly could bring together believers in divine revelation, and guide them in efforts to rectify the appalling injustices in the world, which in Nursi's view spring from present-day civilization's "not truly heeding the revealed religions," was the adoption and practice of principles — he calls them "fundamental laws"— taken from divine revelation. It was only through the general application of such principles that "true civilization" could be established and universal peace be brought about. In describing them, he analyzes society and diagnoses a number of prevalent ills and their sources in either "principles of human origin" or the neglect of revelational values, and shows how their harm can be reversed by revelational principles. For example, he suggests such principles as frugality and endeavour, taken from Qur'anic verses, to counter the wastefulness

30 Vahide, *The Author of the Risale-i Nur*, pp. 353-4.

31 Nursi, *Emirdag Lahikasi*, ii, p. 54.

32 Nursi, *Emirdag Lahikasi*, ii, p. 181.

33 Nursi, *Emirdag Lahikasi*, i, p. 211.

and extravagance encouraged by modern civilization; and the payment of *zakat* (the purification tax) and prohibition of usury and interest, disregard for which had led to serious social imbalances and ultimately to the revolt of the lower classes and disastrous social upheavals. He points out too that while modern technological wonders should be used "for the benefit of mankind ... four fifths are used on meaningless trivia and encourage idleness and depravity." Furthermore, he diagnoses human problems which have become acute due to the general "awakening" of mankind caused by war and advances in science in particular, and points out that with their proofs of the life of the hereafter they can be solved and "healed" only by the Qur'an and divine revelation.[34]

Conclusion

Three main conclusions may be drawn from this outline of Nursi's views on Christianity and the West:

Firstly is the comprehensiveness of his views and their looking to general reconciliation and universal peace. Nursi considered reconciliation and joint action between pious Muslims and Christians to be part of a universal struggle against the forces of unbelief and irreligion. The co-operation he foresaw would most probably fulfil a function in society similar to that of the *Risale* and its students, that is, countering "the moral and spiritual (*mânevî*) destruction" of aggressive atheism, and "healing" and "repairing" its damage. Following the Second World War, Nursi also supported the political alliance of Turkey and the West, and this was because it was engaged, as representing Christianity—anyway to an extent, in the struggle against communism. From the way he worded his letter about the political alliance of the Baghdad Pact, that is his saying "winning the friendship of 800 million Christians and members of other religions ... [and of] 400 million fellow-Muslims," it may be said that he looked on political alliance as an extension of the co-operation of individual Christians and Muslims. Within this framework, Nursi clearly attached great importance to the reconciliation also of the Islamic world and the West, and particularly to the reforging of links between Turkey and other Muslim countries. Similarly, he laid great emphasis on strengthening the internal unity of the Islamic world, and in his works put forward constructive ideas for settling deep-set differences and conflicts equitably, in the light of the many commonly held beliefs. A further, fundamental element of the reconciliation he envisaged was reconciliation on the level of knowledge, learning, and education, and the disciplines and traditions they represented, the basis of any true and lasting reconciliation. Also, a positive outcome of all the wars and destruction of the twentieth century which gave him hope, was "the awakening" or increased consciousness among a section of mankind of their need for "a true religion,"

---

[34] See Bediuzzaman Said Nursi, *The Damascus Sermon* [Eng. tr. Sükran Vahide], pp. 126-131; also, pp. 29-31; Nursi, *Emirdag Lahikasi*, ii, pp. 98-101; Nursi, *The Words*, pp. 167-8. See also, *Emirdag Lahikasi*, ii, pp. 81-4; ii, pp. 172-5.

which potentially greatly increased the force working to establish justice on the earth in the way he foresaw.

Secondly: The unifying factor in this comprehensive view, or strategy even, of Nursi, is divine revelation and the revealed religions, and broadly speaking, adherence to its principles is the criterion for alliance. In my view, this was an elaboration of the analytical model, based on the counterposing of divine revelation and "man-made" philosophy, which was an important element of the New Said's thought, and shows the development of his ideas in the last period of his life. Furthermore, it offers a model for analyzing future developments and the great changes that occurred with the collapse of communism and raising of the Iron Curtain.

Thirdly: In Nursi's "revelational principles," which significantly he called "fundamental laws," are a way of uniting all believers in divine revelation, whatever their position or rank, in a practical and practicable struggle to reorder their own lives and bring about a transformation of present-day civilization. Only in this way may civilization's virtues come to outweigh its evils, and peace and prosperity be secured for the majority of mankind.

PART III
GLOBALIZATION

Chapter 9

Is Globalization a Threat to Islam? Said Nursi's Response

Oliver Leaman

Said Nursi's concern at the imposition of Western values in Turkey and the rest of the Islamic world, at that time very well based, leads to an interesting discussion in his work of how the Islamic world should react to globalization. Even more interesting is his strong belief that this ideological attack would fail. Nursi saw the problem of globalization as largely coming from within not from without. Local Muslim intellectuals become distrustful of their culture and turn to the West. They feel that Islam is old-fashioned and unable to compete in the market for ideas with the sorts of views emanating from the West. To be modern people in a modern world in a modern country implies rejecting religion, or at least demoting it from the leading position, which it might have had in the local culture.

Nursi's confidence in the success of Islam is based on *sabr* and *tawakkul*, two primary virtues that he sees to reside within Islamic culture.[1] The move from the Old Said to the New Said is from the political to the personal, and these illustrate the significance of patience and trust in God. Relying on political change, as the sole means of improving life is precisely not to be patient nor to trust in God, it is to take measures into one's own hands. Nursi is not advocating political quietism. When it is possible for the personal to be converted into the political, then this should be done, and the sorts of ideas about how people ought to live, what sort of social structure should prevail, these are all worth pursuing when it is feasible to do so.[2]

Nursi saw the greatest threat to Islam being in the private and not the public sphere, in the ways in which individuals think. Globalization results in a

---

[1] Yvonne Haddad (1999) 'Ghurba as a paradigm for Muslim life: A *Risale-i Nur* Worldview', *The Muslim World* (LXXXIX), pp. 297-313.

[2] One of the interesting aspects of globalization is that if Turkey joins the EU it will make the position of religion within Turkey more powerful, since many of the measures presently taken to restrict Islam will be judged anticonstitutional at the European Court when challenged. This is an example of globalization being the very opposite of a threat and another example where Nursi's confidence in the ability of Islam to survive the secular critique appears to be justified.

general scientific attitude to the world, to the idea that the world is ultimately scientifically explicable and that God does not play a significant part in the workings of the world. This belief in the importance of science is not necessarily antagonistic to Islam, Nursi himself insisted on the significance of science, but what he criticized was the belief that science explained everything.[3] Here it is important to address the personal and not the political. On a political level one might agree that God was the creator of everything and science explained the actual nuts and bolts of his creation, but it is not easy to disentangle these beliefs, so that although one says that God is the creator, one really may not believe in his actual power over the world. One says that one believes it, but this is a formal general belief in a principle, not a real belief which one holds personally, something which infuses one's life with meaning. The danger of globalization is that it encourages people not only to live like Westerners, by which he means non-Muslims, but it encourages people to think like them, and the principles which Nursi thought characterized global culture is atheism and materialism.

Is he right? I shall argue that he has his sights on an interesting point here. Globalization as it has taken place over the last century or so is largely the imposition of materialist ideas on cultures, which at least in principle were not materialist. They established within themselves a serious role for God, and within Islam that is illustrated by the lives of Muslims, their practices and beliefs. After globalization the practices and beliefs continue, and yet within a thoroughly changed context, one in which those beliefs and practices no longer have purchase on people's lives. What makes the situation so insidious is that they may well not realize what is happening, since they are behaving in the ways in which they have always behaved, but what that behavior conceals is more revealing than what it displays. What it conceals is a real lack of trust in God, who has been replaced by a crude belief that the world operates in accordance with scientific principles, which serve as the complete explanation of everything, which happens. It is not that God and his role are denied; it is just that he is treated as someone who now exists in the background, someone to whom polite reference is appropriate, but no longer a key player in the business of life.

Why has globalization brought about this attitude? After all, the leading engine of the process is the United States, which in many ways is a deeply religious society, and whose inhabitants would be shocked to learn that their main cultural and economic products are believed to lead to the spread of atheism and materialism. It is certainly not the case that the global products include subtle references to Christianity, for example, and so are designed surreptitiously to convert Muslims. Neither do they contain any direct anti-religious message or advocacy of atheism, and were they to do any of these things they would be less dangerous. What they do is to present a picture of the world in which God is

---

[3] Oliver Leaman (1999) 'Nursi's place in the Ihya` tradition', *The Muslim World* (LXXXIX), pp. 314-24.

absent, he does nothing of significance, he is something added on, as it were, and everything can proceed perfectly normally without him.[4] That is the attitude to which Nursi was objecting, and which he thought so dangerous, and surely he has his finger on an important issue here. It is not enough for people to use a word like "God" for that word to have meaning, or at least to have the meaning they think it has. There is a saying that in the early years of Islam there was a reality which came to be called Sufism but it did not have a name. Now there is a name but no reality corresponding to it!

Walter Benjamin claimed that religion persists despite the existence of mass production because the fragmentation brought about by late capitalism produces in us a desire for sources of transcendence to counter modern industry's secularizing impulses. This transcendence may be replicated, albeit in a far weaker way, by entertainment and the mass media, something which Nursi noticed well before these forces took on their omnipresent form at the start of the twenty first century. He points out that in a Europe which has lost its faith the only way in which people can find a reason to live and have confidence in society is through the ubiquity of short-lived pleasure through the entertainment industry and also, more grimly, through force.[5] After all, society is seen as a state of natural conflict, and only force and authority can stop people attacking each other. There is no overwhelming power to which most people give adherence any more, this was the case when Europe was properly Christian, according to Nursi, but in the twentieth century modernity is characterized far more by blunt economic and military power than it is by spirituality. Hence the identification of modernity of the wrong i.e. materialist kind with the *dajjal*, the Anti-Christ, with his one eye. He is one-dimensional in his concerns, and the materialist state is only interested in matter, in what pleasures it can acquire and pains avoid. Nursi refers to the Qur'an here, 'For the prayer of those without faith is nothing but wandering' (13:14). He contrasts this with the situation of the Muslim, or indeed the sincere Christian, who has confidence in God, and believes that 'To God we belong and to him is our return' (2:156).

This provides an indication of what might be regarded as an authentic version of globalization, the confidence that God is everywhere and as a result we should feel at home anywhere. Tarik, on crossing from Africa to Andalusia in his invasion of the Iberian Peninsula, is supposed to have said, "Every country is our country because it is the country of God." He got his troops to burn their boats. One of the reasons why Islam has been such a successful global religion is based on its ability to become local. This is called globalization, referring to the way in which the global becomes the local[6]. Islam is so different in its various manifestations around the world, and as we know this is often decried as evidence

---

[4] Oliver Leaman (1999) *Brief Introduction to Islamic Philosophy*, Oxford: Polity.

[5] Nursi, *Risale-i Nur*, Seventeenth Flash, Fifth Note.

[6] John Short (2001) *Global Dimensions; Space, Place and the Contemporary World*, London: Reaktion Books.

of a basic lack of unity. But in fact it is a sign of strength, that Islam has been able to latch onto the particular individual cultures and interests of the communities which it has affected, and in turn has converted into a different sort of community, the *umma*, those very diverse collections of individuals. Although what comes about is indeed an *umma*, the *ummat Islam* is hardly homogenous, it is rather still marked by the local, by what preceded Islam. In an indication of this, God transmitted the Qur'an in Arabic, in the language of the *jahaliyya*. He adapted his message to the local, as indeed all messengers and prophets do, since to do otherwise is to invite lack of communication. So the contrast between the global and the local is really not a meaningful contrast at all, the global can only spread around the world if it is capable of becoming local, and the local can only survive as local if it is prepared to link up with the global.[7]

The Internet is creating another language, which is neither written nor oral, a world wide web made of images, sounds and written words.[8] *Dawa* on the Internet has proved to be very effective, so globalization has positive aspects for Islam also. In particular, the possibilities for the development of Islamic education are exciting, excellent teaching materials can be effortlessly acquired and used, and a wide gamut of different sorts of teaching techniques can be explored through this medium. One might worry that the very variety of material which can be accessed by computer makes globalization dangerous, the student who has visited some Islamic sites can also visit other sites which have no religious purpose or even an anti-religious purpose. As Nursi would put it, the forces of modernity have a dark side, the emphasis on materialism and human competition and conflict often gets in the way of the general message of scientific advance and intellectual enquiry, and these forces need to be fought. It is no good ignoring them and hoping that they will go away, if God wanted us to avoid such conflicts he would not have sent us to earth as his *khalifa*. When the angels are told to bow down to Adam they predict that if human beings are sent to earth and allowed to do as they wish, they will cause all sorts of problems and prove to be poor representatives of the divinity. It is clear from the surat al-baqarah (30-39) that God intends human beings to take charge not only of themselves but also of the world as a whole. The angels quite correctly pointed out that if human beings are allowed to be free this will result in corruption and bloodshed. Yet God still puts humanity in charge since he knew that we had the innate ability to manage our affairs appropriately. He provided guidance to human beings, which they required even more when they were consigned to this world, and their ability to sin became even greater, since in this world they were partially at least under the influence of Satan. We are free but we

---

[7] This is perhaps one of the reasons why we should be wary of the label *salafi*. It implies that there is something especially important about a particular set of local conditions, which of course there is, but what is important about those local conditions is really that they can be made global.

[8] Naomi Sakr (2001) *Satellite Realms: Transnational Television, Globalization and the Middle East*, London: I.B. Tauris.

need to restrain ourselves, and if we do not then violence can easily result. In fact, Satan refers to enmity as being something, which is going to characterize life in this world. The interesting question, which arises, is how one can reduce this conflict, which seems to arise naturally from life in this world and what it involves. Of course, as we know the angels were right, but God still sent us to earth, taught Adam the names of everything, which exists there and sent guidance to humanity so that we might live well and in the right sort of way.

We often talk of globalization as though it were something very new, but it is not at all, the process of increasing in knowledge inevitably brings with it the possibility of acquiring knowledge which is not really worth having, knowledge which in fact may interfere with the primary process of acquiring knowledge, which is to know God, in so far as we can. This is not a novel problem but something which has characterized Islamic culture right from the beginning. Every generation thinks that the problems which confront it are unique and have never been seen before, but their predecessors knew this was not the case, the precise nature of the problems may be distinct but their presence and general form is all too familiar. God expects us to resolve these problems, with his guidance, and there is no reason to think that we are unable to do so. It is worth recalling here a Qur'anic passage of which Nursi was very fond,'God is enough for us, and how excellent a guardian he is' (3:173).

This might be regarded as being unduly optimistic. After all, globalization is linked with hegemony and homogenization.And perhaps what has so far been argued is based on globalization as part of modernity, not postmodernity. Yet as Canlini argues, there is a big difference between modernity and postmodernity. The former is territorial and usually monolinguistic, while the latter is transterritorial and multilinguistic.[9] Nursi clearly has in mind modern forms of globalization, not the postmodern. Postmodern forms of globalization are even more persistent and irresistible than the modern varieties. But there is no reason to think that the local has lost its significance even within postmodern society, unless the media images of globalization make sense to the local context, they will fail to have purchase in any case. When in the documentary film *Runaway*, Mrs Shirazi threatens a man that if he fails to treat a girl properly, and she runs away, she will take him to the International Court in the Hague,[10] the fact that Mrs Shirazi knows that there are other forms of legislation apart from the Islamic law of Iran is a result of globalization, but it is not essentially threatening to Islam. It is only threatening if adherence to Islam is so fragile that it is maintained through ignorance of any alternatives, and that is hardly a form of adherence, which one would want to defend. Nursi is quite right to be confident of the ability of Islam to resist the forces of globalization, and indeed were he to be alive today he would

---

[9] *Consumers and Citizens*, N.G. Canclini, (2001) trans. G. Yudice, Minneapolis: University of Minnesota Press.

[10] *Runaway*, directed by Kim Longnotto and Ziba Mir-Hosseini, Women Make Movies, London, 2001.

welcome the role which Islam is now playing in presenting itself globally to a wide range of audiences. In fact, the culture of postmodernity is precisely appropriate to Islam, given its universal and inclusivist message, and Nursi would see globalization as presenting the Islamic world with more possibilities than problems.

Chapter 10

Bediuzzaman Said Nursi's Historical Self-Consciousness

Mahan H. Mirza

Introduction

This chapter discusses Bediuzzaman Said Nursi's (1876-1960) perception of his own place in the historical process, paying special attention to the 'end of history'. The 'end of history' has different connotations depending upon whether the perspective is philosophical (evolutionary; within the natural course of history) or eschatological (events imposed on history by Divine intervention towards the end of time). Although it is largely the eschatological tradition within Islam that delineates the parameters for Said Nursi's understanding, his inclination to make this tradition philosophically plausible with respect to the world around him plays an important role in the development and articulation of his ideas. This tendency to mix tradition with pragmatism has played a key role in Said Nursi's appeal to a broad segment of Turkish society. According to Kernal Karpat in his article in *The Encyclopedia of Islam*, "Nursi's teachings lacked the dogmatism and rigidity that infected many other fundamentalist movements and appeared at times to say many things at once. This vagueness appealed to a variety of groups, ranging from modernists to moderate conservatives to dedicated Islamists".[1]

Said Nursi lived a long life during which he witnessed European colonial rule over Muslim lands, two World Wars, the collapse of the Ottoman Empire followed by its radical secularization, the formation and failure of the League of Nations, its reconstitution in the form of the United Nations, and the beginnings of the Cold War. He also witnessed dramatic changes in humanity's conceptualization of the world, such as the articulation of the theory of relativity, the birth of flight and even the spawning of the space-race. He played many roles in these times as a scholar, an activist, a soldier, a teacher, and an author. He was a contemporary of epochal Muslim thinkers such as Iqbal (d. 1938), Abduh (d. 1905), and Mawdudi (d. 1979), and outlived two of them. He came after Enlightenment thinkers of the

[1] Kernal Karpat, "Nursi, Sheykh Badi' al-Zaman Sa'id," in *The Encyclopedia of Islam*, 2nd Ed., Vol. VIII, p. 144. For more on a sociological understanding of Said Nursi's impact in Turkish society, see: Serif Mardin, Religion *and Social Change in Modern Turkey: The Case of Bediüzzaman Said Nursi*, (Albany: State University of New York Press, 1989).

likes of Kant, Hegel and Marx,[2] and must have been aware of the increasing consciousness that "world history travels from the East to West, for Europe is absolutely (*schlechthin*) the end of world history, Asia the beginning".[3] What was his response to this consciousness and how did he appropriate his own life within the context of world history? Before turning to Said Nursi, however, it is prudent to first provide a brief survey of the Islamic 'end of time' tradition.

The Islamic 'End of Time' Tradition

Anyone who has read even a small portion of the Qur'an has noticed constant references to another life. Such allusions clearly create a sense of finitude about things related to earthly existence. For example, the very opening *sura* (chapter) addresses God as "Master of the day of judgment" (1:3), and the beginning of the second *sura*, while describing the characteristic traits of the believers, describes them as "those who have complete certainty in the hereafter" (2:4).[4] There are other verses of the Qur'an that are more explicit about the fleeting nature of worldly existence: "The life of this world is nothing more than entertainment and play. It is the life of the hereafter that is the ultimate living [reality], if they but knew" (29:64); "Everything...will perish, and nothing will remain save the face of your Lord, full of Magnificence and Benevolence" (55:26-27); "He has made the sun and the moon subservient, each running its course for a [limited] term" (31:29); and "God has created the heavens and the earth and all that is between them with a purpose (*bil-haqq*) and for a [limited] term" (30:8). Although these and numerous other references in the Qur'an demonstrate that the world will end and that there is an 'end' to history, these references are eschatological, meaning

---

[2] These Muslim and Western authors are mentioned only to show the spirit of the age in which he lived. Although Nursi's biography suggests that he was extremely well read in Western philosophy and the Islamic tradition, I have not researched which particular authors he benefited from most. It should be noted that according to Karpat, Nursi's studies were mostly in the physical and natural sciences, and this is what Nursi means when he refers to his study of "philosophy" (p. 143).

[3] Joseph McCarney, *Routledge Philosophy Guidebook to Hegel on History*, Ed. Jim Crane, (London: Routledge, 2000), p. 173. Contrary to this, many Muslims believe the end of world history will be with the triumph of Islam. They base this on a number of traditions (briefly discussed in this chapter below). An alignment has thus emerged between some philosophical trends in the study of history and religious ideas inasmuch as both suggest an 'end'. According to Francis Fukuyama: "Both Hegel and Marx believed that the evolution of human societies was not open ended, but would end when mankind had achieved a form of society that satisfied its deepest and most fundamental longings. Both thinkers thus posited an 'end of history': for Hegel this was the liberal state, while for Marx it was a communist society" (Francis Fukuyama, *The End of History and the Last Man*, (New York: The Free Press, 1992), p. xii.

[4] This 'certainty' is to be contrasted with mere 'belief' in God, His messengers, and other dimensions of the unseen realm of reality; compare with Qur'an 2:2.

that cataclysmic events will be imposed on the natural course of history. Note the following as further elaboration:

> When the sun is shrouded in darkness; and when the stars lose their light; and when the mountains are made to vanish; and when she-camels big with young, about to give birth, are left untended; and when all beasts are gathered together; and when the seas boil over; and when all human beings are coupled [with their deeds]; and when the girl child that was buried alive is made to ask; for what crime she had been slain...(81:1-9).

Even in its eschatological narratives, the Qur'an is reluctant to give specific signs of the inevitable apocalypse within the framework of conventional history.[5] The *hadith* literature (traditions from the Prophet's life) tends to be far more specific about things to watch for towards the end of time.[6] Two key figures in the *hadith* literature dealing with the end of time are *Dajjal* (the great imposter)[7] and *Mahdi* (the renewer of the faith)[8], whose armies will be pitched in battle with

---

[5] Some references have been gleaned by many interpreters, such as the coming together of the children of Israel as a "motley crowd" (*lafifa*) at the end of time as the creation of the state of Israel from a cosmopolitan Jewish population (17:104), or second coming of Christ (3:46 and 43:61).

[6] Here are some eye-catching examples in light of contemporary events: "The final hour will not be established until the Euphrates discloses a mountain of Gold that will be fought over. Ninety-nine out of hundred people will be killed, but every one of them will say, 'Perhaps I'll be the one to be saved" (Abu Zakariyya Yahya b. Sharaf, *Riyad al-Salihin*, 1st Ed., Hadith No. 1822, (Riyadh: Dar al-Salam, 1996), p. 822); "He [Gabriel] said, "Tell me about the final hour," and he [Muhammad] replied, "The one questioned about it knows no better than the questioner!" [Gabriel] said, "Then tell me about its signs". [Muhammad] said, "That the slave-girl will give birth to her mistress, and that you will see the barefooted, naked, destitute herdsmen competing in constructing lofty buildings" (Muhammad Manzur Nu'mnni, *Ma'arif al-hadith*, Vol. 1, (Karachi: Dar al-Isha'at, 2001), p. 54); "How will you be when Jesus, the son of Mary, descends in your midst and your leader will be from amongst your ranks" (Muhammad Fu'ad 'Abd al-Baqi, *al-Lu'lu'u wal-marjan fi-ma ittafaqa 'alayhi al-shaykhan*, 1st Ed., Kitab al-Iman, (Riyadh: Dar al-Salam, 1996), p. 66); "The final hour will not arrive until the sun rises from the west. When it does so, and the people see it, all of them will come to believe! Yet, that will be a time when their faith does them no good" ('Abd al-Baqi, *al-Lu'lu'u wal-marjan*, p. 67). Some of these traditions have been taken literally, but some have also been interpreted allegorically. For example, considering the sun rising from the west as the rise of Islam in the western world, the gold of the Euphrates as the oil of Iraq, and the competition to build lofty buildings by barefooted herdsmen as the recent prosperity in the Gulf States.

[7] Lit. "great imposter", but often translated as the "anti-Christ".

[8] According to tradition, God sends a renewer of the teachings of Islam at the end (or beginning) of every century, the last of these being the *Mahdi* (the guided one). For a study on the development of the concept in early Islamic history see Wilferd Madelung's detailed article in *The Encyclopedia of Islam* (2nd Ed.). For a summary with special attention to the place of Said Nursi, see: Hamid Algar, "The Centennial Renewer: Bediuzzaman Said Nursi

each other when Jesus will descend only to join arms with *Mahdi* and kill *Dajjal*.[9] The *hadiths* on the circumstances of these events are surprisingly detailed at times, naming places, describing the physical features of *Dajjal* and even the manner of Jesus's descent. Here are some selected excerpts from a lengthy tradition of the Prophet as a good example:

> If he [*Dajjal*] appears while I am amongst you, I will take care of him for you, but if he emerges while I am not amongst you, then every man for himself...he is a young man with curly hair, blind of one eye, resembling 'Abd al-'Uzza b. Qatan...he will emerge from the area between Syria and Iraq...[his stay in the world will be] forty days – one day like a year, and one day like a month...[he will travel through the earth] like clouds moving on wind, and he will come to a people and summon them, and they will believe in him, and they will respond to him, so he will command the sky and it will pour down rain, and [likewise] the earth and it will sprout...until he comes to a people and summons them and they reject him, so he will turn away from them, and they will find [their land] turning barren, without anything remaining of the wealth they used to possess...and this is how it will be when God, the Exalted, makes the Messiah, son of Mary, descend. He will come down near two white minarets in a yellow robe in east Damascus, his hands resting on the shoulders of two angels. When he lowers his head, it drips, and when he raises it, drops fall from it like pearls...[10]

The entire narration is profoundly fertile for the speculative imagination of theologians, particularly if they are given to allegorical interpretation.[11] Other narrations speak of the historical events as culminating with a victory of Islam before the final apocalypse. For example, the messenger of God is reported to have said: "Indeed God folded up for me the earth, so I saw its 'easts' and 'wests', and indeed the rule of my *umma* will reach all of the places that were shown to me."[12] It is in the shadow of such a tradition that Said Nursi operates.

---

and the Tradition of *Tajdid*," in *Journal of Islamic Studies*, 12:3, (Oxford: Oxford Center for Islamic Studies, 2001), pp. 291-311.

[9] These traditions have been incorporated and interpreted differently by different groups within Islam throughout history. In this chapter I follow the generally accepted views of 'modern traditionalists' or mainstream sunni Muslims, which is consistent with Nursi's own approach.

[10] Yahya b. Sharaf, *Riyad al-salihin*, p. 871-873, narrated on the authority of Muslim.

[11] Allegorically, *Dajjal* has sometimes been taken to be more than a person, but also a 'phenomenon' manifesting itself in as a civilization built upon a one-eyed (materialist) epistemology, blind of the eye of spirituality.

[12] Israr Ahmad, *Musalman ummaton ka mazi, hal, aur mustaqbil, aur musalmanan-i Pakistan ki khususi zimma dariyan* (Lahore: Markazi Anjuman Khuddamul Qur'an, 1996), p. 12. In translation, the title of this Urdu work reads: *The Past, Present and Future of the Muslim Communities, and the Exclusive Obligations of the Muslims of Pakistan*. This work is available from the same publisher in more of an English rendering of ideas rather than a direct translation under the title: *Lessons from History: Reflections on the Past, Present, and Future of Two Muslim Communities*.

Said Nursi And The End Of Time

In the first part of his career that involved events preceding the First World War, Said Nursi was preoccupied with western philosophy and the need to build a university in east Turkey that combined traditional Islamic learning with modern science. He was a vigorous proponent of constitutionalism, which is to say that political life should be regulated by the rule of law as laid out in a constitution, through mutual consultation and the debating of opposing ideas. Said Nursi was confident that enlightened believers could live a life faithful to the *shari'a* (Divine law) through the democratic process: "The consensus of the community constitutes a certain proof in the *shari'a*. The opinion of the mass of the people forms a fundamental principle in the *shari'a*. The public wish is esteemed and respected in the *shari'a*".[13] Such a democratic spirit goes hand in hand with the notion of freedom and a free society. Nursi did not shy away from this conclusion. He embraced it, calling for the same spirit amongst scholars and students. He strongly believed in the legitimising activity of the collective over and above individual brilliance and indicated that this was one of the features distinguishing the past from the future.[14]

The spirit of mutual consultation and cooperation entails a fundamental belief that 'the truth' or the correct way can be gleaned from bits of truths that come together through the process of an open and free discourse. This sets the terms for his interaction with western civilization and its relation to the Islamic civilization in the context of world history. Nursi was adamant at taking and appropriating the best of what Europe had to offer within an Islamic worldview: "...there are numerous virtues in [modern] civilization, but they are neither the property of Christianity, nor the creation of Europe, nor the work of this century. Rather, they are the property of all. They arise from the combined thought of mankind".[15] This is what caused him to conclude as early as 1908: "The Ottoman State is pregnant with Europe, and it will give birth to an European state one day. And Europe is pregnant with Islam; one day it will give birth to an Islamic state".[16] This thesis was elaborated in the celebrated Damascus Sermon in 1911: "...in the future when reason, science and technology prevail, of a certainty that will be the time the Qur'an will gain ascendancy, which relies on rational proofs and invites

[13] Sukran Vahide, *The Biography of Bediuzzaman Said Nursi*, p. 60. All references to the Biography and Said Nursi's works are from the CD-Rom, *Risale-i Nur* 1.0, (2000).

[14] He even applied the same principle towards understanding the Qur'an: "Thus, in the modern age when the cosmos is being opened up and its workings are being revealed by science, commentaries on the Qur'an must keep pace with these giant strides science is taking. Bediuzzaman points out that it is beyond the capacity of an individual or even a small group to be familiar with all the sciences, and a commentary should therefore be written by a committee of scholars who are specialists in a number of sciences, both religious and modern" (Vahide, *Biography*, p. 126).

[15] Vahide, *Biography*, p. 158.

[16] Vahide, *Biography*, p. 67.

the reason to confirm its pronouncements".[17] Thus, Nursi was clearly aware of being in a global age whose consciousness was rapidly evolving as a natural historical process towards affirming God's revelation as the ultimate guiding principle for life on earth.

With the emergence of the 'New Said' post World War I, during troubled times in prison and exile, came the transformation from a preoccupation with western philosophy to a fixation with the Qur'an and the need for 'certain' faith.[18] It was a period in which "the ascetic spiritual 'new' Said replaced the activist worldly 'old' Said". This quest ultimately led towards the emanation of the *Risale-*

---

[17] Nursi, *Damascus Sermon*, p. 32. In such a teleological reading of history, one sees an overlap between religion and philosophy. Although it is possible to claim philosophically and even anthropologically that the flow of history is directional, as many a scientist have done, to suggest an 'end' assumes that a sort of absolute truth is attainable, at least theoretically. Perhaps this is why it is here that philosophically minded theologians and religious minded philosophers find common ground. McCarney explains in his *Guidebook to Hegel on History*: "[Engels] argues that Hegel 'was compelled to make a system', and, hence, to accord with traditional requirements, had to conclude with 'some sort of absolute truth'. So far as the historical process is concerned, this implied an 'end' (*das Ende der Geschichte*) that involves, on the one hand, humanity's arrival at 'the cognition of the absolute Idea', and, on the other, its carrying out of the Idea into reality" (p. 170). For more on this, see for example: Emil L. Fackenheim, *The Religious Dimension in Hegel's Thought*, (Bloomington: Indiana University Press, 1967).

[18] In a manner reminiscent of al-Ghazali (1058-1111), Nursi reflects on this pivotal moment towards the end of his life: "Sixty years ago, I was searching for a way to reach the truth and reality at the present time. That is, I was searching for a short way to obtain firm faith and belief and a complete understanding of Islam which would not be shaken by the attacks of the numerous negative and damaging currents. Firstly, I had recourse to the way of the philosophers; I wanted to reach the truth with just the reason. I reached it only twice with extreme difficulty. I looked and saw that even the greatest geniuses of mankind had gone only half the way, only one or two had been able to reach the truth by means of the reason alone. Then I said: 'A way which even the greatest geniuses had been unable to take cannot be made general for everyone', and I gave it up. For numerous philosophers, even Ibn-i Sina [Avicenna], Farabi, Aristotle and others had only got half way. I saw that only one or two had been able to rise to the truth. Then I understood that a path and way by which not even the great geniuses had been able to rise, could not be the way for everyone. Then I had recourse to the way of Sufism and studied it. I saw that it was most luminous and effulgent, but that it needed the greatest caution. Only the highest of the elite could take that way. And so, saying, neither can this way be a way for everyone at this time, I sought help from the Qur'an. And thanks be to God, the *Risale-i Nur* was bestowed on me, which at this time is a sound and short way of the Qur'an for the believers" (Vahide, *Biography*, p. 168). This key passage gives us helpful tools for analyzing and appreciating the *Risale-i Nur*. It was not meant to be a philosophically rigorous work with universal assumptions, but an inspiration for the masses of Muslims who were trying to make sense of the rapidly changing world in light of God's revelation. For a discussion on Nursi's method, see: Oliver Leaman, "Nursi's Place in the *Ihya* Tradition," in *The Muslim World*, Vol. LXXXIX, No. 3-4, July-October, (Hartford: The Duncan Black McDonanld Center at the Hartford Seminary, 1999), pp. 314-324.

i Nur from Nursi's heart as an exposition of the Qur'an in a manner that made it relevant for the modern Muslim.[19]

There are many references to the 'end of time' traditions in the *Risale-i Nur*, most extensively in the 'Fifth Ray' where he sets out his exegetical principles. Nursi begins: "Like allegorical verses of the Qur'an, some *hadiths* about the events of the end of time have profound meanings", but are not easily interpreted, since "their meaning, interpretation and what is intended by them is only understood after the event".[20] He emphasized the allegorical nature of some of these traditions, cautioning that if taken literally, they are "not comfortable with reality".[21] Although keen to interpret these traditions with reference to contemporary events, thereby placing himself within the context of the last age, Said Nursi cautions that it is not possible to ever know this with certainty.[22]

Nursi's tendency to interpret the signs of the end of time in light of contemporary events remains consistent within the *Risale-i Nur*. For example, amongst the attributes of *Dajjal* that are mentioned in the traditions are that he will travel the world rapidly and that the entire world will hear of his coming. Explaining the tradition, Said Nursi says:

> As for the part, "When the Dajjal appears, all the world will hear of it," the telegraph and radio have solved this. As for his traveling the world in forty days, the railway and aeroplane, which are his mounts, have solved. Deniers who formerly considered these two statements to be impossible, now see them as commonplace![23]

By explaining the allusions to the circumstances surrounding the appearance of *Dajjal* at the end of time with events that were taking place in his own time, Said Nursi wants to show that the end of time is near. His words: "At a time when my old age was warning me of my own departure amid the events of the end of time, which in turn give me warning of the end of the world"[24], state the point explicitly. This conviction of Nursi gives us valuable insights on the way he perceived his

---

[19] Karpat, "Nursi," in EI^2, p. 143.
[20] Nursi, *The Rays*, pp. 97-98.
[21] Nursi, *The Rays*, p. 99.
[22] He approves of this ambiguity within the traditional narrations and justifies it as being rooted in the words of wisdom of the eminent traditionalist Jalal al-Din Suyuti (1445-1505), that because of this ambiguity one remains "aware that the end of the world may occur in any age, or that it may continue, and so works for eternal life within the transitoriness of this world, and strives to build the world as though he was never going to die" (Nursi, *The Rays*, p. 100). Nursi proceeds in the 'Second Station of the Fifth Ray' to interpret twenty-three matters. Although preceding every one of his interpretations with "Allah knows best", Said Nursi relates virtually all of the signs of the end of time to his contemporary environment, such as the mandatory change of head-gear, the call to prayer in Turkish, and even the proximity of the schools and jails with respect to each other.
[23] Nursi, *The Words*, p. 354.
[24] Nursi, *The Rays*, p. 83.

own efforts and the *Risale-i-Nur* movement. On the one hand, he sees the global historical process culminating in an Islamic consciousness, and on the other hand he sees signs of the last days within the Islamic eschatological tradition unfolding before his very eyes.

In one instance, Said Nursi explicitly interprets his own life as a landmark event indicating the imminence of the end of time. When asked whether he himself might be the prophesied *Mahdi* sent to revive the *umma* at the end of time, he flatly rejected the idea in a literal sense, but partly accepted it in a metaphorical sense:

> The collective personality of the sacred community which the Mahdi descended from God's Messenger will represent will have three functions: to save belief, to revive the marks of Islam under the title of the caliphate of Muhammad (PBUH), and to modify to some extent the laws of the *shari'a* of Muhammad (PBUH). He will attempt to carry out this vast duty. Since the Risale-i Nur students see the first duty completely in the Risale-i Nur, saying that the second and third duties are in second and third place, they rightly suppose the Risale-i Nur's collective personality to be a sort of Mahdi.[25]

This is a conclusive statement of Nursi's historical self-consciousness – the perception of his own movement as a collective personification of the *Mahdi*. This interpretation is consistent with the way Nursi construes Jesus and *Dajjal*, with Jesus being personified in his true followers and *Daijal* in the iniquitous culture of materialism:[26]

> It will be the truly pious followers of Jesus who will kill the gigantic collective personality of materialism and irreligion which the Dajjal will form – for the Dajjal will be killed by Jesus' (PUH) sword – and destroy the ideas of disbelief, which are atheistic. Those true pious Christians will blend the essence of true Christianity with the essence of Islam and rout the Dajjal with their combined strength, in effect killing him.[27]

It is not difficult to conclude that Said Nursi saw himself as playing a central role in the revitalization of Islam and the Muslims that would lead to the ascendancy of Islam before the end of the world – a moment in history when humanity is capable of intellectually grasping the truths of Islam. Accordingly, the *Risale-i Nur* exemplifies Nursi's realization that the real struggle or *jihad* for the glory of Islam was in the realm of ideas.[28]

---

[25] Nursi, *The Rays*, p. 439.

[26] Nursi does not abolish the literal reading of these traditions that *Mahdi*, *Dajjal*, and Jesus will all be persons, but he adds another dimension by his interpretation of them as social phenomena or movements.

[27] Nursi, *The Rays*, p. 108.

[28] Sükran Vahide surmises that the *Risale-i Nur* was "a Qur'anic commentary proving the truths of belief by a method…which blends science and the truths of religion and uniquely addresses the mentality of the modern man" (Vahide, *Biography*, p. viii).

Conclusion

This chapter presents Said Nursi's self-consciousness with respect to the historical process within the context of the 'end of time' scenario in the Islamic tradition. Nursi believed in a teleological notion of history, with Islam as its culmination. He felt strongly about the spirit of cooperation amongst peoples and nations, thus harboring a firm democratic spirit that would be worthwhile for modern Islamic movements to consider. However, this picture raises other complex issues that should be covered in further studies. For example, in a democratic Islam, what are the consequences if Muslims collectively choose a way of life that transgresses the *shari'a*? Furthermore, if human consciousness is evolving towards realizing Islam as the perfect intellectual, spiritual, social, moral, political, and economic system for humanity, then what does this say about the ideal caliphate immediately following the Prophet? If it was indeed ideal, why was it unable to sustain itself?[29] Is it possible to meet the intellectual and spiritual needs of modern Muslims without systematically addressing such issues?

An absence of a critical discussion here indicates that the guiding principle in the *Risale-i Nur* was the Islamic traditional narrative rather than nagging questions on the philosophy of history. It is likely that this approach was a pragmatic one, because Nursi's intention was to strengthen (or save) the faith of those who already believed by helping them make sense of their tradition in a rapidly modernizing world. Consequently, Said Nursi developed the self-understanding that his intellectual and spiritual movement was the centerpiece of Islamic revival at the tail end of human history.

---

[29] A related question arises from the tension between the teleological approach to history that Nursi adopts and the Islamic tradition as exhibited in the following saying of the Prophet: "The end of the world will not occur so long as there remain on the earth those who say, Allah! Allah!" When Nursi was asked to comment on this tradition, he said: "[W]hen the end of the world is close an atheistic current will again appear and become dominant. According to the rule, "The word is with the majority," no one will remain on the earth who says, "Allah! Allah!;" that is, "Allah! Allah!" will not be uttered by a significant group which holds an important position on the earth" (Nursi, *The Letters*, p. 80). The question is that if Islam is to gain supremacy at the end of time as the result of a historical process, then what will cause its adherents to be reduced to an insignificant minority before the end of the world?

Chapter 11

Globalization in the Light of Bediuzzaman Said Nursi's *Risale-i-Nur*: An Exposition

Amer Al-Roubaie and Shaifiq Alvi

Introduction

During the past three decades, the term globalization has been widely discussed in academic journals, newspapers, electronic media, satellite broadcasts, institutions and various other bodies both nationally and internationally. The euphoria about globalization reflects the fears that people worldwide are expressing about the potential impact that new global trends may have on their societies. Bearing in mind that globalization is a multidimensional concept, it is likely that its effects will have far reaching consequences on all aspects of human relations. In non-Western societies the process of globalization introduces undifferentiated cultural products and social relations that may violate the fundamental principles of the indigenous way of life. The underlying objective of globalization is to standardize global rule of conduct by imposing secular ideologies and cultural by-products, mainly of Western origin. However, endorsing such materialistic and individualistic practices may not necessarily be suitable for development in non-Western societies. For example, the Islamic worldview contains Divine guidelines that cannot be subject to change or modification. Thus, penetration of globalization without scrutiny into Muslim societies may produce undesirable social, political, and cultural consequences leading to the loss of individual identity, weakening of the national sovereignty, a social divide, poverty, income inequality, and political instability. In addition to being universal, Islam is a dynamic religion. It contains all the ingredients for scientific advancement and rapid progress. As Nursi explains: "The truths of Islam are able to progress materially, and in moral and non-material matters, and possess a prefect capacity to do so."[1] The significance of Nursi's statement reflects the fact that Islam does not need to draw on others to promote development and sustain progress. As a way of life, Islam constitutes

---

[1] Bediuzzaman Said Nursi, *The Damascus Sermon*, (Istanbul: Sözler Nesriyat, 1989), p. 14.

moral and ethical fundamentals, which do not change or cannot be modified owing to their Divine contents. Similarly, the Islamic worldview includes universal principles such as the meaning of God, the Prophet and man, which cannot draw on others to reconstruct the social organization of Muslim societies. Globalization is a product of Western modernization over the past five centuries of their history and therefore cannot be a substitute for development in Muslim societies. However, globalization constitutes scientific means and technological features that Muslims are able to benefit from. Similarly, economic globalization could enhance the capability of Muslims to improve the socio-economic condition of their societies by increasing productivity and promoting growth.

Due to the limited scope of this paper, our main concern will be directed at interpreting some of the issues currently discussed with regard to globalization in the light of Nursi's *Risale-i Nur*. The relevance of Nursi's teachings constitutes important grounds for examining the principles of globalization and their impact on Muslim societies. Globalization poses challenges for the main determinants of the Islamic worldview by diffusing secular ideas and spreading undifferentiated cultural values.

Globalization And Religion

Globalization, as mentioned earlier, is a product of modernization, which is closely associated with the transformation of western societies over the past few centuries. As a process of social change, the development of Western societies has been built upon the principle of separation of religion from state implying that the Church plays no active role in the evolution of the socio-economic and political formation of these countries. Religion is limited only to the preservation of individual freedom of worship, whereas the formulation of legal, social, political and matters concerning the society at large are entrusted to elected members of the society. As Martin Gerhard Giesbrecht explains:

> The response of the people to the Church's sickness was, on the one hand, a turning away from religion – a secularization – and, on the other, a reform of religion itself. Both of these responses were instrumental in turning society into new directions of progress. The secularization laid fertile grounds for the growth of the philosophy of humanism, the glory of being an individual human being. For humanists, the observation of nature in all its beauty, perhaps even more than simple religious faith, brought revelation and truth. [2]

In other words, man himself has been elevated to the status of sovereign being superceding God's power on earth. Such authority was also based on the notion that God dissociated Himself from the rest of His creation and decided to have an eternal rest after six days of work. In contrast, in Islam, whereas man is

---

[2] Giesbrecht, Martin, *The Evolution of Economic Society* (W. H. Freeman and Company: San Francisco, 1972), p. 37.

given the responsibility to implement God's commands as a viceregent, in Christianity man took over the responsibility of commandments making profane decisions marginalizing the sacred. As explained by Anis Ahmad:

> The Qur'an introduces a responsible and global role for man in the world. It defines man, not as a developed form of animal, but as Allah's creation, created in his own rights as man. The purpose of man's creation is highlighted as Allah's vicegerent on earth. This vicegerency stands for an ethical role of man. It allows man to exercise authority, freedom of the will, and his judgment in personal, social, economic, political, legal and cultural matters.[3]

Therefore, societal transformation is left to changes over time and circumstances with regard to issues concerning the public interest or public pressure for reform. However, such separation between religion and state is rejected in Islam on the basis that man cannot sustain himself without the Divine commandments laid out in the Shari'a. As Nursi explains:

> For if man does not recognize God and place his trust in Him, he becomes extremely weak and impotent, needy and impoverished, a suffering, grieving and ephemeral animal, exposed to endless misfortunes. Suffering continuously the pain of separation from all the objects of love and attachment, he will ultimately abandon all of his loved ones and go alone to the darkness of the grave.[4]

What Nursi affirms here is that man is not capable to conduct his worldly affairs by himself alone because of his weakness and that without spiritual guidance and Divine interference man is ultimately the loser. He goes on to say: "In regard to his acts and deeds and his labour man is a weak animal, an impotent creature. The extent of his power of disposal and ownership in this respect is so narrow that it is no greater than as far as his hand can reach."[5] To depend on the commandments of God to furnish man's path in life of this world means that the message of Islam is universal in the sense that all mankind was invited to follow the same path drawn by the same Creator. The Islamic mission is to free man from all forms of worldly worship, oppressions, slavery, and exploitation that cause the degradation of man status as God's vicegerent. In the Hereafter man will be judged not on the basis of color, race or religion but on the basis of Taqwa or good deeds. Globalization on the other hand, means to change the role of religion in society by imposing a global set of rules to be applied by all. As pointed out by Inoue Nobutaka:

> Since religion enjoys a different status in different places around the globe, the concept of religion itself is forced to undergo transformation as part of the process of globalization. These processes, however, should not be understood merely as a

---

[3] Ahmad, Anis, *Dawah*, Vol. VIII, Issue-IV, April 1997, p. 5.

[4] Nursi, Bediuzzaman Said, *The Tongues of Reality* (Istanbul: Sözler Nesriyat, 1994), p. 98.

[5] Nursi, Bediuzzaman Said, *Belief and Man* (Istanbul: Sözler Nesriyat, 1992), p. 40.

> breakdown of tradition, and which must therefore be inhibited. The globalization processes do not proceed in specific fields or areas, but function as a rearrangement of world systems. [6]

Secularization is often interpreted as a rejection of the past by applying modern Western methodology that is based on the separation of church and state to transform non-western societies. Historically, western countries have not only dissociated themselves from the activities of the church but also rejected religion as a part of their worldly affairs and have opted for humanism and sciences to endorse the process of social and political transformation. The Muslim opposition to western secularism is due to the "nature of the Christian religion" which "recognized the division of life into what belonged to God and what belonged to Caesar."[7] "For Muslims, this identity crisis often draws them closer to the religion into which they were socialized as children. Their religion acts as an anchor, alleviates their fears, and gives them a sense of stability, direction, and faith in the future. Therefore, Islam, as both a historical and an organic religion, is especially significant in the modernizing Muslim world."[8]

Globalism Vs. Universalism

To understand the relationship between globalization and Islam, it is important to reflect on the concept of the universality of Islam. The message of Islam is far from being limited to a particular region or place, rather it is universal in the sense that it is directed at "everything that exist everywhere" including stars and planets. The Qur'an addresses the Prophet by saying, "We send you mercy to all worlds", implying that the finality of God's messages is one and covers the whole universe. The universal meaning of Islam is directly linked to the concept of Tawhid or the Oneness of God, Whose sovereignty and power over the universe determines the movements of everything in it including that of man's actions. As Malcolm Waters argues:

> ...the claims of universalistic religions that the world was created by a single God and that humanity is a common forum of existence in relation to that God is a primary long-run driving force in the direction of globalization. It leads to the argument that humanity constitutes a single community that disvalues geographical localities and political territories. ... This is most explicit in Islam. [9]

---

[6] Nobutaka, Inoue, *The Information Age and Globalization of Religion, In Globalization and Indigenous Culture*, Institute of Japan Culture and Classics, 1997, p. 96.

[7] Tamimi, Azzam, The Origins of Arab Secularism, in Azzam Tamim and John Esposito, (eds.), *Islam and Secularism in the Middle East* (London: Hurst & Company, 2000), p. 16.

[8] Husain, Mir Zohair, *Global Islamic Politics* (New York: Harper Collins Collage Publishers, 1995), p. 165

[9] Malcolm Waters, *Globalization* (London: Routledge, 1995), p. 127.

Thus the knowledge of God is an essential guide for man in implementing God's commandments on earth. Similarly, the Qur'an states that the only religion accepted by God on earth is Islam and therefore, Islam is already a global religion and there is no need to be globalized. Globalization, on the other hand is a process of worldly affairs with no connection to any religious principles. These processes are man made rules influenced by man's desire to exercise authority over others, make profit, to have control over markets, resources and their exploitation.

Within the universal system of Islam human relations, coexistence and understanding are enhanced owing to the preservation of nations and groups identity. Despite the fact that Muslims are highly diversified in their cultural, social and linguistic features, they are united in the universality of the Islamic faith. Such Islamic fundamentals as freedom, justice, equality, ethical and moral conducts are applied to all people in spite of their diversity. In doing so, the Islam rejects cultural homogeneity propagated by globalization. Allah (SWT) says in the Qur'an:

> O mankind! We created you from a single (pair) of a male and a female, and made you into nations and tribes that you may know each other (not that you may despise each other). Verily the most honored of you in the sight of Allah is (he who is) the most righteous of you.[10]

The Islamic Worldview

Globalization aims to influence the worldviews of various groups and nations affecting in the process some of the basic fundamentals concerning religious, social, cultural and political aspects. The pluralistic nature of world societies makes difference among groups a natural feature reflecting the variability in their environment, way of life, customs, traditions, religion, and the social organization. What this simply means is that people tend to develop some attachment to practices and norms of relations and conducts drawn from their own worldview. Among other things, religious belief and cultural matters are perhaps the most important features, which define the worldview of various groups. This is certainly the case with the Islamic worldview where religion has a decisive input in shaping the overall elements with regard to behavioral patterns, rules of conducts and other factors governing human relations among Muslims. Professor Syed Muhammad Naquib Al-Attas explains:

> Since Islam is the religion which transcends the influences of human evolution and historicity, the values embodied in it are absolute; and this means that Islam has its own absolute vision of God, of the Universe, of Reality, of Man; its own ontological, cosmological, psychological interpretation of reality; its own worldview and vision of the Hereafter having a final significance for mankind.[11]

---

[10] Qur'an, 49:13.

[11] Muhammad Al-Attas, Syed Naquib, *Islam and Secularism* (Kuala Lumpur: Muslim Youth Movement of Malaysia, 1978), p. 28.

This implies that the Islamic worldview encompasses all the Islamic fundamentals outlined in the Quran and the Sunnah of the Prophet (PBUH). It is thus incumbent upon all Muslims to follow and implement these fundamentals in relation to their day to day activities and in dealing with others. However, the Shari'a guidelines represent the truth and are Divine in nature. Therefore, Islamic fundamentals that represent the main components of the worldview of Islam cannot draw on others for change or modifications. Nursi clearly states that "the Shari'a's injunctions do not change in consequence of purposes or instances of wisdom: they look to the true reason."[12] As outlined by professor Omar Jah, the worldview of Islam consists of: (1) believing in the Oneness of Allah as the Omnipotent, Omniscient, and Omnipresent, (2) believing that Allah is the creator of the universe, (3) believing that Allah is the sustainer of the worlds, (4) believing in the unseen realties, and in the life to come, (5) recognition of the holy Prophet Muhammad (PBUH) as the messenger of Allah and (6) belief in the angels of Allah and acknowledgment of the Quran as the book of divine guidelines and the authority that defines the truth.[13]

As a world system, globalization attempts to introduce a new set of relations having a multidimensional facet, which will affect not only the relations governing production and finance but also the main fundamentals of the social organization in Muslim societies. Globalization constitutes cultural, educational, scientific and technological dimensions that will have a direct impact on the patterns of conduct, of groups and nations, especially those concerning individual religious belief, identity, ideology, social relations, and lifestyle. However, if Muslims want to be part of the "global village", then they have to make considerable efforts to filter the materials passed into their own societies via modern technologies. They must ensure that the cultural identity and religious fundamentals are safeguarded against the invasion of Western secular products speared by globalization. In Rasel-i Nur Nursi made it very clear as far as the Islamic teaching and the implementation of the Shari'a guidelines in the Muslim daily life. For Nursi the Oneness of Allah, the teaching of the Prophet, and other components of the Islamic worldview listed above are not subject to compromise in any form. He explains:

> And since the Prophethood of Muhammad (PBUH) and the Qur'anic revelation are like the spirit and intelligence of life, it may be said that their truth is as certain as the existence of life... If the light of the Prophethood of Muhammad (PBUH) was to depart from the universe, the universe would die. If the Qurian was to depart, the universe would go mad, the earth would lose its head and its reason it

[12] Bediuzzaman Said Nursi, *The Flashes Collection* (Istanbul: Sözler Nesriyat, 1995), Vol. 3, p. 63.

[13] Omar Jah, Globalization and Socio-Cultural Change in the Muslim World, Unpublished Paper, 2001.

> would even strike its now unconscious head on a planet and Doomsday would occur. [14]

Being products of Western civilization, Nursi could have rejected the new global trends on the basis of their violation of Islamic ethical rules of conducts, particularly the sovereignty of Allah and His absolute power. Nursi is critical of Western civilization because of its orientation towards self-interest, conflict, and aggression.

Bediuzzaman Nursi clearly states that Western civilization is based on secular principles in the sense that European literature "regards the universe not as Divine art, but from the point of view of nature, it prompts materialism and the worship of nature."[15] Furthermore he clearly state that injustices are inherent in Western civilization by having the wealthy classes dominate economic life and oppress the poor, which are the causes of social disorder and political insecurity. He also argues that to maintain public order and preserve peace requires bridging the gap between various classes in society. In this respect, it is interesting to mention that globalization were to create divisions within nations globally based on wealth accumulation and technological advancement. It is argued that globalization is selective in terms of production and labour demand creating in the process different classes and an unbalanced development from which the poor, the unskilled, women, and the non-privileged individuals and regions are to suffer. The solution to remedy the injustices and inequalities of Western civilization lies, according to Nursi, in "making the payment of zakat obligatory and prohibiting interest"[16] which will bring harmony and justice to various groups in society.

Globalizatıon And Culture

Globalization hopes to spread homogeneous elements and lifestyles, mainly of Western origin, which are not necessarily suitable for the development of Muslim societies. Some of these cultural elements are materialistic and individualistic in nature containing music, songs, ideological, religious, social and political messages that violate the norm of ethical and moral conduct of the Islamic worldwide. By allowing these secular elements to be circulated and practiced could cause lose of identity, a generation gap, a social divides and a cultural shock. From an Islamic point of view, culture is defined as "customs, civilization, and refined understanding of the intellectual development of man, made in the light of, and in accordance with rules and laws ordained by the Supreme Being."[17]

It is worth mentioning that in non-Muslim societies religion is viewed as a product of culture itself and is defined as ritual practices conducted along other

---

[14], Bediuzzaman Said Nursi, *The Flashes Collection* (Istanbul: Sözler Nesriyat, 1995), Vol. 3, pp. 434-435.

[15] Ibid. pp. 159-60

[16] Ibid. pp. 160-161

[17] Javed Malik, *Dawah Highlights*, Vol. XII, Issue – V, May 2001, p. 32.

social customs and traditions. In other words, culture tends to evolve and change depending on the transformation of the society and its connection to the outside world. In Islam, however, such an interpretation of the meaning of culture is totally rejected on the basis that culture itself is a product of religion and not the other way around. Thus, the Islamic culture constitutes conduct, values, social relations, customs and a lifestyle that is based on knowledge of the religion of Islam. Not only are material products essential to a Muslim, but also spiritual guidance, the acquisition of knowledge and worship are important for man's action and behavioral attitude.

Nursi maintains that the knowledge of God is what guides man's life not only as a vicegerent in fulfilling his duties and responsibilities but also in his personal relationships and behavioral conduct. Culture, which constitutes the various activities, relationships, contacts, social habits, food, pleasure, and arts, is inherent in the religion of Islam making religion itself a basis for defining culture. Man cannot survive on his own creation or on the adoption from others to attain happiness and become satisfied with life of this world. As explained by Nursi:

> Man is helpless and exposed to numerous misfortunes. He is indigent, and his needs are numerous. He is weak, and the burden of life is most heavy. If he does not rely on the Omnipotent One of Glory, place his trust in Him and confidently submit to Him, his conscience will always be troubled. Fruitless torments, pains and regrets will overwhelm him and intoxicate him, or turn him into a beast.[18]

Thus the danger of globalization on the Muslim way of life comes mainly form the penetration of a materialistic, Western, secular, ideological into Muslim societies. However, globalization is posing challenges far beyond the sphere of socio-cultural life to include political, social, scientific, technological, educational and institutional foundations, which are still lacking in most Muslim states. To overcome these difficulties, substantial efforts and resources on behalf of Muslims need to be devoted towards the reformation of the social organization, and to sustain economic and technological change. As a matter of fact, most of the recent demand for change in the Muslim World includes improvement in the sector of economic development.

Unlike present day globalization, Islam throughout history did not interfere with people's cultural and social life by imposing a new set of alien practices. The undifferentiated process of globalization promotes homogeneity of culture, which tends to weaken and fragment human relations between groups, regions and nations. With respect to being sovereign to preserve the cultural identity and promote national integrity Nursi stress the fact that 'sovereignty is a station of dignity'[19]

---

[18] Bediuzzman Said Nursi, *Fruits from the Tree of Light* (Istanbul: Sözler Nesriyat, 1993), p. 40.

[19] Bediuzzaman Said Nursi, *The Supreme Sign* (Istanbul, Sözler Nesriyat), 1993, p. 105

There is no doubt that globalization has dramatically increased the flow of people, ideas, information, capital, lifestyles, and cultural products among nations via compressing time and space, travel, satellite broadcasting, mobile telephone, the Internet and other forms of information technology. Such rapid interconnections make it difficult for countries or groups to control the flow of information into their territories owing to the lack of financial, scientific and technological means. The developing countries including Muslim countries are not in a position to respond effectively to the cultural materials and secular ideologies penetrating their boarders. The mainly Western origin publicity of such expressions, as liberal democracy, human rights, population control, nationalism, freedom, and the environment, are in one way or another in contradiction with the prevailing socio-cultural set up in non-industrialized societies. In Muslim societies, some of these issues are equally important but are defined within the framework of the Islamic system that relies on the Shari'a to derive its injunctions and legal interpretations. As a global economic system, globalization is guided by the principles of capitalism that depends on market transactions where interest rates are key to the functioning of the market. Economic and financial transactions based on interest rates or Riba have been condemned in Islam and therefore globalization cannot provide an alternative for development in Muslim societies because of its violation of the Islamic ethical norms of business and trade. Nursi has been very clear on this issue by declaring Riba unethical and that those who deal with it must be condemned. Similarly, globalization attempts to create unbalanced development by allocating resources to promote external trade paying less attention to domestic economic problems. As a consequence, inequalities and poverty are likely to increase in relation to global integration. Recent statistical data by the World Bank clearly indicates that the income gap between nations has been so severely widened to the extent that the non-industrialized world with more that 80 percent of the world population received only 14 percent of the total world income in 2000. Such disparities happened over the past three decades during which the process of globalization to propagate is in full swing.

Ethics In Islam

In Islam ethics is crucial in that it is directly linked to the concept of Tawhid or the Oneness of God. In its vertical dimension, ethics signifies the relationship between man and God implying that man's conduct and place in the universe is a derivative of God's choice. In other words, if man has to obey and worship God, he must then follow the path drawn by God in order to achieve Falah in order to gain God's reward in the Hereafter. The Qur'an clearly states that the whole purpose behind the creation of man was for glorifying and worshiping Allah. In doing so man has to conduct his entire day to day activities in accordance with the Divine guidelines as stated in the Qur'an and the Tradition of the Prophet. These guidelines represent the core of ethical principles governing man's behavioral functions to conduct his worship. In other words, man's life in this world is guided by Divine instruction any deviation will violate the ethical code of conduct. That is to say, as aforementioned, Islam cannot draw on other religions to define the path of conduct nor is it possible to change or modify the Divine fundamentals. For example in Western civilization, over the past several centuries of their development religion was completely removed from the process of change. For them God simply rested after the creation of the heavens and earth. Therefore man began to assume the role of God on earth becoming arrogant and selfish in his attitude towards other men, nature and the universe. The secularization of Western societies brought about a complete deviation from any religious guidance. The entire principles governing man's conduct including the moral and ethical aspects are man -made, which keep changing in response to changes in social, political and economic fields. As Nursi explains:

> The All-Wise Creator of the universe made the universe like a tree with conscious beings as its most perfect fruit, and among conscious beings He made man its most comprehensive fruit. And man's most important fruit, rather, the result of his creation, the aim of his nature, and the fruit of his life are his thanks and worship. Would that Absolute Sovereign and Independent ruler, that Single One of Unity, Who creates the universe in order to make Himself known and loved, give away to others man, who is the fruit of the whole universe, and man's thanks and worship, which are his most elevated fruit? [20]

It is important to keep in mind that Islam does not confine itself to religious matters only but also a way of life in the sense that it governs man's day to day social, economic and community activities. This springs from the fact that one of the meanings of Islam itself implies submission to God's commandments. In this respect, man's entire activities in this world rest upon the principle of Tawhid or the Oneness of God. By accepting the sovereignty of God implies that man must follow God's commandments in all aspects of life, which also underlines the main fundamentals of the Islamic worldview.

Knowledge in Islam is the means to understanding ethics and human conduct, without which it would not be possible for man to perform worship in a correct manner. In the Quran and the Tradition of the Prophet, striving to learn knowledge is directly linked to the process of Ibada or worship. This implies that ethics cannot be separated from religion, and is to be acquired through learning and the acquisition of knowledge of God as stated by Nursi. In contrast, globalization is not linked by any means to the knowledge of God, rather it is worldly practices derived from man experience throughout history. Being a product of Western modernity, globalization enforces a different set of worldly materialistic, individualistic, and secular principles created within man's environment and influenced by social change and political desire. According to Nursi, man's salvation can only be achieved through the knowledge of God, a notion globalization rejects completely rejects. He argues:

---

[20] Bediuzzaman Said Nursi, *Nature: Cause or Effect,* (Istanbul: Sözler Nesriyat, 1989), p. 37.

> The multiple existences and stages of each species and each member of each species, existing in Divine knowledge, from a chain of being in God's knowledge, and like its external existence, its existence in God's knowledge is a manifestation of universal life that draws all the aspects of its life from these meaningful and vital Tablets of Divine Determining.[21]

Being concerned only with worldly affairs, globalization does not contain a spiritual dimension, which is essential for man's progress and happiness. It has been greatly emphasized that man cannot live by material means alone and that spiritual means are equally important for his happiness and progress. Globalization is a process of a worldly nature aimed at increasing man's material gain without any attachment to his spiritual needs. In Islam the ultimate objective of man is to seek the pleasure of Allah by means of ethical conduct. This conduct involves worship, which is the main source of man spiritual satisfaction because it gives peace of mind and makes him a good man. As a matter of fact, man's conducts in both his worldly affairs and his spiritual needs are ultimately meant to guide him to attain the best life in the hereafter since temporal life is limited only by man's physical existence.

It is important to mention again that in Western tradition, religion has been classified of being part of the society's culture, whereas in Islam such a distinction is rejected on the basis that culture is influenced by religion and not the other way around. As mentioned above, human conduct, including the principle of ethics, are products of the religion of Islam. Muslims may live in different geographical areas, speak different languages and practice a variety of socio-cultural customs yet they still follow the Islamic norm with regard to conducts in their daily activities.

Conclusion

The purpose of this chapter is to explain the present trends spread by globalization in the light of Bediuzzaman Said Nursi's Risale-i-Nur. The teaching of Risale-i-Nur comprises a Divine guidance to promote man's spiritual and material happiness both in this world and the hereafter. By doing so, Nursi made it clear that man cannot earn the pleasure of Allah unless he is guided by the principles of the Shari'a. The implementation of these principles contains ethical and moral conducts in order to assist man achieving justice, freedom, and peace. On the other hand, globalization is a worldly affair based on secular principles with the objective of standardizing human culture and establishing a "global village" society. In the new society, religion is reduced to a personal matter with no role to play in decisions governing the society. The Islamic worldview, which contains the teaching of divine guidelines, cannot draw on globalization to promote development and increase man's happiness. However, Islam provides the incentive

[21] Bediuzzaman Said Nursi, *The Flashes Collection*, (Istanbul: Sözler Nesriyat, 1995), Vol. 3, p. 435.

for Muslims to acquire knowledge to enhance their material well-beings. In this regard, globalization could be beneficial if Muslims learn how to make use of its scientific and technological contents in the advancement of their own societies.

Chapter 12

Globalization: Its Meaning, Scope and Impact in the Light of Bediuzzaman Said Nursi's Damascus Sermon

Fred A. Reed

Let us begin with three questions. What does globalization mean? What are its scope and impact? And, most important to this eminent International Symposium, how can the perspective laid down in the sermon delivered by Bediuzzaman Said Nursi at the Umayyad Mosque in Damascus ninety years ago, and revisited by the author shortly before his death, help men and women today understand and confront this seemingly inevitable phenomenon.

I argue that we cannot accept the inevitability of any process or action that belongs to the political or economic domain, that is to say, that of man and society. Marxism-Leninism, the pseudo-religion of materialism, produced a dogma of historical inevitability. It is instructive to take note of the fate and failure of that dogma.

Globalization promises to be little different. Like the collapse of Argentina or the acute social and economic crisis shaking Turkey, it is anything but a fatality. Argentina and Turkey are not, of course, isolated cases. They should be seen rather as evidence of an underlying disorder.

Globalization, we are assured, is a supra-natural force as powerful and arbitrary as time or the tide, located beyond human understanding, in a realm of pure, unbounded necessity. But at closer look, we see two things. First, globalization is a product of an age of radical unbelief. No divine agency is or can be claimed for its rise and promised triumph. Rather, it attempts to portray itself as a semi-Darwinian realm sprung from the primeval ooze, where only the fittest survive; as a state of nature that is characterized by the war of all against all, as "the end of history."

Second, paradoxically, the proponents of globalization also claim for it semi-divine attributes. As an expression of materialism reduced and refined to a state of extreme purity, it alone holds the promise of future happiness, fulfillment and general well being, not in some abstract hereafter, but here and now.

We would not be amiss, in fact, in describing the dogma of globalization as fundamentalism of a particularly insidious type, whose god is the absolute supremacy of the market; as the apotheosis of materialism.

In fact, it reminds us of Marxism-Leninism in its deterministic single-mindedness, and also in its astonishing capacity for self-deception. For the promised happiness and general well-being is always just around the corner, always receding at the same speed at which we advance, or worse, receding more rapidly than we can advance.

As the crowning achievement of Western culture, a culture which has turned its back on any notion of divine agency, globalization must be understood as a phenomenon that is no longer restrained or limited by the imperatives of revelation and the religious beliefs that derive from it. In fact, it posits no limits and no restraints whatsoever, and in this regard, is perhaps unique in human history in its absolutist aspirations.

Back to our opening questions: Today, globalization stands revealed in radical terms. Its agenda can be stated thus: to impose a homogenizing vision upon all aspects of life and society, from the most intimate to the most broadly public. All belongs to it, all refers to it; nothing can exist outside it.

This new, global system acts in three ways: first, it establishes a system of absolute economic domination; second, it creates an ideological structure which, being unseen, cannot be questioned; third, it legitimizes the unrestricted application of violence on whatever scale is deemed necessary to enforce its globalizing will.

The system of absolute economic domination is now all but in place. Few countries remain outside the World Trade Organization, one of the three international agencies that presume to order and dictate the natures of the societies we live in and the beliefs we cherish. The World Bank and the International Monetary Fund are the other two.

Two decades into the unrestricted application of the new dogma, standards of living and employment rates are falling except among a tiny, possessing minority concentrated in a handful of major economic powers colloquially known as the G8 and their allies in countries such as Turkey. Mass layoffs of productive workers reflect the imperatives of financial markets, not public need for goods and services, especially essential social services, education, healthcare, clean air and water.

In countries of the insolvent South, such meager social programs as once existed have been destroyed not by the malfeasance of governments, but by the IMF directives that impose structural adjustment programs. The purpose of such plans is to divert and channel wealth from the deprived to the wealthy, from poor nations to rich ones. And now, in the prosperous North, existing social programs are under attack, singled out for privatization by the same planners who devised the doctrine of structural adjustment. World wide, between 1991 and 1995, publicly traded corporations employing more than 5000 workers eliminated 3.3 million jobs.

Everywhere, the gap between the richest and poorest is growing. Despite the growing public frustration, political leaders no longer pretend to respond to the desires of their electorate. They must, instead, respond to the demands of their masters. Several years aso Hans Tietmeyer, then-president of Germany's Bundesbank put it this way: "You political leaders must realize that from now on, you are under the control of financial markets."

The recent bankruptcy and collapse of the Enron pyramid scheme in the United States revealed not only the extent of control of political leaders by financial markets, but the criminal involvement of these financial markets in transfering wealth from small shareholders and pension funds to a handful of fabulously wealthy insiders.

Globalization doctrine claims that higher profits and lower wages, the aim of structural adjustment programs, promote growth and employment. The withdrawal of the state, argue its theoreticians, will bring about prosperity.

Some figures: the portion of international Gross Domestic Product of the richest 20 percent grew from 70% to 85% between 1960 and 1993, while that of the poorest dropped from 2.3% to 1.4%. The world's three richest men possess a fortune greater than the total wealth of the 48 poorest states. The share of the 200 leading multinationals in the world's Gross Domestic Product climbed from 17% in the sixties to over 30% in the nineties.

For there to be globalization, in its cruel fact as opposed to its seductive fiction, there must exist not Adam Smith's "invisible hand," but a conscious hands-on policy formulated by what can be termed the Global Directorate. This directorate brings together the heads of the largest transnational corporations and political leaders purchased by them to carry out their will. It meets both formally, in places like Seattle and Genoa, and informally. It is not the product of a conspiracy theory; it is a fact.

Its program for the developing world has been and is structural adjustment, a tried-and-true formula for poverty, social collapse, disease and morbidity. For the developed countries, it includes four key concepts: 1) the reduction of taxes for the wealthy and for corporations on the pretext of job creation; 2) the elimination of obstacles to corporate profitability through deregulation; 3) the opening up of new areas of potential profit through privatization of public services; 4) the destruction of social programs.

Ultimately, as taxes assessed against the wealthiest individuals and most powerful corporations are slashed, budget deficits soar and the state can no longer fund social services. These must then be privatized.

Deregulation has brought the deadly impact of "mad cow disease" in England and France, the collapse of the deep sea fishery, the Enron pyramid scandal in the United States, global warming, and now, the present danger of nuclear war driven by the addiction to petroleum.

The Multilateral Agreement on Investment may have been temporarily sidetracked at Seattle but remains the key to the globalizing agenda. Under its provisions, which are in force in the North American Free Trade Area, private firms can now take supposedly sovereign states to court if a government or a public action — such as a boycott, a strike or civil unrest — puts their interest at risk.

The second prong of the global strategy is ideological. The message of globalization is so thoroughly integrated into public discourse by mass media owned by the globalizers themselves, a phenomenon known as convergence. The result is resignation and demobilization. That is precisely its design: to demonstrate that no other form of discourse is possible.

According to this ideology, markets are not only the natural state of existence, but are objective, impersonal favor no particular player, and generate wealth for all. The operative sub-doctrine here is that of the "open door" and the "level playing field" in which the ant and the elephant revel equally in the thrill and mutual benefit of competition. Competition, we are assured, is the natural state. As inherent in the structure of existence as is the concept of natural selection in the emergence of the immensely wealthy, as the promoters of social Darwinism so grotesquely argue. Competition, however, has one goal only: to eliminate all rivals, establish monopoly, corner the market, then charge all the traffic will bear. Merely a complex of modalities, it is utterly devoid of any social or moral content.

The prophet of Neoliberalism, the economic doctrine that underpins the globalization agenda, Freidrich Hayek, wrote: "Man has no choice but to adapt himself to what seems to him to be the blind forces of social progress." For Hayek, social progress meant the triumph of competition.

Alongside the notion of competition as the driving force of progress, that of "liberty" is essential to understanding globalization and the forces that propell it. Liberty, as understood by the Global Directorate, means the economic liberty of those forces, which derive immense profit from the exploitation of the inhabitants of poor countries, and from the manipulation of financial markets that generate no productive activity. The private sphere, locus of the same interests that collide in mortal competition, is held to constitute "civil society." It is understood that the state is no longer capable of representing the needs of its citizens, let alone of protecting them. It can only act to repress them when they act to challenge globalization and its local and global impacts.

The ideologues of globalization present liberty as the ultimate ethical criterion, the supreme authority for what constitutes what is good and what is just. In reality, however, the liberty of the globalizers is nothing more than a vulgar annex of property.

Globalizationists are today striving to wipe away the last vestiges of social achievement. But despite their hatred of 'government', their avowed enemy is not the state itself. Paradoxically, it remains necessary to enforce at the local or national level the decisions taken behind closed doors by the Global Directorate. Though the state has been disqualified from regulating markets, its monopoly of violence will increasingly be used to safeguard the immunity of unregulated market forces from the outrage of the citizens.

The third aspect of globalization is that of enforcement. After the events of September 11, 2001, this aspect has become more visible. To protect the interests of the Global Directorate, a reliable security apparatus is needed. Having toyed with the idea of handing this mission to NATO, the United States has concluded that it need not encumber itself with alliances in which it must share decision-making powers. The attack against Iraq, likely to be followed by an assault on Iran, has convinced Washington that it no longer need seek either advice or permission.

The United States seems now convinced that it has the capacity to head up a contemporary version of the universal empire, in which its vassals will submit willingly to its authority. If they do not, they risk being simply "ended", as US Under-secretary of Defense Paul Wolfowitz puts it.

There are to be few limitations on American power, and none on the ability to use it. Mr. Wolfowitz's superior, Defense Secretary Donald Rumsfeld, recently sketched out how his government intends to behave: "Now we must act to acquire dissuasive capacity in four major theatres of operation...(and to) prevail over two aggressors simultaneously while being prepared to launch a major counter-offensive to occupy an enemy capital and install a new regime."[1] Let us take careful note of that last phrase.

As the United States prepares to operate in four major theatres, it stigmatizes as "terrorism" all opposition to its policies, and promises to attack the states that support it. Today, the United States military planners are building more overseas bases from which they will be able to destroy that which they define as terrorist or enemy sanctuaries; they are moving rapidly to protect access to space and to the American space potential; even more ominously, they now threaten pre-emptive unilateral nuclear war.

In the post-September 11 environment, the United States has declared that the use of force to attain its objectives has become both necessary and legitimate. It cannot have escaped us that globalization has come to resemble the foreign policy and commercial agenda of the United States. Long praised as a universal phenomenon, which knows no borders, globalization is the ideological cloak under which American imperal interests are to be advanced.

Professor Riccardo Petrella of the Catholic University of Louvain, in Belgium, has identified the central aspect of globalization as the affirmation that the United States is the sole superpower in military, technological, economic, political and cultural terms.[2]

In fact, globalization today can be viewed as the product of American economic and military power, and can be precisely defined as "the ideological, technological, military and economic americanization of today's world society." We should not be surprised that anti-globalization protests are seen as expressions of opposition to the global order, and to the United States itself, as its supreme regulator. It would be naive to be surprised when they are defined as "terrorism."

In the United States, what was once whispered in private is now being discussed openly. "The rich world, writes an American commentator, increasingly

---

[1] Paul-Marie de la Gorce, "Bombing to Control" in *Le Monde Diplomatique*, March 2002, pp. 10-11.

[2] "Criminalizing Contestation" in *Le Monde Diplomatique*, August 2001, p. 6.

realizes that its interests are threatened by chaos, and that it lacks the tools to fix the problem."

"Now U.S. foreign policy must respond to these circumstances," he continues. "The logic of neo-imperialism is too compelling for the Bush administration to resist. The chaos in the world is too threatening to ignore. A new imperial moment has arrived, and by virtue of its power, America is bound to play the leading role. The question is not whether the U.S. will seek to fill the void created by the demise of European empires, but whether it will acknowledge that this is what it is doing."[3]

An interesting slippage has taken place. Chaos in the world is too threatening to ignore. But it has been amply demonstrated that the "failed states" which have become the source of chaos are quite precisely the first victims of globalization.

There are many similarities between today's world and that in which Bediuzzaman Said Nursi made his way. He was born in eastern Anatolia, a region known for its spiritual richness, and for the devotion of its inhabitants to their Islamic beliefs. At the end of the nineteenth century of the Christian era, an earlier wave of globalization was having an impact on even the remotest villages of the region.

Aggressively proselytizing Protestant sects were combing the Ottoman Empire, a kind of ideological advance guard for the expansion of the Western powers. In Anatolia, the most determined and effective resistance came from the *ulama* in general, and from the sheikhs of the Naqshbandi order in particular. These were the men who provided Said with the spiritual compass that was never to fail him.

Now, as then, the principal characteristics of globalization were its ability to present itself as inevitable, along with its economic power, and ultimately, the military force it could bring to bear to impose its will. By the early years of the twentieth century, Western control over the Ottoman state had become decisive. Foreign banks controlled the state treasury, and Ottoman policy often seemed to be drafted in London. Great Britain, at the time, saw the maintenance of the empire as being in its interests. By the same token, when those interests shifted, the empire suddenly became expendable.

When Said Nursi traveled to Damascus in early 1911, the wave of globalization that had been launched by Britain to expand its world economic domination was reaching a peak. And competition among contenders for a portion of the spoils was sharpening.

"The nations of Europe had divided up the African continent among themselves. Some of them were now hungry for new conquests. (...) Much of the

[3] Sebastian Mallaby, "The Reluctant Imperialist" in *Foreign Affairs*, March-April 2002, pp. 2-7.

surface of the globe was already taken: a quarter by the British Empire and a sixth by the Russian Empire. (...) The Middle East was the only vulnerable region left."[4]

They were to be given priceless assistance by nationalism, the dominant European creed. Intellectuals among the Turkish and Arabic-speaking people of the Empire flocked to the new ideology, seeking to discover in it the keys to a new political identity. Of course, it escapes no one's attention that one of the most effective and virulent of these movements did not arise within the confines of the Empire, but was to impact upon it, and upon the Middle East with deadly precision decades later.

As these storm clouds were forming, from the *minbar* in the Umayyad Mosque Said Nursi, that great Warner, reminded the 10,000 faithful who had crowded into the vast prayer hall to hear him, that the prescription for a sick age and an ailing nation...is to follow the Qur'an. And for an illustrious though hapless state, a noble though ownerless people, the prescription is Islamic Unity.[5] We need only reflect briefly on these words to realize how timely they are, how accurately they describe the torments of the region today.

Several years later, in an addendum to the Damascus Sermon called "Seeds of Reality",[6] Bediuzzaman Said Nursi wrote:

> Tyranny has donned the hat of justice; treachery has clothed itself in the garment of patriotism; *jihad* has been given the name of rebellion; captivity has been called freedom! Opposites have changed forms!

Presciently, he had defined not only globalization, but identified its ideological underpinnings. Though he was referring to the specific conditions that prevailed in the Ottoman Empire immediately prior to World War I, he put his finger squarely upon the deceit, distortion and concealment that are the ideological weapons of globalization.

The United States, today's purveyor of globalization, presents itself as a model of justice, yet it unilaterally withdraws from its international commitments and abrogates its signature on the treaty establishing the International Criminal Court which would give the victims of its policies recourse against its tormentors. Instead, under the aegis of globalization an international culture of immunity for the perpetrators of crimes against individuals, against societies and against the environment has arisen. And alongside it, a culture of impunity.

The patriotism of globalization is reserved for the leader of the Global Directorate. But this patriotism is a mockery of the national conscience of other countries, who are informed that "if you are not with us, you are against us."

Jihad, in both its minor and major forms, is not only depicted as rebellion. It is slandered as terrorism and singled out for military action. The violent

---

[4] David Fromkin, *A Peace to End All Peace: The Fall of the Ottoman Empire and the Creation of the Modern Middle East*, New York, Avon Books, 1989, p. 45.

[5] Said Nursi, "Seeds of Reality", in *The Damascus Sermon*, Sözler, Istanbul, 1989, p. 96.

[6] Said Nursi, "Seeds of Reality," in *The Damascus Sermon*, Sözler, Istanbul, 1989, p. 102.

dispossession of the Palestinian people is the most outrageous example of how the right of resistance to oppression has been redefined, under the distorting glass of the global ideology, as terror.

At the same time, it is essential to underscore that the noble concept of *jihad* has also been seized, in our day, by a cohort of international desperados whose behavior a man of unbending principle like Bediuzzaman would powerfully reject. For, if he was one of the signatories to the *jihad fatwa* that engaged the Ottoman state in its war of defense against the onslaught of Great Britain, his entire career was dedicated to the greater *jihad* of spiritual self-perfection.

Most penetrating of all was Said Nursi's insight that captivity has been called freedom. Indeed, the ideology of globalization promises mankind a future of unprecedented liberty. But, as we have seen, this liberty means enslavement to the imperatives of global finance and commerce. "Politics which revolves around benefit is savagery," he said then. That statement remains powerfully true today.

Said Nursi's "Seeds of Reality" is a treasure chest of penetrating aphorisms, each one more apposite to our current situation than the preceding one. The Global Directorate meets in secret to decide the policies to be promulgated and enforced by its economic, ideological and military agencies. The effect and impact of its decisions mirror what he wrote then:

> So long as honor and good things are to be obtained from a thing, they offer it to the upper classes, but if it is a bad thing, they divide it among the ordinary people."
> "The Qur'an," he wrote, "which is a mercy for mankind, only accepts a civilization that comprises the happiness of all, or at least of the majority. Modern civilization has been founded on five negative principles:
>
> 1) Its point of support is force, the mark of which is aggression;
> 2) Its aim and goal is benefit, the mark of which is jostling and tussling;
> 3) Its principle in life is conflict, the mark of which is strife;
> 4) The bond between the masses is racialism and negative nationalism, which is nourished through devouring others; its mark is collision;
> 5) Its enticing service is inciting lust and passion and gratifying the desires. But lust transforms man into a beast.

He went on to conclude that the civilization that flows from the *Shari'a* supports truth against force, and that the mark of truth is justice and harmony. In place of benefit, it offers virtue, the mark of which is love and attraction. In place of racialism and nationalism, it offers sincere brotherhood. In life, the principle of mutual assistance takes the place of conflict.

> And it offers guidance instead of lust, the mark of which is human progress and spiritual advancement.[7]

---

[7] Said Nursi, "Seeds of Reality", in *The Damascus Sermon*, Sözler, Istanbul, 1989, p. 105.

Said Nursi's description of Western civilization remains as pertinent and accurate today as it was nearly a century ago. The only difference between then and now is one of degree.

Today, in the West, courageous voices can be heard. Voices, which are as critical of the failings and excesses of its culture and civilization as was Said Nursi of those of the Islamic world. If, I might add parenthetically, this paper does not dwell on the obligations of Muslims as laid down by Said Nursi, it is because the author's first obligation, as a Westerner, is to be critical of his own culture.

Bediuzzaman's proposal to treat the ills he identified is no less accurate than his diagnosis. If we accept that globalization is not a creation of nature — and certainly not of God — but of men, if we accept that it masks the quest for world domination by a single dominant power, then it is easier for us to understand why the prime target of globalization, and its last significant obstacle, is Islam itself: the ultimate barrier, the hard core of resistance which Bediuzzaman Saïd Nursi so powerfully contributed to defending and revitalizing.

Having clearly identified the ills of the age, Said Nursi offered in Damascus and refined down through the years a vision founded not in withdrawal, isolation and fear, but on an appeal to brotherhood, common humanity and cultural dialogue. For running like a gold thread through his life and work is an overflowing sense of hope and confidence not only in the power of providence, but in humanity's ability to receive and act upon the Divine message.

When we understand this much, we realize why his Damascus Sermon and the documents that accompany it, offer a sovereign key to confronting, resisting and reversing the world disorder called Globalization and to replacing it with another, brighter dispensation.

Chapter 13

Virtue vs. Decadence: The Struggle of Civilizations within the Global Village*

Necati Aydin

Introduction

With the spread of communication and information technologies, the resultant shrinking world has become "a global village." With this spread, economic, social, cultural, and political relations are being globalized, and continue to spread to even the remotest corners of the Earth. People are engaged in a fierce struggle to become citizens of this village. As the village leader, America makes its commanding presence felt and tries to define relations between the villagers. Now that communism has been effectively consigned to history, America's trinity of capitalist ideology, laicism and secularism strives to convey its message to all residents of the global village; to divest them of all vestiges of their histories, traditions and cultures, and to "help" them to become "modern."

The tempest of global capitalism blows through the entire world sweeping away any debris in its path, and its hurricane-force gales pound the enduring dam of Islam. Although Islam appears to be immeasurably sturdier than other remains of the past, if the storm overcomes this dam, the capitalist world-view will reinforce its role as the primary determinant of the life style within this village. Perhaps, the world has become too small to sustain more than one world-view. The struggle between different worldviews has intensified. Doubtless, among those who confront the hurricane, Bediuzzaman Said Nursi was one of the most successful. His use of the concept "global village" in the early 1920s as though foreseeing the present storm, "This decadent** civilization, which has made the globe of the earth into a village" (Nursi, *Mesnevi-i Nûriye*, 123) - shows that he

---

* The first edition of this paper was presented at the Sixth International Symposium on Bediuzzaman Said Nursi, entitled 'Globalization and Ethics in the Light of the *Risale-i Nur*,' held in Istanbul 22-24 September, 2002.

** Sükran Vahide, the translator of Nursi's *Nur Collection*, uses "dissolute" for Turkish word "*sefahet*". However, I think the word "decadent" is more appropriate, therefore, I prefer to use decadent throughout this paper.

was aware of the dangers posed by modern civilization. Then, when in Fred Reed's words, the Kemalist project set Turkey on the road to modernization, "This powerless man employed no force, relied on the strength of no army, and had no worldly possessions other than a prayer-rug on which to prostrate and a tea-pot and kettle." Yet, his movement and his works represented "the triumph of humility over pride, of wisdom over force, of sincerity over sycophancy, of belief over disbelief, and impotence over power" (Reed, 1999).

In my opinion, Nursi's views on present-day civilization are not well-understood, despite his being a leading Islamic thinker who looked to the future and addressed "the new generation." The primary reason for this is that the related concepts used in the *Nursi's Nur Collection* are unfamiliar to today's reader. For example, his concepts of the First and Second Europe and their civilizations are neither known by ordinary people, nor understood by intellectuals. This paper aims to rectify this if only to an extent, and to include Bediuzzaman in the debates on Islamic civilization and Western civilization, which have again gained currency since September 11th. The paper consists of two main parts. The first consists of a summary of the arguments in the relevant literature related to global capitalism, while in the second, Bediuzzaman's ideas on Western civilization and Islamic civilization will be studied within the framework of the concepts of "decadent civilization" and "virtuous civilization."

The Rise of Global Capitalism

The seminal work on the sociological and historical roots of capitalism is by Weber (1953). Entitled *The Protestant Ethic and the Spirit of Capitalism*, it links the appearance of capitalism in the West to Protestant ethics. Weber argues that the spirit of Protestantism instilled in its adherents gave rise to capitalism and so changed the course of history.[1] Weber's mission is continued today by Francis Fukuyama, who has gone even further to predict that capitalism and liberal democracy signal the end of history.

In *The End of History and the Last Man* (1992), Fukuyama explicitly announces the triumph of liberal democracy and capitalism. In his view, mankind's historical search has concluded with the finding of the best system. He shows the demise of communism, capitalism's strongest rival, as powerful proof of his claim. Fukuyama argues that the whole world would eventually accept the liberal-capitalist system.

While social scientists were debating this book, he published another one, entitled *The Great Disruption: Human Nature and the Reconstitution of the Social Order* (Fukuyama, 1999), which contains arguments contradictory to his thesis of *The End of History*. He claims that "the Great Disruption" has been experienced in countries governed by liberal democracy and capitalism. In these countries, crimes

[1] If Weber's thesis is correct, history is witnessing a bitter truth: present-day Christianity, including Protestantism, is suffering the pangs of death in the grasp of capitalism, to which it gave birth.

rates have soared, the use of drugs has drastically increased, family relations, which reinforce social ties, have weakened, the institution of marriage heads for the rocks, and trust in society has disappeared. If the necessary steps were not taken, these social problems, would reach serious proportions, which he calls "the Great Disruption". So that his previous thesis is not proved wrong, Fukuyama offers warnings to the liberal democratic world. If solutions are not found for present problems, it will be the end not of history but of liberal democracy and capitalism.[2]

Huntington is another frequently cited writer whose influential book *The Clash of Civilizations* claims prophecies about the future of civilizations. In Huntington's view, it is too early to proclaim victory. He predicts a new conflict. He points out that the Cold War has come to an end and argues that new blocs will be formed on the basis of civilizations (Huntington, 1996). The rival Islamic and Chinese civilizations confront western civilization, which was born with the baptism of Greco-Roman civilization by Christianity. Clashes will be experienced between these civilizations, rather than between nation-states. It is inevitable that Western civilization and Islamic civilization will clash since the latter is opposed to the homogeneous global values of the Davos culture. Conflict will also be directed against people who resist Western values although they migrate to Western countries. Huntington proposes therefore that as a precautionary measure, those who will not be assimilated should not be allowed into these countries. The immigration policies followed by the Bush government after September 11th show that the government listens to his proposals.

Similarly to Huntington, Benjamin Barber speaks of such a clash. He discusses it in his book *McWorld Versus Jihad*, in which he uses the concept of McWorld to portray global capitalism and the concept of Jihad to represent all movements opposed to this. In Barber's book, Jihad is used in a broad sense, not limited to violent reactionary movements. The Jihad declares against the homogeneous global McWorld culture of pop music, video, TV, theatre, books, amusement parks, certain brand names, film stars, and pop stars. The products and services of America-based giant holding companies, such as Coca-Cola, Marlboro, Nike, Hershey, Levi's, Pepsi, and McDonald's, depend on the spread of McWorld culture. Naturally, people who live the McWorld life-style will demand the products of these companies (Barber, 1996, p. 60). For example, societies which drink tea and coffee have to undergo a cultural change if soft drinks like Cola are going to be sold to it. If a society that does not adopt the McWorld culture, even partially, it could not be expected to give up its drinking habits of centuries. Since the global holding companies are aware of this, they use the media as an effective means of instilling the McWorld culture, so as to create demand for their products and services. According to Barber, Hollywood works for McWorld's world

---

[2] According to Bediuzzaman, decline on both the individual and social levels arises from global capitalism, which is nurtured by decadent civilization. It is interesting that although he sought solutions for the problem in the light of human nature the same as Fukuyama does, as an Islamic thinker he reached different conclusions.

domination by reiterating themes of decadent life-styles, secularism, consumerism, and pacifisms (Barber, 1996).[3]

The Distinction Between Decadent Civilization and Virtuous Civilization

For at least the past three centuries Islamic scholars have debated the attitude to be adopted towards Western civilization. Nursi found himself in the middle of this debate in the 20th century, when Westernizing currents were gaining strength. Some scholars favored taking science and technology from the West while rejecting its culture. Others rejected it outright. The latter argued that partial adoption of Western civilization would lead to total submission, since technology is not independent of culture. In contrast to those who rejected Western civilization *in toto*, Nursi distinguished between two Europes by which he meant the existence of two civilization in the Europe (Nursi, *The Flashes Collection*, 160). The first Europe "follows the sciences which serve justice and right and the industries beneficial for the life of society through the inspiration it has received from true Christianity." Although Churches as religious institutions were the primary obstacles for scientific studies in the middle age, Nursi believes that the revealed messages from God have been the source of ethics and inspiration for "virtuous civilization". He even mentions the miracles of prophets as milestone for scientific studies. Furthermore, he sees science as a tool to disclose the knowledge in the book of universe and therefore to realize the names and attributes of God. The distinguishing mark of First Europe is its being beneficial to humanity. It has been a fountainhead of technological advance and made possible the development of human potentialities, allowed social developments opposed to despotism; it is a part of "virtuous civilization."

In Nursi's works, Islamic civilization is the pillar of "virtuous civilization," since it causes the unfolding through virtue of man's infinite potentialities, whereby he may rise higher than the angels. While Nursi proposes co-operation with the First Europe civilization, which is founded on Christian ethics, against vice and irreligion, he rejects the other civilization he calls the Second Europe, whose source is philosophy rather than religion and claims that mankind can find happiness only in vice; this he calls "decadent civilization." It is because this Second Europe is characterized by its encouragement of vice that Nursi rejects capitalist culture and decadent civilization. As the current leader of western civilization, the United States embraces virtuous as well as decadent civilization. In one hand, the US becomes the engine of technological advancement to serve humanity. On the other hand, it turns the planet into a global theme park in

[3] Decadent civilization and virtuous civilization as discussed in this paper correspond respectively to the concepts of McWorld and Jihad with a significant difference. Bediuzzaman strictly talks about the Jihad in people's heart, which is a non-violent rejection of McWorld. The other difference between the two is about the future of this struggle: unlike Barber, Bediuzzaman argues that the victory will be virtuous civilization's.

which the primary goal of life is sensual pleasure. In this regard, American "popular culture" forms the backbone of global decadent civilization.

Nursi asserts that "absolute vice" is being called civilization. He is severely critical of this "decadent civilization" (*The Rays Collection*, 312). In a letter included in *Emirdag Lahikasi [Emirdag Letters]*, he calls it "low" civilization [lit. "mim'siz" *medeniyet*] (For Eng. trans. see, Nursi, *The Damascus Sermon*, 128). While in *Lema'at*, he says that it casts humanity down to the level of animals:

> ... its alluring service is to excite lust and the appetites of the soul and facilitate the gratification of whims, and their result is vice.
>
> The mark of lust and passion is always this: they transform man into a beast, changing his character; they deform him, perverting his humanity.
>
> If most of these civilized people were turned inside out, you would see their characters in the form of apes and foxes, snakes, bears, and swine.
>
> They appear to the imagination in their pelts and skins! Examples of its products are these"(Nursi, *The Words*, 745). Nursi states that the goal of decadent civilization is "mean self-interest instead of virtue," while virtue is the basis of Qur'anic virtuous civilization (Nursi, *The Words*, 745). Virtuous civilization takes all man's subtle faculties into account, causes him to progress spiritually, and to rise higher than the angels. In his words:
>
> Its aim is virtue instead of self-interest ... Its service takes the form of guidance and direction instead of lust and passion. And the mark of guidance is progress and prosperity in way befitting humanity; the spirit is illumined and perfected in the way it requires (*The Words*, 745-6).

Although the various wars in the Islamic countries in recent years and the terrorist attack on the World Trade Centre confirm to an extent Huntington's theory of the clash of civilizations, according to Bediuzzaman, essentially the clash is between decadent civilization and virtuous civilization. In his view, contrary to Hungtington's theory, Christianity and Islam form the front in virtuous civilization, while secularism, laicism, and capitalism are the three allies on the front of decadent civilization. The fiercest battles take place not on the battlefield but in people's hearts, and the struggle is characterized by its not being limited by geographical boundaries. Similar clashes occur in both Islamic societies and Western societies. Everyone witnesses the battle every day in his own small world.

Decadent Civilization Looks on Man as Consisting of His Instinctual Soul

In Nursi's view, decadent civilization mostly addresses man's instinctual soul. Its pupil's goal is "to satisfy the lusts of the soul, to cunningly seek his own personal interests under the screen of patriotism and self-sacrifice, and work to satisfy his ambition and pride. He loves seriously nothing at all other than himself and sacrifices everything for his own sake" (Nursi, *The Flashes*, 163-4). Decadent civilization looks on life as a sort of amusement and makes the world in to a 'theme park.' It tries to gratify people's instinctual souls through entertainments of all sorts. It is because of this that whenever they can, its pupils organize gatherings for fun and want to experience carnal pleasures of every kind. In contrast to the idea that "life is fun," which sums up decadent American culture and adorns the t-shirts that some Americans wear, Nursi points out that life has more exalted aims. He considers illicit pleasures to be like a poison fatal for human potentiality, and suggests setting aside a limited amount of time for licit entertainments. Where decadent civilization amuses the instinctual soul, virtuous civilization gratifies the spiritual subtle faculties, and chiefly the heart, affording happiness. Nursi expresses the difference between the two civilizations in this way:

> Both give rise to eagerness. But through the eagerness provoked by the foreign literature, the soul becomes excited, the desires are stimulated; its gives no joy to the spirit.
>
> The Qur'an's eagerness, however, fires the spirit, gives rise to a lofty eagerness. It is for this reason that the Shari'a of Muhammad (PBUH) wants no amusements or diversions.
>
> It has forbidden some musical instruments, for amusement, and permitted others. (Nursi, *The Words*, 772).

In the view of virtuous civilization, man is not a rational animal, but a guest of the Most Merciful One, who may attain to the highest perfection. The true purpose of man's life should not be to gratify his lusts and desires, but to develop his innate abilities so to rise higher than the angels. Bediuzzaman is severely critical of those who think it progressive to frequent nightclubs, the breeding-ground of decadent civilization, and to consume alcohol and live a night-life. "Progress is not as the people of misguidance imagine, to plunge into the life of this world in all its minute details and in order to taste every sort of pleasure, even the basest, make subject to the evil-commanding soul all the subtle faculties and the heart and intellect, and make them assist it; to do this is not progress, it is decline." True progress is not to blunt all the senses in service of the soul, but "to turn the heart, spirit, intellect, and even the imagination and other subtle faculties given to man towards eternal life and for each to be occupied with the particular duty of worship worthy of it" (Nursi, *The Words*, 331).

The Most Powerful Means of Decadent civilization: The Multinational Media Organizations

Multinational companies, the product of global capitalism, dominate the international market in vice and the means of decadent living as they do in many fields (Herman-McChesney, 1997). As demanded by capitalist ideology, in order to maximize their profits, these holding companies grow by taking over firms offering related products and services. For example, Hollywood is a centre spewing out films and music for the world market. American Time Warner, Viacom, Walt Disney, Vivendi Universal, and News Corporation and German Bartelsmann AG are giant firms which dominate the whole world in the fields of music, entertainment, and news, as though it were a colony.

These holding companies control the mass communications sector through numerous TV and radio stations, magazines, newspapers, news agencies, and publishers. For example, Viacom owns TV entertainment channels, such as primarily MTV, and VH1, Black Entertainment Television, CBS, and Showtime. Then Walt Disney owns the global amusement parks known as theme parks. Vivendi Universal alone controls 22% of the music market. Although in America there are around 500 TV stations, as though offering viewers a wide range of choice, in fact they consist only of entertainment channels serving the economic, political, and philosophical interests of a handful of large holding companies (McChesney, Monthly Review, 2001).

The TV stations of decadent civilization serve capitalist ideology in many respects. The people who found these firms for capitalist aims utilize every possible means to maximize their profits, the main reason for their existence. A capitalist who deems every means of achieving his Machiavellian political aims, will recognize no ethical values when it comes to maximizing his profit. Maximizing profits depend on achieving maximum sales for minimum outlay. Thus, music and entertainment programs have to reach the largest audiences for the least costs. Most typical of the TV stations of decadent civilization is MTV, whose music programs are watched in 350 million homes every day. Broadcasting stations of this sort have no choice but to reach the largest audiences, since they exist only through income from advertising. Such companies can do this only through taking advantage of people's weaknesses, arising from their instinctual desires. In Nursi's words, they profit from people's animal appetites, subjugating them to the capitalist life-style. McChesney says that such decadent media companies make young people leap about to their frenetic music while emptying their pockets of money (McChesney, 2000).

Decadent Civilization Aims at the Youth

Bediuzzaman makes a distinction between the different categories of society, such as the children, young people, elderly, and the sick, and states that virtuous civilization promises happiness for all of them. Decadent civilization, however, takes the youth as its target group. For instance, the decadent civilization typical channel MTV targets people between the ages of 14 and 34 (Cunningham, PBS, 2001).

McChesney, a professor of communications, describes the activities of the multinational media organizations as "neo-colonialism." All the TV stations are like the modern weapons of these holding companies, which colonize their target groups, exploit them economically, and try to influence them politically and ideologically. Instead of countries, chiefly the youth sector and all social groups, are colonized through being inculcated with the philosophy of global capitalism. Instead of killing people with guns and exploiting their natural resources, they kill with fatal broadcasting all their senses that will resist capitalist consumerism, and apply the strategy of using them to increase profits. McChesney summarizes his views on this question like this: "You should look at it (entertainment companies) like the British or the French empires in the nineteenth century. Teens are like Africa.... their weaponry is films, music, books, CDs, internet access, clothing, amusement parks, sports teams. That's all this weaponry they have to make money off of this market, to colonize this market...." (Quoted from the article by Muehlenberg, *News Weekly*, March 9, 2002).

Bediuzzaman was aware that decadent civilization targeted the youth, and warned young people as follows:

> O sons of this land! Do not try to imitate Europeans! How can you reasonably trust in and follow the vice and invalid, worthless thought of Europe after the boundless tyranny and enmity it has shown you? No! No! You who imitate them in decadence, you are not following them, but unconsciously joining their ranks and putting to death both yourselves and your brothers (Nursi, *The Flashes*, 166).

Since he mentions "vice and invalid, worthless thought," it is clear he is referring to decadent civilization, not the First Europe. He argues science and technology is not the property of Europe, rather it belongs to humanity as a whole. In his speech "Address to Freedom", he suggests that science and technology should be taken from the West, since it is useful for humanity, and offers the Japanese as examples:[4] "We shall take with pleasure the points of Europe-like technology and industry - that will assist us in progress and civilization.... we shall forbid the sins and evils of civilization ......We must imitate the Japanese in acquiring civilization, for in taking only the virtues of civilization from Europe they preserved their national customs, which arc the leaven of every nation's continuance"(Vahide, 2002).

In his work *A Guide For Youth*, Bediuzzaman warns the youth against the pitfalls of decadent civilization. He tells those of them who seek the pleasures of life that true, everlasting, and pain-free pleasure is to be found only in religious belief. The licit is sufficient in this respect. There is no need to deviate into the unlawful. He points out that illicit pleasures are false, painful, and short-lived. He told a group of young people who expressed their fear of the pitfalls of decadent civilization and asked how they might preserve their beliefs: "O you unfortunates who are addicted to the pleasures of the life of this world, and with anxiety at the future, struggle to secure it and your lives! If you want pleasure, delight, happiness,

[4] When it started to follow America after the Second World War, Japan adapted to a large extent the present-day capitalist life-style, and therefore lost its position as a model. It had not yet suffered cultural erosion at the time Bediuzzaman held it up as a model.

and ease in this world, make do with what is licit. That is sufficient for your enjoyment" (Nursi, *The Words*, 157).

Where the ulama (Muslim scholars) of former times deterred people through fear of hellfire, Bediuzzaman tried to save young people from falling into vice by showing the poison in illicit pleasures. Although youths are eager and able to experience pleasure, they can restrain themselves by seeing the poison in apparently pleasurable vice. Virtuous civilization helps them to be aware of this poison. It sees man as the noblest of creatures, with the potentiality to surpass the angels. But decadent civilization claims that men are descended from apes, and addresses their animal emotions. According to Nursi, it reduces man to the level of animals and, from the point of view of pleasure, causes him to fall infinitely lower. For although an animal about to be slaughtered can enjoy its fodder to the utmost, for a person faced with the gallows even the most delicious foods are like poison.

Decadent Civilization Subjugates Man to His Instinctual Soul in the Name of Freedom

One of the most important differences between virtuous civilization and decadent civilization is related to their definitions of freedom and its limits. This arises from their different understandings of human nature. The former posits that under the influence of the soul and Satan, man can act in spite of his reason and heart. It looks on the soul and Satan as inner forces that influence man outside his will. Total freedom is possible through making decisions without being affected by internal or external forces. However, since decadent civilization does not accept the existence of inner forces, it considers that the non-intervention of external forces is sufficient for freedom.

Bediuzzaman said about those who define freedom as doing as one likes so long as one does not harm others: "Such people proclaim not their freedom but their vice and degradation and mutter childish pretexts deliriously. For delicate freedom is instructed and adorned with the good manners of the Shari'a (Islamic laws). Freedom to be decadent and behave scandalously is not freedom; it is animality. It is the tyranny of the Devil. It is to be the slave of the evil-commanding soul. General freedom is the product of the portions of individual freedom. The characteristic of freedom is that one harms neither oneself, nor others" (Nursi, *Münâzarat*, 16). And in *The Damascus Sermon*, he points out that "The freedom outside the bounds of the Shari'a is either despotism, or slavery to the soul, or animality, or savagery" (Nursi, *The Damascus Sermon*, 86).

Since decadent civilization does not recognize the existence of the instinctual soul and Satan, it looks on all man's wishes and desires as "his own," and says that freedom demands that on condition a person does not harm others, he should act as he wishes. Whereas virtuous civilization considers that the soul and Satan are "the other" within man, and that freedom demands that he resist these inner forces as well as external ones. In that matter, while virtuous civilization rejects homosexuality, the decadent civilization sees no harm in recognizing family status for homosexuals.

Through the various means it utilizes, decadent civilization and "its depictions so incite vice that they make the mouth water and the reason cannot remain in control. They whet the appetite, excite desire, so that emotions no longer heed anything" (Nursi, *The Words*, 771). In this sense, a person loses his freedom and feels himself compelled to buy what is advertised or accept what is offered. For instances, on some American radio stations there are 18 minutes of advertisements every hour. In this way, due to the capitalist way of life they have inculcated through their overt and subliminal advertising, the multinational media organizations indirectly force people to buy particular brands of goods. The people therefore lose their freedom in this respect.

Reasons for the Successes of Decadent Civilization

Bediuzzaman examines human nature and explains why decadent civilization has spread so speedily affecting even believers. He considers deficient the definition of man of neo-classical economics, as a rational animal who uses his intellect to choose things that are useful. Such faculties as the soul, Satan, and the heart and conscience all play a part in the taking of decisions. If the instinctual soul predominates, a person may make irrational choices. This view is concealed in the Qur'an's prohibition on doing anything that might lead to fornication, rather than just forbidding fornication itself. Presenting vice mouth-wateringly may make people captives to their instinctual souls. Nursi says that one of the soul's salient characteristics is its preferring an ounce of immediate pleasure to tons of future pleasure. In *The Flashes Collection*, he explains how decadent civilization captivates people:

> ... man's evil-commanding soul prefers an ounce of immediate, present pleasure to a ton of postponed, hidden pleasure; similarly, he shrinks at the fear of an immediate slap more than at a year's torment in the future. Furthermore, if the emotions are dominant in a person, they do not heed the reasoning of the mind. Desires and delusions govern and he prefers the slightest and least significant present pleasure to huge reward in the future. And he shrinks from some minor present distress more than from some terrible postponed torment. For desire, illusions, and emotions do not see the future, indeed, they deny it. And if the soul assists them, the heart, which is the seat of belief, and the mind fall silent and are defeated (Nursi, *The Flashes*, 111).

Also in *The Flashes* is the following simile for those who are defeated by their souls and get carried away by the enticements of decadent civilization:

> ... like a silly child who sells the portion of the Qur'an he is learning to buy a single sweet, in order to flatter his emotions, gratify his senses, and satisfy his appetites, he makes his good deeds, as valuable as diamonds, the means to egotistical pleasures like insignificant fragments of glass, and he loses out in profitable works (Nursi, *The Flashes*, 373).

Nursi mentions the intensive use of amusement as another reason for the successes of decadent civilization despite its bringing pain to people rather than happiness. It prevents people feeling the pain of their situations through its narcotic or stimulant effects, causing heedlessness. Like a drunkard covered in wounds may bellow at his surrounding as though he were fine, so the pupil of decadent civilization, intoxicated and heedless, may be unaware of the pains in his spirit:

> "But in these stormy times, currents which numb the senses and scatter man's attention on peripheral matters, plunging him into them, have deadened his senses and bewildered him. As a result of this the people of misguidance are temporarily unable to feel their torment, while the people of guidance are overwhelmed by heedlessness and cannot truly appreciate its pleasures" (Nursi, *The Rays Collection*, 642).

Decadent Civilization Never Brings True, Permanent Happiness

Bediuzzaman asserts that decadent civilization has dragged humanity into a spiritual whirlpool, rather than bringing peace and happiness. People are temporarily oblivious of this while they enjoying themselves, but when they again face the reality of life they will feel the torments of Hell. To put it another way, people who see the world as good while they are engrossed in their entertainments and suppose that they have captured happiness, continue to suffer spiritually when the entertainments come to an end. The pupils of decadent civilization therefore continually preoccupy themselves with different amusements so as not to feel this pain. It is as though every game offers happiness, and lifelong happiness resembles the story of donkey of the Italian peasant.[5] They rush from pleasure to pleasure thinking "this time I've found it," only to find that they have exerted themselves for nothing.

In *Lema'at*, Nursi calls decadent civilization "fancy," and makes the following analysis:

> ...fancies block out the feelings. This requires solace, it requires feigned unmindfulness, it requires occupation, it requires entertainment. Enchanting desires.
>
> Then it can deceive the conscience and put the spirit to sleep so they feel no pain. Otherwise that grievous suffering scorches the conscience; the pain is unendurable, the despair cannot be borne.

[5] The well-tried way of the Italian peasant to get his donkey to move is to attach some hay to a stick which is then tied to the animal so that it hangs 20 inches in front of its nose. Taking step after step to reach the tasty morsel, when he finally reaches home he realizes his efforts were all for nothing.

> This means, however far one deviates from the Straight Path, to that extent one is affected in that way, causing the conscience to cry out. Within every pleasure is a pain, a taint.
>
> That means glittering civilization, which is a mixture of fancy, lust, amusement, and licentiousness, is a deceptive panacea for the ghastly distress arising from misguidance, a poisonous narcotic.

Virtuous civilization, however, which he calls "guidance," brings true happiness because it gratifies the soul with licit pleasures and satisfies the heart, spirit, and conscience as well:

> ... it imparts a state to the spirit varying in degree according the strength of belief. The body receives pleasure through the spirit, the spirit receives pleasure through the conscience.
>
> An immediate pleasure is felt in the conscience; a spiritual paradise is present in the heart. To think of it is to open it up; while consciousness is marked by its secrets.
>
> Now, however much the heart is aroused, the conscience stimulated, the spirit stirred, it increases the pleasure, transforming fire into light, and winter into spring.
>
> The doors of paradises open up in the conscience, the world becomes a paradise. Within it our spirits take flight, soaring like kites, entreating, praying (Nurşi, *The Words*, 778-9).

Being based on the domination of the instinctual soul, decadent civilization both denies the other human faculties and leaves them unnourished, and cannot therefore offer happiness. While the instinctual soul enjoys itself in a perpetual festival, the other subtle faculties weep, abandoned.

Bediuzzaman depicts the situation of a person who follows decadent civilization with the following allegory: "His situation is thus: behind him stands a lion poised ready to spring on him; before him await the gallows; on his right side a deep wound has opened up; on his left is a suppurating boil; but while in this state, he is sent on a long journey" (Nursi, *Nur'un Ilk Kapisi*, 22). The lion here represents the appointed hour, and the gallows death, while the two wounds allude to man's infinite innate impotence and poverty. The journey is man's lengthy, involuntary journey, which starts in the spirit world and continues to the hereafter. Decadent civilization can never be the means to human happiness so long as it does not banish death, remove all the dangers and harms threatening man, and answer all his physical and spiritual wants and desires.

Bediuzzaman calls out as follows to all those fallen into vice: "O you neglectful people wallowing in misguidance, if you have found a way of removing death from the world and impotence and poverty from man, you can do without religion and its practices. Otherwise be silent! For with their reverberating voices, creational signs such as death, impotence, transitoriness, poverty, and the journey of life all proclaim the necessity of religion and the practice of its marks" (*Nursi, Nur'un Ilk Kapisi*, 24).

Bediuzzaman does not only mention the suffering caused by decadent civilization; he discusses virtuous civilization's elevated pleasures, which address all man's subtle faculties. He asserts even that they receive peace and pleasure from all good works. Perfected people rise above corporeality and animality, so experience these pleasures, while the decadent remain deprived of them:

> A state of mind pleasing to the mature and perfected with their appreciation of meaning, does not gratify the childish, whimsical, and decadent.
>
> It does not entertain them. In consequence, those raised amid base, decadent, carnal and lusty pleasures will not experience spiritual pleasure (Nursi, *The Words*, 770).

He says too that permanent, pain free pleasure is found within the sphere of virtuous civilization in this world too:

> ... know certainly that true pleasure in the life of this world lies in belief and the sphere of belief. And there is an immaterial pleasure to be found in all good works. The *Risale-i Nur* has proved with hundreds of decisive evidences that even in this world most bitter and grievous suffering is present in vice and misguidance. I myself have experienced on numerous occasions as certainly as seeing it with my own eyes that present in belief is a seed of Paradise while in vice and misguidance is a seed of Hell. This truth is repeated many times in the *Risale-i Nur* (Nursi, *The Flashes*, 264-5).

And it is a fact that despite 28 years of prison and exile, Bediuzzaman knew himself to be happy. He signed himself "Your most fortunate brother" in his letters to his students even in the harsh circumstances of prison.

> Just as through virtuous civilization man's physical organs like his eyes, mouth, nose and ears and hands profit from physical pleasures, so the spiritual organs and senses unfold: " ... not the ten or so human members like the eyes, ears, and heart, but the hundred members in the form of an extremely long arm which believers may extend each according to his degree, to those two tables of the Most Merciful, to gather in the bounties from all sides (Nursi, *The Flashes*, 319).

Nursi pointed out that man is connected to the past and future with his reason, heart, and memory, and said that he can be truly happy only when his true nature is known and satisfied. A person who recalls the pains of the past with his memory can be consoled only through the light of belief. For the more he thinks of all those he loves who have died, the more even his present pleasures are transformed into pain. He may capture happiness only when his "intense desire for immortality" is satisfied. Since decadent civilization offers only present animal pleasures, it cannot satisfy the spirit. It can provide no permanent joy even if it busies a person temporarily. Just as since the 1960s in America incomes have increased twofold, people are not noticeably happier — although according to indicators of affluence like cars, air-conditioned houses, and washing machines, the average American is doubly better off. However, during the same period, divorce rates have doubled, suicides among young people have increased threefold, while cases of depression have increased tenfold (*Newsweek*, 2002).

The Most Effective Defense Against Decadent Civilization

According to Nursi, it is not enough merely to believe in God and the hereafter to be saved from the captivation of decadent civilization. And for the most part it is ineffective in inducing people to give up vice, to frighten them with the thought of Hellfire. Even the believers may say: "God is forgiving and compassionate, and Hell is a long way off,' and continue in their dissipation. Their hearts and spirits are overcome by their emotions" (Nursi, *The Rays*, 640). This is indicated by the verse, "Let not then this present life deceive you, nor let the Chief Deceiver deceive you about God" (Qur'an, 31:33). For this reason, at the present time the most effective way of preserving believers from decadent civilization is "to show them the pain present in their pleasure and to defeat their emotions. Although they are aware of the diamond-like bounties and pleasures of the hereafter, as the verse, 'They deem lovable the life of this world' (Qur'an, 14:3) indicates, while being believers, the people of misguidance choose worldly pleasures, which are like pieces of glass soon to be shattered. The only way of saving them from this love of the world and from the danger of succumbing to it is by showing them the hellish torments and pains they suffer even in this world" (Nursi, *The Rays*, 640).

In the allegorical comparisons in the Sixth, Seventh, and Eighth Words, and Third Stopping-Place of the Thirty-Second Word Nursi points out the fearsome pains suffered by who follow decadent civilization seeking its pleasures, and the permanent happiness of those who take the path set out by the Qur'an. Depicting with these comparisons the poisons within the enticements of decadent civilization, he urges the sensible among its followers to repent.

Bediuzzaman says that true, permanent, and pain free pleasure is found only in the sphere of belief and he invites people to such happiness but points out that they have to avoid vice if they are to find it. "As for the medicine of belief, it shows its effects though your carrying out your religious obligations as far as is possible. Heedlessness, vice, the lusts of the soul, and illicit amusements prevent the effectiveness of the remedy" (Nursi, *The Flashes*, 285).

Decadent Civilization will Cause the End of the World

Bediuzzaman stated that the sins of decadent civilization would be a cause of the End of the World. He says that due to mass communications, the means of decadent civilization, one sin becomes manifold through its reaching millions of people. Thus personal sins that could be committed only in a lifetime of thousands of years, gain universality through the media, reaching proportions that may cause the end of the world (Nursi, *Kastamonu Lahikasi* in *RNK*, ii, 1615).

The causal relationship Bediuzzaman points out between the end of the world and the sins of decadent civilization rests on the thesis of "the purpose of creation." According to this, God created the world from nothing in order to make Himself known to conscious beings and to man in particular. So long as man acts in conformity with this purpose, He continues the existence of the world. Since decadent civilization generally neglects this underlying purpose of creation, no reason remains for the universe's continued existence. In the past, divine wrath destroyed peoples who acted contrarily to this purpose, and at the end of time it will cause Doomsday to break forth at a time decadent civilization has become widespread and most people have become sinful and rebellious.

Conclusion

If decadent civilization and virtuous civilization are compared theoretically and conceptually in the light of Bediuzzaman's views, the following conclusions may be reached from the present essay:

Firstly, Bediuzzaman includes within the concept of virtuous civilization the First Europe, which sprang from Christianity and has produced things useful for humanity. The Second Europe is a civilization the primary aim of which is licentiousness rather than virtue. In other words, while the former takes into consideration man's reason, heart, and other faculties and aims for their development through virtue, the latter's main aim is to serve man's instinctual soul, encouraging decadent living rather than virtue. The struggle between these two civilizations has been continuing since the first man and will intensify at the end of time.

Secondly, Bediuzzaman accepts the struggle between decadent civilization and virtuous civilization, but he firmly rejects the inevitable clash between the civilizations of east and west predicted by Huntington. He proposes co-operation with the part of Western civilization that has sprung from Christianity and whose aim is virtue, against decadent civilization and irreligion. Although decreasing spirituality suggest that the Christian world's resistance in this struggle is weakening, the Islamic world continues to withstand global capitalism.

Thirdly, in comparison with Bediuzzaman's ideas about the dangers of irreligion, his ideas related to decadent civilization have not been studied, as they deserve. As an external, open enemy, communism alerted and awakened people, whereas the dangers of decadent civilization, concealed behind a pleasanter, friendlier mask, is not well understood. Bediuzzaman, however, predicted that the sins of decadent civilization would become so great as to cause the end of the world.

Fourthly, Bediuzzaman put forward a new method for achieving a successful outcome in the struggle between the two civilizations, different to former scholars (ulama). He suggested that the struggle could be won by demonstrating with proofs that contrarily to what is claimed, decadent civilization brings humanity only false, fleeting happiness, whereas virtuous civilization provides true, permanent happiness.

References

Cunningham,Todd (2001): an interview at http://www.pbs.org/wgbh/pages/frontline/shows/cool/interviews/cunningham.html (published 20.12.2001.)

Fukuyama, Francis (1992): *The End of History and the Last Man*, New York: Maxwell Macmillan International.

Fukuyama, Francis (1999): *The Great Disruption: Human Nature and the Reconstitution of Social Order*, New York: The Free Press.

Herman, Edward S. and McChesney, Robert W. (1997): *The Global Media: The New Missionaries of Corporate Capitalism*, Washington, D.C.

Huntington, Samuel P. (1996): *The Cash of Civilizations and the Remaking of World Order*, New York: Simon & Schuster.

Mabry, Tristan James (1998): "Modernization, Nationalism, and Islam: an examination of Ernest Gellner's writing on Muslim society with reference to Indonesia and Malaysia", *Ethics and Racial Studies*, v 21, no 1.

McChesney, Robert W. (2000): *Rich Media, Poor Democracy*, The New Press 2000.

McChesney, Robert W. (2001): "Global Media, Neoliberalism, and Imperialism", *Monthly Review*, v.52, 10, 1.

Muehlenberg, Bill (2002): "Culture: How the media exploits the US$150 billion American youth market", *News Weekly*, March 6, 2002.

Newsweek, September 16, 2002.

Nursi, Bediuzzaman Said, *The Letters* 1928-1932 [Eng. tr.], Istanbul: Sözler Publications, new edn., 1997.

Nursi, Bediuzzaman Said, *Mesnevi-i Nûriye* [Turk. trans. Abdülmecid Nursî], Istanbul: Sözler Yayinevi, 1980.

Nursî, Bediuzzaman Said, Nursi, *Münâzarat*. Istanbul: Sözler Yayinevi, 1991.

Nursi, Bediuzzaman Said, *Nur'un Ilk Kapisi*, Istanbul: Sözler Yayinevi, 1991.

Nursi, Bediuzzaman Said, *The Damascus Sermon* [Eng. trans.], Istanbul: 1996.

Nursi, Bediuzzaman Said, *The Flashes Collection* [Eng. trans.], Istanbul: Sözler Publications, 1995.

Nursi, Bediuzzaman Said, *The Rays Collection*, [Eng. trans.], Sözler Publications, 1998.

Nursi, Bediuzzaman Said, *The Words* [Eng. trans.], Istanbul: Sözler Publications, new ed., 1998.

Nursi, Bediuzzaman Said, *Kastamonu Lahikasi* in *Risale-i Nur Kulliyati*, II, Istanbul: Nesil Yayinevi, 4 edition, 1997.

Qur`an, English Translation by Abdullah Yusuf Ali.

Reed, Fred A. (1999): *Anatolia Junction*, TalonBooks, Canada.

Vahide, Sükran: *Bediüzzaman Said Nursi: The Author of the Risale-i Nur*, Istanbul: Sözler Publications, 1992.

Weber, Max (1958): *The Protestant Ethics and the Spirit of Capitalism*, trans. by Talcott Parsons. New York: Scribners.

Chapter 14

Islam and Modernity

Durmus Hocaoglu

This chapter states by identifying nine features that will be developed further.

1. There are signs that the Modern Age is coming to a close and that humanity is on the threshold of a new age.
2. This 'new age' will not reject modernity; it will be an age of 'neo-modernity', which transcends it.
3. History has loaded a heavy burden on the shoulders of Muslims in this matter. For in founding this neo-modernity, there are many things that are not 'historical Islam,' otherwise known as 'phenomenal Islam,' which has been formed in the course of history, but 'pure Islam,' also known as 'noumenal Islam,' has the potential to do, and that it has to do.
4. Neo-modernity has to be founded by Muslims in a *Muslim manner*. For all the varieties of modernity lack compassion, crushing those who lag behind. Western modernity overwhelmed all societies that remained outside itself together with their cultures, religions, and civilizations.
5. If this neo-modernity emerges from within Western modernity, which at present is the sole modernity, Islam, not as a religion but as a culture and civilization, will receive a blow so severe it will be unable to sustain it, and it will be crushed more severely than it has up to now.
6. In conclusion we may say that the pride and dignity of Islam and Muslims is dependent on founding an **Islamic modernity** which transcends the modernity of the present, offers joint and necessary values for all humanity, has no alternative, affords no right of choosing any other, to which all roads lead, and whose foundations are established on the universal spirit of Islam.
7. One of the primary conditions of founding this modernity is becoming 'worldly.'
8. And the primary condition for becoming worldly is 'acquitting' and 'legitimizing' the world in the minds of Muslims.
9. The Qur'an shows the world to be licit. The aim of this chapter is to demonstrate this briefly and concisely.

MODERNITY AND POST-MODERNITY

Modernity

Modernity is a much-disputed concept. Two main groups have emerged in these discussions: 'positive' and 'negative.' The supporters of 'positive' modernity see modernity to be the most important milestone in mankind's progress, while the supporters of 'negative' modernity put forward the opposing view that modernity has gained for mankind less than it has lost for them, and that it has led to a decline.

The main ideas of the supporters of *'negative' modernity* may be summarized as follows:

- Modernity is a way of life restricted to the physical and material (*res materialis*), which has relegated the spiritual (*res spiritualis*) to a secondary position.
- For this reason modernity looks on nature as a field of exploitation, lacking all respect for it and destroying it.
- Man's wholeness, consisting of the fusion of matter and meaning, has suffered in consequence of this restriction of the view to the physical.
- Similarly, religion was banished from the life of society and confined to the conscience, and frequently it did not stop at that; the attempt was made to root religion out of the conscience too.
- In view of this, modernity is an anti-religious movement.

Because of the Western character of modernity, the supporters of negative modernity in non-Western societies add their own particular problems to the negative views listed above. These anti-modernity views, which have been especially influential in recent times, add the following to the criticisms of modernity in the West:

- Modernity has been imposed by the West. It is political, economic, and cultural oppression by the West of non-Western societies, that is, a sort of colonialism.
- Modernity, which is identified with the West, tends to destroy the beliefs of the followers of all religions, and particularly those of Muslims.
- For this reason, it is 'misguidance' and 'imperialism.'
- In particular, modernism is modernity in the form of a despotic ideology, and in this form is a sort of 'atheism', which is the reverse of religion.

The main ideas of the supporters of **positive modernity** may be summarized like this:

- Modernity is one of the most important stages in mankind's progress.

- According to some people, modernity is not only one of the most important stages in mankind's progress in the general sense, in its particular, concrete form Western modernity forms the final point of man's progress. This idea is present in Fukuyama's works, who discusses the concept of "the end of history," and in those of Huntingdon, although here it appears to be the opposite of this.
- Modernity is man's ceasing to be passive in the physical world and his becoming active. It means his domination over the physical world.
- Modernity brought humanity power and wealth. In modernizing societies this increased man's worth and value. For it should be noted that the highly valuable mechanism of democracy is essentially the product of modernity.
- Broadly speaking, it is true that modernity made religion passive, but this is the fault of religion, not modernity. Religion (particularly Christianity) is opposed to man's inborn nature, so if it dominates him, it prevents the advance of humanity, abasing and pauperizing men.

Post-Modernity

Post-modernity is a recently-coined expression, based on the hypothesis that modernity is drawing to a close. Its end is in sight. For the industrial age, with which modernity is identified, is coming to an end. Humanity is now on the threshold of a new era.

If the preliminaries of post-modernity may be summarized briefly in this way, it has so far been unsuccessful in putting forward anything clear to succeed it. Post-modernity is the general name for the view that what follows modernity is an age of decomposition and falling-apart. But according to our thesis, post-modernity merely consists of the footsteps of another modernity. It is because of this that some people call it "hyper-modernity."

INTRODUCTION TO THE THESIS: MAIN PRECONCEPTIONS

Modernity Generally

In western philosophy, modernity is first dealt with as an abstract concept, and being reformulated, is defined as follows: modernity is a new situation, qualitatively and radically different to the previous social condition of humanity, following no previous model or example, at a more advanced level. According to this definition, agriculture is modern compared with the tending of sheep, for it is not the same as shepherding and is more advanced. Similarly, industry is more advanced than agriculture.

According to this definition, in order to be able to define any social situation as 'modern,' it should not be the same as any existing situation or quantatively more advanced; just the opposite, it should coincide with a qualitative change.

Western Modernity

According to this definition, there is only one modernity at the present time: Western modernity. Particularly for us, as the intellectuals of a nation that for centuries has had relations with the West, has suffered its tyranny, whose civilization and culture have been overwhelmed by the West, and that is encircled by enemies, it is a bitter fact hard to accept; but facts are facts. This statement is true. On referring to the definition above, it is not possible to reach any other conclusion.

The chief characteristic of modernity and the one that makes it 'modern' are the relations between man and things being ordered in accordance with 'industrial civilization' and its new world situation, which has the meaning of being ordered in a way radically different to all previous stages of civilization.

The Surpassing of Modernities

According to our thesis, any modernity can be surpassed only by another modernity. Briefly, here surpass refers to the term 'hyper-modernity' being included within the definition of modernity. According to this, for a modernity to be surpassed, a more advanced modernity has to be created.

Thus, post-modernity makes no claim to surpass modernity. From this point of view, the term, which cannot be asserted in respect of either extension or intension, has the quality of being a reaction against modernity. The sources feeding this reaction are the views of negative modernity which we attempted to summarize above.

THESIS: NEO-MODERNITY AND ISLAMIC MODERNITY

Neo-Modernity

Here we assert the following as our hypothesis: Western modernity, which is still existent and effective, can be surpassed only by a formation which is more advanced than itself and is *modern* in the true meaning. We call this **neo-modernity**.

Neo-modernity may be better understood by setting out the sum total of what modernity has given to humanity and what it has taken from it.

1. The most important thing modernity has given humanity, its greatest gain for humanity, and what makes it modernity, is its completely re-forming the relations between man and things, in a way totally dissimilar to anything that preceded them. In essence these are as follows:

   a) Philosophically: man's sovereignty over 'things,' that is, his domination over things.
   b) Its concrete manifestation: Industrial civilization.
2. On the other hand modernity deprived humanity of many things, the chief of which was its destruction of the balance between spirit and matter. Here, we should briefly say this: the spoiling of the balance between spirit and matter was not the fault of modernity alone. For this balance had always been the most difficult balance to maintain. With few rare exceptions, at virtually no time in human history had it been perfectly established. Basically, by tending to dominate things, modernity pushed 'meaning' into second place. It built a world stripped of the sacred to the greatest extent possible. In doing this, modernity weighed the balance in favour of 'matter', which in the Middle Ages had proponderated towards 'meaning.' Or to put it more clearly, rather than spoiling the existing balance, what modernity did was to change the imbalance from one extreme to the other.

However, despite the efforts to defunctionalize the sacred, modernity increased man's worth immeasurably. Perhaps never previously had man been accorded so much importance. Out of all its institutions, democracy should be seen as the best example of this.

Thus, since neo-modernity can be established only by surpassing existent modernity, in spite of everything, modernity, or with its full name Western modernity, should be seen as an important stage in mankind's development, and these points should be noted:

- Man's sovereignty over things, and his gaining worth, that is, his winning freedom, are facts which are irreversible and the reversal of which would not be right. They are what modernity has gained for humanity.
- However, the serious destruction of the natural environment, and more importantly, the relegation of 'meaning' to a position subordinate to 'matter,' and the defunctionalizing of the sacred are matters that should be counted as 'minuses' since they have impoverished mankind.

Since this is so, in essence neo-modernity must be this: man's dominance over matter and his winning of freedom should be taken further, but in doing this, the balance between 'meaning' and 'matter,' spoiled by Western modernity in favour of 'matter,' should be re-established authentically, and the sacred should be refunctionalized in order to do this.

Islamic Modernity

At this point 'noumenal Islam' opens up broad horizons. It is the thing we deem suitable to call 'Islamic modernity.'

By the term Islamic modernity is meant the project of universal world rule which establishes the balance between 'matter' and 'meaning,' restores the function of the sacred, completely re-orders the relations between men and between man and things, and in essence is based on the Qur'an, that is, its point of reference is the Qur'an (Islam). Islamic modernity makes the following two things (simultaneously) imperative: the re-reading of Islam and the present age; the renewal and revival of Islam, the ordering of the world according to a universal system that will be established in accordance with the Book. The re-reading of Islam will be possible by taking the Qur'an as the source of reference. For which reason Islamic modernity also has the meaning of Qur'anic modernity.

From a universal world rule project we may move on to this: Islamic modernity or Qur'anic modernity means also the Islamization of the world or making Islam 'worldly.' However, the Islamization of the world does not mean the whole world accepting the religion of Islam, nor does making Islam 'worldly' mean a 'reform' of Islam. What is meant by the two terms is this: a way of existence without alternative springing from a system whose basic principles are Qur'anic but in which everyone Muslim and non-Muslim may participate, and to which the whole world is bound to submit either willingly or unwillingly.

For sure, it is not possible to supply any details at the moment for such a project. That is, to put it more clearly, the realization of this project should be left to time. For to attempt to define this project categorically, which looks to many years in the future, means determining history, and that is impossible. Here, we shall investigate briefly the answer to the following question: is the realization of such a civilizational project possible within the framework of the Qur'an?

We set out with the belief that the answer to this question will be affirmative, and say this: with its perpetual youth, the Qur'an shows the following important potentialities, which will form the basis of the construction of neo-modernity. Firstly, a basis should be sought for the legitimisation of man's dominion over 'things.' This is given by the Qur'an in this way:

- Individually (as a person) man is transitory and his home is the hereafter; but in respect of society (humanity) he is permanent and his home is this world.
- Man was sent to this world, not as a monk who abandons the world, but to rule the world. The world has been promised to man(kind), and is therefore a 'promised land.'

These two matters not only legitimise man establishing dominance over things; they indicate something more than this: they charge man with the obligation of being God's vicegerent of the earth, and with establishing rule over "everything between the heavens and the earth."

However, as an individual, man is a stranger in this world whose home is the hereafter. Individual man's essence is spirit, and spirit is from the world of the Divine command. Thus, since essentially man is a stranger in this physical world, he can only be happy in the true sense when these two sides of him are in harmony.

This is what we called the balance between matter and meaning, which can be established only with reference to the sacred. For Muslims, the Qur'an is the sole, perfect, matchless reference in this matter.

The main matter to be discussed in this chapter is this: in order for the Qur'an-based world rule project to be realized, the possibility has to be investigated of acquitting world dominion and becoming worldly' from the Qur'anic point of view. It is an historical question, whether or not this has been done up to the present. That is to say, the author is proposing that the legitimization of 'becoming worldly' should be sought not in 'historical (phenomenal) Islam,' but that the worldview of 'noumenal Islam,' that is, of the Qur'an, should be investigated. The author's starting point is this: Muslims today have as much right and freedom to interpret the Qur'an as the Muslims who lived in the past. It is essential to always keep in mind the Qur'anic understandings and interpretations of the Muslims of the past, and how they lived it, and to respect these, but we should not forget that one person's understanding, perception, and interpretation cannot be binding on another person. It is the Qur'an which is most certainly binding on a believer, followed by the Prophet's *Sunna* and Hadiths, according to their degree.

* * *

We shall now discuss the concept of 'worldiness,' which is important in my thesis of Islamic modernity.

The Concept(s) of 'Worldliness-Becoming Worldly' Generally

Here, it will be useful to define in general terms the concept of 'worldliness.' The main purpose of this is to state the truth, and secondly to prevent error. For in many cases it is not enough merely to put what is right; what is wrong has also to be eliminated. Because one of the inadequacies of the intellectuals in our country, which makes itself felt in many fields, is the tendency to judge like an ideologue, rather than investigating concepts like a true intellectual and trying to understand them. Similarly, many conservative intellectuals and academics look on modernity as being opposed to religion, and consider 'worldliness' to be 'materialism,' then condemn them outright.

Thus, here we want to study briefly the problem of 'worldliness' in the sense we use it, with the concepts of what it is not (negative definition) and what it is (positive definition), and to reformulate it. 'Worldliness' does not only mean making this world an object of interest and knowledge. That might be known as 'absolute worldliness.' Absolute worldliness is primarily and necessarily focussed on a theoretical problem: ontologically, its starting point is by tending towards monism, the construction of a monobloc globe of existence, and positing that existence consists only of this world, no other reality may be accepted outside this or above it. The chief characteristic of absolute worldliness is, by not accepting any field of reality outside this world, its being an 'ontological monism' in respect of the physical field of existence (*res extensia*); and by in the final analysis reducing this monism to a single substance, its being 'materialism;' and by not accepting any field of reality above this world, its being 'atheism.'

Parallel to and dependent on this ontological analysis, the second main characteristic of absolute worldliness is the rooting out axiologically of belief in God and the hereafter, and parallel to this extirpation of belief making this world, by which we are addressed only between our births and deaths, into a sort of object of worship. However, worldliness in the sense we use it is radically different to 'absolute worldliness.' Thus: as an ontological problem, 'worldliness' is not based on the thesis that this world is the sole area of existence. That is to say, contrarily to absolute worldliness, worldliness does not tend towards an ontological monism. Essentially, it is based on the thesis of the acceptance ontologically of the reality of this world in which we live as axiologically a legitimate field of existence, in other words, that this world should be 'acquitted.'

Generally speaking, the reality of this world does not necessitate at the first stage of the ontological analysis the rejection of another field of existence (the metaphysical world). Similarly, it does not necessitate the rejection of the existence of a superior transcendental being (God). However, as is discussed below, from the point of view of the Qur'an, which forms the basis of Islamic philosophy, this first stage of the ontological analysis is inadequate and a second stage is necessary. Essentially this second stage of analysis is its existing not 'of itself', but 'in itself.'

However, again from the point of view of the Qur'an, that is, God's Word, the basis of Islamic philosophy, the stage which truly demonstrates 'worldliness' is the stage of axiological analysis. This analysis shows that this world, which is a reality, is not illicit, unclean, and the source of sin, from which one should therefore distance onself or give up altogether, or even execrate; on the contrary, that it is licit and clean; that of itself it is not foul and the source of sin, but that its uncleanness arises only from man's conduct. Since that is the case, life in this world, or to put it technically 'worldly life,' in the pure sense, is legitimate. Acceptance of the legitimacy of worldly life necessitates acceptance of the legitimacy of striving and endeavour in relation to it.

Islam and Worldliness

In my opinion, mature philosophy should have these two basic aims: worldliness and humanity.

Worldliness (The conquest of the outside world; material conquest). This means total dominance over the outside world (this world, *physis*). From the Islamic point of view, this is to acknowledge God's promise not to individual man, but to humanity, and to carry out the mission of the Divine vicegerency with which God has charged it.

Humanity (Conquest of the inner world, spiritual conquest). Man's conquest of himself means his return to himself. In Islamic terminology this is to acknowledge what God has promised to man.

That is to say, the outside world has to be conquered, which is an obligation laid on man. On the one hand this is a fundamental difference between himself and the other beings in the universe, and on the other it is a mission with which he has been charged. However, man should not lose the seat of his sovereignty during this conquest along the frontiers, and this means establishing a sensitive balance between himself and nature, and between himself and his Object of Worship.

The success of Western civilization lay in its victory in the field of 'worldliness' (*dünyexîleşme*), while its weakness and fault was its defeat in the field of humanity (*insanîleşme*). We may say that to a certain extent Western civilization 'became savage while becoming worldly.' As Max Scheller put it, in Western civilization man was defeated in the inner world while conquering the outer world.

The Concept of 'World Rule'

The conquest of the outer world may be expressed with the term 'world rule.' Although traditionally we mostly use this term in the political sense, the concept as we use it here has the meaning of 'man's domination over things.'

'World Rule,' 'Worldliness,' and 'Legitimacy'

In order to be able to realize the project of 'world rule,' which is the conquest of the outer world (material conquest), the outer world, that is, the cosmos, or with its other name, 'this world' has to legitimised axiologically firstly in the minds of Islamic societies, that is, in Islamic thought (which is also called 'phenomenal Islam'), which may be defined briefly as 'the understanding and interpretation of Islam that has been formed in the course of time.' According to this, on the one hand this world has to be acquired as a means of sovereignty, and on the other this process has to be legitimised.

Ruling the world is to become 'worldly.' Or to put it the other way round, to become worldly means gaining sovereignty of the world. But basically we, that is we human beings as individuals, are not originally from this world. Everything in this world other than man belongs to this world. This is where the concept of legitimisation emerges as an important concept from the philosophical point of view. We are bound to prove that we have the right to rule a field of existence that does not belong to us, otherwise the conquest will lack an ethical basis. Then the conquest would an occupation, a seizure, which would an illicit act without any ethical basis. It would only be a misdeed, an act of aggression and tyranny.

The conquest of the world has to be legitimised from two points of view.

As a theoretical ethic: Man is also a moral being. Morality is concerned with not with what is, but with what should be. According to the latter, since morality is particular to man, the conquest of the outer world that we shall attempt should be human, and this is only by being moral, and the condition of this is the legitimacy of the conquest.

As a practical ethic: This legitimacy at the same time holds a special meaning and importance for Muslims. The legitimisation of the conquest of the outer world will prevent the bifurcation of our inner, spirit, worlds, will speed up our conquests, and pave the way for establishing our modernity. To reiterate, the chief primary condition of Islamic modernity is a world rule based on Islam, and that will be possible only by legitimising the world in the minds of Muslims.

Worldliness and Islam

What is meant by the phrase "legitimising the world in Islam" is in very clear words, firstly making this world licit in the eyes of Muslims in order to be able to be sovereign over it as the world in which we live and its physical entity, and to be able to carry this out within the framework of an Islamic world order.

As a term, the phrase 'an Islamic world order' means the conjugation of two concepts, which are 'Islamic worldliness' on the one hand, and 'worldly Islam' on the other. Islamic worldliness means the world achieving a universal system of Islamic origin, and the most important condition of this is the enactment of the concept of 'worldly Islam.' 'Worldliness' is a very novel concept in Islamic thought and difficult to accept. There is always the danger of its being understood as materialism, for which reason is a new concept that might easily be branded as being non-Islamic and be given a heterodox meaning. I therefore feel the need to emphasize that it should not be understood as an experiment in 'reforming' Islam. Worldly Islam means the careful extricating of elements which hold Muslims back from the world yet are ascribed to Islam, and the discovery of worldly elements in Islam and putting them into practice. Thus, worldly Islam may also be understood as 'the rediscovery of Islam.'

At this point it will be useful to offer further brief discussion of the concept of 'worldliness.' We said that in this paper we use this concept in two complementary meanings: cosmic worldliness and social worldliness.

Cosmic Worldliness (worldliness in the broadest sense)

The following meanings are included in this general worldliness, which may be defined as 'worldliness in the widest and most comprehensive sense,' and may also be known as 'cosmological worldliness:'

- The reordering of the existence and value of the cosmos: the legitimisation and 'acquittal' both ontologically and axiologically of the physical environment in which we live, the cosmos, or this world, or briefly, the world, and its existence and value.
- The resituating of man in the cosmos: the ethical legitimisation of 'worldly life' as an operation and the idea of laying claim to the world.
- The reordering of man's relations with the world: the reorganizing of the relations between man and things, putting into practice the idea of man's rule over things (the world).

Social Worldliness (worldliness in the narrow and particular sense)

'This worldliness,' which may be called social worldliness, means the reordering of relations between man and things by actualizing the idea of man's sovereignty over the world, and in addition securing a harmony and co-ordination between society, political organization and belief systems, and the goal of this, the ordering of social life, the life of this world, which up to the present has generally been denigrated, appropriately to the world or in accordance with the idea of world rule.

The concept of worldliness comprising two different but complementary meanings arises from the fact that the concept of 'the world' comprises two meanings. In the first sense, it is the world which is the field of physical existence and is studied by the physical sciences, and in its second sense it is a field of social existence which is studied by disciplines like axiology and ethics. If noted carefully, it will be seen that there is a profound and close tie between the two.

We speak of the world in the first sense as the cosmos, the universe, or the world without man, while we call the second one this world or man's world, and so on. At this point we should discuss briefly the Qur'anic view of the cosmos.

The Universe (Cosmos) in the Qur'an

Broadly, we may see the Qur'anic view of the cosmos as twofold: the cosmos without man, and the cosmos with man.

The cosmos without man. This is usually expressed in the Qur'an by the phrase "the heavens and the earth," it is treated as a sheer being devoid of contents, as a physical being. The cosmos without man, that is, pure *res extensia*, is presented in the Qur'an as a faultless, perfect, noble, auspicious field of existence. At the same time, this is the Qur'an's 'sacralization of the cosmos.'

The cosmos with man. Generally this is described with term 'the world,' and here it is not sheer as a being, that is, it is not empty; its contents is man, in which case the cosmos with man is treated not as a sheer being devoid of man, but together with him. While the cosmos described by phrase "the heavens and earth" is solely a field of physical existence, the cosmo-physical field of existence expressed by the term 'the world' is transformed into a sociological field of existence. That is to say, although the cosmos is 'in itself,' it is not 'for itself.' In order to understand better the relationship between man and the cosmos, we shall touch briefly on man and his place in it.

Man and His Place in the Cosmos

Man has two complementary places in the cosmos. These are his 'individual' and his 'social' places. In the first, man is only a person, an individual. While in the second, he is treated as a being with an historical and social meaning and content, as an historical and social being.

Man as an Individual and the Cosmos

The cosmos is a purely physical being, and because it is only physical, it is 'singular,' it is a field of singularity. Whereas man as an individual is not a 'singular' being, but a 'double' being. This 'twoness' is formed by the togetherness of spirit and matter, and has both dualistic and dichotomic characteristics. In respect of his essence, man does not belong to this world of physical existence, the Manifest World; he was sent here for a specified time, then he will be taken back to his original abode, the World of the Divine Command. Thus, as an individual, man, to use a much-used Sufi expression, is "a guest" in this world.

Man as Society (Humanity) and the Cosmos

As regards his place in the cosmos, there are various differences between man as a single individual and men as society. When considered as an individual, essentially his original home is the hereafter and his basic character is *spiritual*, but when considered as society, his basic character is transformed into a *worldly* one. The term 'worldly' here is not restricted to the material. Nothing in which man is found can be purely material. What is meant by worldliness here is this: men as individuals are born, they live, and they die. Their true home is the hereafter, where they came from. They will return there. However, humanity, which is constituted by the coming together of human beings, is undying until the resurrection of the dead and Last Day. Humanity is born in this world, it lives in this world, and as a being belongs to this world. Individual man's mark is to be a 'true person.' The characteristic of humanity however is to be a 'legal person (body).' The one whose true home is the next world is the true person, that is, individual man. While the one whose true home and original abode in this world is humanity. The profound and radical difference between the two has virtually always escaped notice in the history of Islamic thought.

To come to the idea of 'man ruling the world,' this holds meaning not for individual men, but for society(ies) and for humanity in the widest sense. Although due to his original home being not this world but the next, individual man is a stranger and guest in this world, humanity is not a guest in this world; its original home is this world. Individual man is 'otherworldly.' Society-man is 'this worldly.' To use a metaphor, humanity resembles an organism whose single cells are individual men. Just as the cells continuously change, while the organism is permanent until it dies as a whole; so despite the deaths of individual men, its single cells, humanity is permanent until the day it will die as a totality. For which reason, for practical purposes humanity is considered to be immortal. To summarize: Individual man is a 'true person,' his true home is the hereafter, that is, he is 'otherworldly' and mortal. Whereas humanity is 'worldly' since its true home is this world, and it is immortal.

Up to the present in 'phenomenal' Islamic thought, man's relations with the cosmos have virtually always been dealt with in the context of individual man. Our thesis however is that man-cosmos relations should be considered within the framework of this double understanding of the concept of man. There are two reasons for this. According to our thesis, theoretically the nature of 'noumenal Islam' itself commands this, and practically this offers a radical solution to something it is vitally necessary to solve. That is to say, in the opinion of the writer of these lines, Islamic thought can bring about a fundamental revolution in this respect. So long as man's relations with the cosmos are not considered as 'mankind's relations with the cosmos,' as much as they are 'the individual's relations with the cosmos' Muslims will continue to live with a perpetual 'death phobia'. Whereas man was sent to this world to live, not to die.

The Relations Between Man And The Cosmos

Humanity's Relations with the Cosmos: Anthropocentric Teleology and the World

It should be mentioned that the Qur'an offers an 'anthropocentric teleology.' That is, the cosmos was not given existence for no purpose; it has a purpose and that is man. Contrary to what Christianity teaches, the cosmos is not an accursed place of exile where man was cast out to in order to be punished. It is 'the promised land' for man. Man was sent to the cosmos as God's vicegerent, to rule it and be sovereign over it. The meaning of this is the idea of 'world rule.' The importance of dealing with man's relations with the cosmos as humanity's relations as much as the individual's relations here becomes clear. For on considering rule over the cosmos as an idea concerning immortal humanity rather than mortal man, that is, the individual, it will acquire a sounder meaning.

The Individual's Relations with the Cosmos: 'the Clean World' and 'the Unclean World'

In this situation then, the cosmos is generally considered in two ways in respect of man's relations with it, and these do not negate, but complement each other.

The Clean World In the first, the world is 'the clean world.' For sure man was sent to the cosmos to rule as God's vicegerent, that is, to be sovereign over nature, but he does this not in his own name, but in God's name and as His deputy. While ruling the cosmos man should know that it is in trust to him, and should not spoil it. He should rule it in God's name and as His vicegerent and deputy. This applies to both humanity and individual man. Moreover, individual man, the true person, is mortal. He will die, and will attain to a perpetual life in place of this transient one. And that perpetual life is to be won here in the cosmos. Thus, man's life in the cosmos, that is, 'man's relations with the cosmos,' is called in the Qur'an 'worldly life' or just 'the world.' And if his life is in conformity with the basic aims of his existence, with God's commands and prohibitions, these relations will be 'clean' (laudable, acceptable). Then man's relations with the cosmos, that is, worldly life, or briefly 'the world,' will be sacralized and legitimized. This, briefly, is what Islam calls 'the clean world.'

The Unclean World If worldly life, that is, the product of what man does in this world, which constitute man's relations with the cosmos, is not in conformity with the basic aim of his existence, with God's commands and prohibitions, his relations are 'unclean' (reproved, detestable), in which case, his relations with the cosmos, that is, worldly life, or the world, are not sacralized or legitimized; on the contrary, they are execrated and illicit. This is what we call 'the unclean world.' Again, this applies both to humanity and to individual man.

That is to say, what may be 'unclean' is not this world itself (physical existence), but the world created by man in consequence of his relations with it. Thus, in conclusion we may say that contrarily to what many people assert, Islam is not opposed to worldliness; just the reverse, it is in favor of worldliness. What is important here, is that starting from this point, it should be able to throw open new horizons for Muslims and all humanity.

Islamic Modernity And Bediuzzaman Said Nursi

Bediuzzaman and Degenerate Negative Modernity

Bediuzzaman was always opposed to **degenerate modernity**, which is an understanding of modernity that is imitative, characterless, coercive, and modernist in a way that destroys the basic elements of culture. That is to say, what he was opposed to may be summarized as firstly, with the stance of a dignified thinker, by man inclining everywhere in the world towards the purely material alone, the damaging of man's place in the sphere of existence; and secondly, with a more concrete and particular stance, the defeat of Islamic culture and civilization before the West turning into serious destruction.

Before there was any discussion in Turkey of the problem of modernity and it was unknown what it was, it was conceived of as a simple, trite, low-quality parroting of the West. This drove Bediuzzaman to indignant rebellion, as it did all religiously-minded conservative intellectuals. In the final paragraph of the Fifth Note of the Seventeenth Flash, Bediuzzaman says:

> O sons of this land! Do not try to imitate Europeans! How can you reasonably trust in and follow the vice and invalid, worthless thought of Europe after the boundless tyranny and enmity it has shown you? No! No! You who imitate them in dissoluteness, you are not following them, but unconsciously joining their ranks and putting to death both yourselves and your brothers.[1]

While the following warning corroborates also what we said above:

[1] Nursi, Bediuzzaman Said, Lem'alar (Istanbul: Sözler Yayınevi, 1990), p. 116, *The Flashes Collection* [Eng. trans.] (Istanbul: Sözler Publications, 1995), p. 166.

> O miserable pseudo-patriot who fervently encourages Muslims to embrace this world and forcibly drives them to European industry and progress! Beware, do not let the bonds with which certain members of this nation are tied to religion be broken![2]

For apart from this, Bediuzzaman was not opposed to either material civilization or technology. Moreover, the importance he afforded technology and the modern physical sciences was so great that his students who have followed on in his path have played a truly significant role in legitimising the physical sciences in our country from the religious point of view. Although it would be superfluous to dwell too much on this since it is not directly concerned with our subject, I want to say this briefly: this close interest in the physical sciences has given rise to a current of 'fideistic scientism' in almost all of the various groups of the *Risale-i Nur* school of thought.

Bediuzzaman Said Nursi and the World

In the *Risale-i Nur*, Bediuzzaman Said Nursi dwelt mostly on the question of belief. He has no work therefore that may be said to be directly an analysis of modernity. Nevertheless, scattered unsystematically throughout the *Risale-i Nur* are numerous references to the matters we have spoken of. We may divide into two his discussion of the world, in accordance with texts of the *Risale-i Nur* and related to our subject: 'the clean world' and 'the unclean world.'

The Clean (acceptable, approved) World

In Bediuzzaman's philosophy this world in the sheer sense is a clean being. The reasons for this may be reduced to two:

- This world is the work of God, it receives its existence from Him. It is also evidence for His existence.
- This world was given to men by God so that they might win clean livelihoods from it.

We now examine these more closely.

The World as Ontological Evidence

In Bediuzzaman's philosophy the world, that is, the field of physical existence, is a reality, a sheer truth. There is no debate in the *Risale-i Nur* of a philosophical or theological (*kelâmî*) nature concerning scepticism. That is, the outer reality we perceive through our senses is accepted as 'in itself existent'. The sentences,

---

[2] Lem'alar, 117, The *Flashes Collection*, p. 168.

"Since there is a reality, a truth, in this world, most certainly there is true mercy"[3] show that rather than opening debate about the reality of the world, Nursi thought that by taking it as 'given,' it would lead to proof of the Necessarily Existent. This is the 'cold cosmology' side of Nursi's cosmological philosophy. However, he does not pay overmuch attention to this cold side; his main area of interest is the warm side of the cosmos, that is, according to our definition, 'warm cosmology.' Even in *Isharat al-I'jaz*, which he assigned to the questions of physics, 'warm cosmology' is given greater importance than 'cold cosmology.'

The main purpose of Nursi's warm cosmology is proof of the Necessarily Existent. In this respect, he reads the cosmos as though it were a book. However, his reading is different to that of a physicist or a world-conqueror. The underlying aim of his reading is to reach what lies beyond it, that is, "to pass from the work to the one who worked it." Thus, the proof he most frequently employs for proof of the Necessarily Existent is the cosmological evidence or proof called in technical philosophical terms "passing from the work called the cosmos to its maker, God." Bediuzzaman almost never uses the ontological proof for proof of the Necessarily Existent, and he uses the cosmological proof more than the teleological and ethical proofs.

Sufficient as examples of this subject, which are superabundantly present in virtually all his works, are the proofs for everlasting happiness:

> *First Point:* If observed carefully, it will be seen that a perfect and intentional order embraces the whole universe. ...
>
> *Second Point:* Total wisdom is apparent in the universe. ...
>
> *Third Point:* Through the testimony of reason, wisdom, induction, and experience, the absence of futility and absence of waste in the creation of beings, which is constant, indicate eternal happiness. ...
>
> *Seventh Point:* All the exquisiteness, all the virtues, all the perfections, all the attraction, all the yearning, all the compassion known and seen in the universe are meanings, significations, immaterial words. They necessarily and self-evidently show to the heart and thrust in the mind's eye the manifestations of the All-Glorious Maker's favour and kindness, benevolence and munificence. Since there is a truth, a reality, in this world, most certainly there is true mercy. And since there is true mercy, there will be eternal happiness...[4]

Therefore, the "perfect and intentional order [which] embraces the whole universe" and is mentioned in the First Point is the principle of 'regularity' in the universe. According to Bediuzzaman, this regularity is "perfect" and "intentional." That is, he first notes that there is the most perfect order in the cosmos, and passes from its

---

[3] Bediuzzaman Said Nursi, Sözler (Istanbul: Envar Neşriyat, 1996), pp. 521-2 / *The Words* [Eng. trans.] (Istanbul: Sözler Publications, new. edn. 1998), p. 541.

[4] Sözler, pp. 518-522, The *Words*, pp. 538-541.

perfection to intention. This intention indicates that the order of the cosmos is not from itself, but from outside itself.

As for the "total wisdom ... apparent in the universe" in the Second Point, this recalls the regulation of the cosmos and raises it to the level of wisdom and purpose.

As for the Third Point, "the testimony of reason, wisdom, induction, and experience" and "the absence of futility and absence of waste in the creation of beings" and its moving from there to proof of the Necessarily Existent, all demonstrate this:

- There is an "absence of futility and absence of waste" in the universe. That is to say, physical existence is not meaningless (pointless, absurd). It is also free of wastefulness (unnecessary conditions, excesses). If the first of these (the absence of futility) gives meaning to the universe, the second (the absence of waste) shows how it should be, its demonstrates that there is such a being.

- Setting out from the absence of futility and absence of waste in the universe, he bases proof of the hereafter, that is, the resurrection of the dead, which is one pillar of proof of the Necessarily Existent, on rational, philosophical, inductive, and empirical evidences. A further conclusion is drawn from this, that reason, wisdom, induction, and experience are all legitimate as sources of sound argumentation.

In the Seventh Point is shown that all the things in the universe which are exquisite, virtuous, attractive, perfect, yearning, and compassionate are evidences for God's existence, and that the hereafter is a reality. Bediuzzaman considers that the universe resembles "a clock or a regular machine,"[5] "a great clock" (God's great clock known as the earth),[6] "a Divine machine" (a dominical machine), and cites the machine's regularity as evidence for God's existence, that is, he proceeds from the cosmic regularity to proof of the Necessarily Existent:

> The heedless who disregard the testimony to a perfect will, all-encompassing knowledge, and total power, of all the benefits and purposes in the order of the world...[7]
>
> The thing they call nature is a press, not the printer. ... Therefore, looking at it superficially and in second place, a man with an untaught conscience and intellect might deem it possible that nature, which is constant and continuous, has an

---

[5], Bediüzzaman Said Nursi, İşârâtü'l-İ'caz (Istanbul: Sözler Yayınevi, 1978), p. 213.

[6] Sözler, p. 520, *The Words*, p. 539.

[7] İşârâtü'l-İ'caz, p. 100.

effective external existence. "In short: Nature is the art-work of God and His law of creation.[8]

Similarly, things being "existent and full of art" is certain evidence for the existence of a Maker, "Since things exist and they are full of art, they surely have a maker."[9] One of the most powerful cosmological proofs is set out splendidly in *Şualar* (*The Rays Collection*).[10] Moreover, besides being a machine, the universe is also "a book."[11] As for the Qur'an, it is "the pre-eternal interpreter"[12] of the cosmos, which is also known as "the book of the universe," and is described in some places as "the mighty book of the universe."[13]

Like all books, the great book of the universe should be read. Describing the cosmos as a book in a way that recalls Descartes' "Le grand livre du monde," Bediuzzaman told the schoolboys who complained when visiting him that their teachers showed no interest in religion: "All the sciences you study continuously speak of God and make known the Creator, each with its own particular tongue. Do not listen to your teachers, listen to them,"[14] showing that he considered it sufficient that they read this book.

The World Given to Men as a Clean Place to Earn Their Livelihoods

In Nursi's philosophy, the world is a place all beings win their livelihoods. See for example, his "Supplication" in the Third Ray:

> Yes, there is not one of the stones to be found in mountains, or the various substances used as remedies for illness, or the varieties of metals and minerals, which are essential for living beings and especially man, or the species of plants that adorn the mountains and plains with their flowers and fruits, but through the wisdom, order, and fine creation it displays, which is impossible to ascribe to chance, it testifies to the necessary existence of an infinitely Powerful, Wise, Compassionate, and Munificent Maker. This is especially true of substances found in the mountains like salt, potassium oxalate, quinine sulphate, and alum, which superficially resemble each other, but whose tastes are totally dissimilar; and particularly of all the varieties of plants, and the great diversity of their flowers and fruits. Moreover, through their being administered and managed as a totality, and their origins, situations, creation, and art all being similar, and the ease, speed, and cheapness in their making they testify to the unity and oneness of their Maker. ...

---

[8] İşârâtü'l-İ'caz, p. 101.

[9] Sözler, 473, *The Words*, p. 488.

[10] Nursi, Bediuzzaman Said, Şualar (Istanbul: Sözler Yayınevi, 1992) 65 ff., *The Rays Collection* [Eng. trans.] (Istanbul: Sözler Publications, 1998), p. 84 ff.

[11] Sözler, 547, *The Words*, p. 570.

[12] Sözler, 367, *The Words*, p. 376.

[13] Sözler, 242, *The Words*, p. 250.

[14] Sözler, 156, *The Words*, p. 169.

> Also, the mountains -both their surfaces and their interiors- being filled in orderly fashion with trees, plants, and minerals to meet the innumerable needs of all the living creatures on the earth, and even to supply the remedies for their many different illnesses, and gratify their various appetites and tastes, and these being displayed for those who need them, indicates the infinite breadth of Your mercy and infinite extent of Your sovereignty...
>
> Also, the lofty mountains holding stored up in orderly fashion the reserves to meet the future needs of the travellers in the guest-house of this world, and their being stores stocked up with all the treasures necessary for life, indicates, indeed, testifies, that the Maker Who is thus Munificent and hospitable, All-Wise and Compassionate, Powerful and nurturing, surely possesses eternal treasuries for His never-ending bestowal in an everlasting realm, for His guests Whom He clearly loves.[15]

The point to note here is Bediuzzaman's deducing a teleological conclusion from this 'clean' quality of the world, and according to the above, reaching "the Maker's unity and oneness."

The Unclean (detestable, reproved) World

Thus, this world as a field of existence, that is, as a thing, is not unclean (despicable). That is to say, the world's uncleanness is not on the 'outside' that is, on it as an object; it is on its inside, that is, on it in respect of its relations. The world is of itself clean, but the relations man forms with it, make it either clean or unclean.

This question, which is also mentioned above, is perhaps the most emphasized point in Nursi's philosophy. Among the many places it is mentioned is the Second Ray. Important clues about Bediuzzaman's philosophy of man are also to be found here in compressed form:

> "Through the mystery of Divine unity, among all creatures man may attain to the highest perfections, and become the most valuable fruit of the universe, the most perfect and refined of creatures, the most fortunate and happy of animate beings, and the addressee and friend of the world's Creator. Indeed, all man's perfections and his lofty aims are tied to the affirmation of Divine unity and find existence through its meaning. For if there was no unity, man would be the most unhappy of creatures, the lowest of beings, the most wretched of the animals, the most suffering and sorrowful of intelligent beings. For together with his infinite impotence, his innumerable enemies, his boundless want, and endless needs, he has been decked out with a great many faculties and senses, so that he feels innumerable sorts of pains and experiences countless sorts of pleasures. He has such aims and desires that one who does not govern the whole universe at once cannot bring about those desires."[16]

[15] Şualar, 44-5, *The Rays Collection*, pp. 60-1.

[16] Şualar, 14 , *The Rays Collection*, p. 23.

Thus, man has a position within the universe bestowed by the Creator and a role determined by Him. The world's legitimacy should be sought in this position and role. Because the man who acts in conformity with these will have fulfilled the purpose of his creation, he will not dirty the world, or to put it another way, the world will not be unclean (blameworthy, despicable) for man.

Bediuzzaman mentions the acceptable, laudable, praiseworthy side of the world, and describes its detestable, blameworthy aspect, with the concept we have named "pure worldliness:"

> O my soul! If you make the life of this world the aim of your life and work constantly for that, you will become like the lowest sparrow.[17]

Then in the Eleventh Word, he warns that "gratifying the physical appetites"[18], cannot be the function of life, and in disparaging fashion describes a life directed solely towards the life of this world as gaining "worldly life like an animal."[19] On the following page Nursi summarizes in nine points the aims of life, and by characterizing a view of life which looks only to worldly life as "an animal life," he condemns it roundly, and says:

> O my soul and my friend! Come to your senses! Do not spend the capital and potentialities of your life on pleasures of the flesh and this fleeting life like an animal, or even lower. Otherwise, although you are fifty times superior with regard to capital than the highest animal, you will fall fifty times lower than the lowest.[20]

It is clear what Nursi is leading to with all these arguments. Like all beings, when considered on his own, that is as apart from God, man only 'exists.' But this is not a 'valuable existence,' because it is only a superficial ontological analysis.

It is an ontological analysis, but it is superficial because despite being 'in himself,' he is not 'of himself,' that is, his existence did not arise from his own self. Moreover, this analysis of existence and man within existence will be inadequate because it lacks ethical-axiological analyses. What gains meaning for existence is not 'only existence,' there has to be something more than that. It is in consequence of this that following the way of classical *kalam*, he wants to connect man with God, the greatest and truest existent (*ontos*). Only in this way can both 'being' in the broadest sense, and man's existence be given meaning. In another place this meaning of existence is explained suitably to tradition with the theory of **trial and examination**:

> As eternal benevolence and pre-eternal wisdom necessitated, the Pre-Eternally All-Wise One created this world to be a place of trial, an arena of examination, a mirror

[17] Sözler, 24, *The Words*, p. 35.
[18] Sözler, 126, *The Words*, p. 139.
[19] Sözler, 126, *The Words*, p. 139.
[20] Sözler, 127, *The Words*, pp. 139-40.

to His Most Beautiful Names, and a page for the pen of Divine Determining and power. Now, trial and examination are the cause of growth and development...[21]

Conclusion

In which case, we may say this:

- The Qur'an gives us the basic means of legitimising a modernity aimed at man's rule over things, that is, sovereignty of the world. These means are the facts that the world is a being that has been subjugated to man; that it is not itself unclean, but possesses the potential to become unclean in respect of man's relations with it; and that although individual man is mortal, society-man is this-worldly and immortal.

- In being a clean (laudable, acceptable) and even praiseworthy field of existence, the world depicted in Bediuzzaman Said Nursi's philosophy is not accursed and blameworthy. What makes it unclean (detestable, blameworthy) is man's situation, which are his relations and the degree of his distance. In many places he emphasizes its unclean aspect more that its clean side, but this may be explained to a great extent on the one hand by the tradition in which he was raised, and on the other by the grievous atmosphere created by the stormy times in which he lived and the destruction wrought throughout the Islamic and Turkish world by the collapsing empire, and the grievously wounded civilization which was on the point of collapse, and by Western culture. Nevertheless, despite all this, Bediuzzaman's understanding of the world may form a basis of the concept of Islamic modernity, which we have attempted to develop, and hold up a light to.

[21] Sözler, p. 532, *The Words*, p. 553.

Chapter 15

The Gesture of Said Nursi as a Challenge to Modernity**

Wolf D. Ahmed Aries

Introduction

In the West people often complain that Islam did not develop its philosophical and theological system so that the believer could orientate himself easily in modern times. Although there exists a broad discourse in Islamic Societies which concentrates on the so-called Western challenges - technical development, medical standards, sciences, unions, social security, etc, there is a background question that does need discussion. This background question is: whether the Islamic countries could adapt to these standards without being forced to pay the tribute which Western nations paid and do pay? This, of course, is how King Faisal formulated the issue.

No doubt these debates are necessary for the Orient as well as for the Occident. But there exists another level, which we should consider. It is the spiritual one. I do not mean laicism or secularism. In this context these just touch on the surface.

First, a preliminary comment about my approach: I intend to focus on the discussion Said Nursi led when he stated, "Belief comes first." I believe that in order to keep Nursi's focus on the future, it is necessary for succeeding generations to continue his work. And this is not only the published papers, the *Risale-i Nur*, we have to look also at his gesture, his way of life, and his unshakeable courage to accept the challenges of human thinking. Work and life belong together. They form an integrated unity, which is still a provocation; because he was not fascinated by the possibilities of calculability, feasibility, or changeability of worldly events or the world itself. As a Muslim he did not tire of uttering that the whole is creation for which he stays accountable. No science or policy, however, can determine the values behind any accountability. Science and policies do not tell us to whom we are accountable.

Said Nursi's biography and work asked and answered this question without any hesitation: All evidence refers to the ONE. Are we not under the same obligation? I think the *Risale-i Nur* is not an Islamic museum but a workshop to meet coming tasks. My task in this chapter is to continue the work of the *Risale-i*

Nur. Two further remarks are necessary. My own background is as a West European intellectual whose roots go back to the Prussian minority and to the 1960s. Thus my scientific attitude has a twofold origin.

The second remark is a question: I always wondered why Said Nursi's personality and his work attracted such a lot of people in Turkey but not abroad? His language might have been a barrier, but also his special subject. In contrast to the general tendency to marginalize religious and spiritual issues, our thinker insisted on a discourse which put these themes in the centre of his reflections. "In the view of reality, the most important and the greatest [matter] is the question of belief." In a modern way of expression: Man has to acknowledge his anthropological transcendental openness and find his personal answer to it and society should draw its consequences from that.

My translation points to a certain problem. Our respected thinker was moulded by conflicts and differences between technical and scientific development of the western world and the decline of the empire. The coping with this phenomenon was a decisive element of his reflections which had some social psychological as well as political aspects. He concentrated, however, on the transcendental question in a very special manner which still challenges thinking without having used psycho-analytical terms or the results of social sciences. Modern discourses in humanities, however, cannot be thought in another language than that of these social sciences. In consequence of that there will be a certain tension in my own reflections between the discussion which Said Nursi led and my research - specially for those who are not used to applying sociological terms over our thinker's work.

This is not the place to begin with a discourse on the structure of modern, and post-modern societies. Therefore I would like to summarize some characteristics, which can be found in literature. I chose five perspectives. The first one is the political one. What constitutes the political perspective in (post-) modernity?

- Any kind and social form of coping by which the individual finds an answer to his anthropological transcendental openness is his very personal challenge and decision.
- Any form of practised power or rule needs rational grounds.
- The necessary social co-operation is built up on a minimal set of rules which is represented through human rights.
- Political power is bound to people's sovereignty.

The cultural perspective may be described by the following aspects:

- o The empirical sciences entered a continuing learning process.
- o The point in all moral and legal discourses is to find generally accepted reasons for social actions and life.
- o Arts are autonomous.

The social perspective has three additional aspects:

- o The capitalistic enterprise is based on rational rendering of accounts.
- o The bureaucratic state administration is built on reliable legal decisions and administrative structures.
- o Societies form nation-states.

The philosophical perspective:

- o Every tradition and norm must be open to questioning and has to be defended in an open social discourse by rational arguments.
- o Group norms have to be substantiated through universal norms.
- o The socialization of a personality, the social structures in which the individual grows up lead to an abstract ego-personality.

Miscellaneous aspects:

- o It is the individual's will to quote whatever he wants to quote and to combine what he quotes.
- With regard to the multi-cultural structure of societies all non-universal norms are relative. The individual who changes between different groups changes not only his loyalty but also the normative frame of references.
- The necessary radical openness leads to fundamental unreliability and uncertainty.
- The individual will stand for the behaviour only which society demands of.

This scenario is completely different to that which Said Nursi had in mind when he wrote the *Risale-i Nur*. His thinking was challenged by the contrast between technology and religion, the apparent contradiction of feasibility, calculability, and creation. One of his answers was learning as he thought that knowledge could never stand against belief Today this question is obsolete. Modernity does not care. It just ignores the possibility that the present world could have been created. Societies as well as research-fellows question a development, a problem or any matter in discourse for its rational reasons. People do not ask for truth but for successful handling. Thus the question of belief or atheism is simply irrelevant.

The generally accepted hypothesis is that man can decide and act without referring to transcendence. In order to find the answer of our thinker we should not only look to his work but to his life also and the sociological development in the twenties and thirties. At that time the official policy tried to turn society into a worldly nation-state. Said Nursi did not only start to argue against this public tendency but - forced to do so or not - lived the alternative. He turned to the anthropological transcendental openness in writing "The First Word," which was: "Bismillah, In the Name of God, is the start of all things good." In doing so he lived the alternative axiom to the one of public life. These axioms were:

- There is no being beyond human perceptual frontiers.
- The existing being reveals itself and is a creator, my creator.

Neither the first nor the second sentence can be rationally proven, but the individual can decide himself in favour of one and thus "close" the anthropological openness.

Said Nursi did not take up any discourse of whether the first axiom could make sense or not; he demonstrated by his life and writing how senseful it is to look at the world as a creation. The *Risale-i Nur* is full of examples in which he fitted events, scientific results and human experience together to a single proof: the transcendental openness can be sensefully closed by evidence: THE ONE does exist.

Thus the citation from above continues in the following manner: "... Just as this blessed phrase is a mark of Islam, so too it is constantly recited by all beings through their tongues of disposition..." As a Muslim, Said Nursi did the only thing possible; he took the verbal revealings as evident predicaments. In Islamic language, one would say: Our thinker took the Qur'an as the *Sirat al-mustaqim* (right path) through life and world.

From a modern point of view this remarkable decision provokes the question why such a movement could happen. A question which leads to life-span developmental psychology. Its research identified puberty as the phase when the individual has to decide on the different aspects of his openness. The range of challenges goes from looking for an own standpoint to the organization and planning of the own life up to the questions: "Who am I? What shall I become?" One moment within this broad range goes to the transcendental openness: "Is there any possibility of a being beyond the bounds of my reason and possibilities of perception?"

We know that it is not necessary to put the question or feel the impact. Man can ignore the fact of his transcendental openness. But if the individual accepts and decides on the subject he/she will influence the statics of his/her identity. The consequence of the acceptance that there is a being, what theologians call "belief," is the acknowledgement of a creator, a creation, and within Islam the acceptance of the oneness, unity etc. of a being, God, Allah. Our thinker therefore demanded to "renew belief by means of 'There is no god but GOD.'" On this background the individual is so embedded in the world that his personality does not move into the direction of an abstract ego-development. On the contrary the Islamic system of duties can form a structure which resists disembedding. May I remind you of the imprisonments. Said Nursi prayed and brought others to do so. John Lifton showed in his research on the process of brainwashing in which the personality is reduced to substantial structures that turning to one's own transcendental decision erects a wall against attacks.

In post-modern social development the individual changes the circles of identity within hours, days or weeks. Some of them might even belong to quite different cultures; but if the individual has decided on the axiom of Oneness this decision works like an (perceptual) anchor... All beings recite the blessed name. These reflections refer to a political aspect. Today we know that the liberal state cannot prove the foundations, axioms, on which it is built. More than this, in order to secure its own liberalism the liberal society has to convince its members to decide on their own which axioms will fit as base for their personal lives. Out of such a commitment grows the only chance for a stabilized order. Universal norms and a lot of group norms cannot be enforced completely; between states there exists no force at all, which could do so as the political events demonstrate. Who does care? Said Nursi's answer would have been the one, which he discussed, in his first Words: the hereafter. In his work *The Flashes*, he wrote:

> Just as the penalties of those perpetrating small crimes are delivered locally, and serious crimes are sent to the high courts, so too, according to the rule, the small errors of believers and close friends are punished swiftly and in part in this world, in order to quickly purify them. But the crimes of the people of misguidance are so great that since their punishments cannot be obtained in this brief worldly life, as required by justice they are referred to the Supreme Tribunal in the eternal realm, and most do not receive any punishment here.

This does mean that the individual stays accountable even if worldly institutions do not give any judgement. A probably ironic reference to Stalin who asked how many divisions the Pope had, or to any long lasting ill behaviour do not meet his argument. The term 'hereafter' based on the axiom of a transcendental being supposes a time dimension which does not transgress lifetime but embeds it like an envelope enfolds a subject. If we look through the contexts in which Said Nursi uses the term we should see that he draws from it a strategy which out-manoeuvres all other positions. Even post-modern attitudes are kept within bounds. You cannot quote without any reference. If one follows up this construct you might deduce that the autonomy of an artist has its limits. The intellectual and practical problem is who among men decides on the limits. Are these stable or on which conditions do they change?

These questions lead to a central term of modern development: learning. The statement - sciences have entered a continuous learning process - maintains that no predicament can be taken for sure, right or true. As Popper said: knowledge is progressed by falsifying an hypothesis.. Thus scholars must always be ready to correct or improve a theory. Research in the West, however, is not done today solely in the quest for truth, but looked at under the perspective whether the proposed hypothesis leads to a successful manipulation, which allows a predictable control for further industrial use. Although, Said Nursi was happy with an instrumental view of science, he was also committed to the discovery of truth. As a Muslim, he was sure that science could not discover anything that would contradict the Qur'an.

The situation changes if, as the social sciences do, man is treated in the same manner as a natural science subject. With regard to ethical limits social scientists do not do this literally. However, their gesture of observance tend in that direction. This is one side of the coin; on the other we might describe the situation as man observes himself like the Greek Narcissus, who fell in love with himself while looking at his reflection in the water. It is the endless regression of man, who observes how he observes himself and so on. Video-artists have imitated this structure by putting two televisions opposite each other.

At the same time everybody is forced to realize that the systematic observation of human behaviour revealed some remarkable results on the nature of ourselves, our structures, our growing up, our references and social engagement. As far as I can see, Said Nursi would never have refused to do such a research. But he would have interpreted all results as signs of how conditioned human existence is, conditioned by HIM, GOD. "The true nature of all beings is mirror-like. They are subject to Divine creation through pre-eternal power." And this is a reference to the Qur'anic verse: *And He is Powerful over all things.* The result is that whatever the research done connected with the social sciences, it is certain to show us a meaningful facet of His creation.

With this attitude, our thinker makes frequent references to axioms related to human thought, and recalls to everyone their consequences related to thought, behaviour, and action. It is for this reason that his phrase "Belief comes first" is like a constant challenge to modern or post-modern thinkers, who reject the anthropological openness, which has a place in anthropological structures. Some people consider the phrase to be an attack on secularism or laicism. But to either reject it with modern or post-modern logic, or see it as supporting the spiritual side of the body-spirit distinction, both represent wrong views, even if they appear to offer two completely different solutions to the same problem. These two views surfaced together with the question of who would succeed to the collapsing Roman Empire and who would take its place. It was also the question of whether the political leader would succeed, or the spiritual one. That is, would it be the German king, or the Pontifex Maximus, the Pope? The dispute continued for centuries, and finally Western Europe remained face to face with two solutions:

- The Roman Catholics were ultimately forced to live with this answer: political institutions are compelled to be dominant over spiritual institutions. The course of time brought the result of the present partnership of state and church. But it was a partnership in which the state held clear dominance. And this went as far as severe suppression of any other form of spiritual life.
- The Lutheran-Protestant German regions developed the so-called "governmental tolerance" (Toleranz von oben). During the 19th century it changed into a marriage-like partnership, which developed into mutual assistance after 1945.
- Both solutions were possible because there were two distinct organizations with clear hierarchies and clear structure forms to

> express power and will. Islamic societies never found a 'breakthrough' to an independent church-like structure, not to mention the Christian possibility of a body under public law, as for example the round about thirty churches in the Federal Republic of Germany did. (Hirtenbrief, Denkschriften, Sozialwerke)

Islam does not know any theological option for a clerical structure of it. Muslims do not need a theological institution which says who should intercede on behalf of him. If Western Europeans want to understand Said Nursi's attitude and gesture we have to go back to this remarkable condition. It is the *conditio humana Islamica*. Under such a perspective there is no theological difference if someone bows in front of a wall, which is part of a prison, a marvellously built mosque, or human existence. Having in mind to answer to the transcendental openness it is just decisive to perform the gesture, i.e. in Islam to pray and recite. It is that that Said Nursi permanently did. He lived the Islamic alternative to the separation of belief and world. At this point I regret that we do not have a biography at our disposal, which was written from the psychoanalytical point of view, as Erikson published a work on Martin Luther.

Westerners as well as Muslims often overlook the consequences of a churchless community. As one consequence these believers have to organize another way to hand down belief, traditions, behaviour, etc. One option goes with the family and the other refers to the archetype of the teacher who internalized norms and interpretations as well as history. Such inner directed personalities function like social anchors in times when critical events happen or a society tends to become outer-directed as (post-)modern societies do. At his time when wars turned things upside down, every day behaviour had to change, and heavy losses had to be deplored as well the challenge of foreign visible and invisible, intellectual colonialism, assaults, developments, and intensively inner directed personality becomes easily a symbolic figure. If this individual is endowed with an outstanding intellect, character, and eloquence - as our remarkable thinker was - he will become an outstanding figure. Such an inner-directed character might be looked at as a natural counterpoint to the (post-)modern issue of the abstract ego-personality.

Conclusion

In conclusion, Said Nursi provides an embodied model of engagement with modernity. Utterly convinced of the truth of Islam, he calls for a commitment to learning and research that can provide a much needed antidote to the western relativism and post-modern scepticism. Muslims today need the same attitude. They need to ground their commitment to science, learning and peaceful political coexistence on the truth of the Qur'an.

** Original English text.

Chapter 16

Rethinking Globalization: Hardt and Negri in Conversation with Said Nursi

Ian S. Markham

Introduction

This chapter will start with a brief examination of the meaning of the word 'globalization'. I shall defend the view that it is important to retain at the heart of the word the idea of market capitalism as the main framework for economic activity. This, I shall suggest, partly explains why globalization is such an issue today. The paper will then look at Hardt and Negri's *Empire*. This book is a postmodern Marxist response to the economic dynamic underpinning globalization. It will be noted that there are dangers in confining the conversation about globalization to advocates and opponents of free market capitalism writing largely in the European and American context.

At this point, we shall identify four themes in the work of Bediuzzaman Said Nursi's *Risale-i Nur*. These four points reintroduce the centrality of the ethical and religious in our dealings with each other in society. From this perspective the paper will suggest we need to recover certain basic ethical insights that shape our behavior with each other. In so doing, globalization can be made to work in a constructive way for society.

What Is Globalization?

Although everyone agrees that 'globalization' is a helpful category, there is considerable disagreement about its precise meaning. Many commentators, while conceding an economic aspect to globalization, want to see it defined much more broadly.. So Roland Robertson, for example, writes:

> For present purposes, globalization may be defined simply as the compression of the world. This notion of compression refers both to increasing sociocultural density *and* to rapidly expanding consciousness. Globalization itself has been a long term process extending over many centuries, although only in recent centuries has it, with increasing rapidity, assumed a particular, discernible form.

> Globalization is, it should be clearly recognized, a multidimensional process. In other words, it is simultaneously cultural, economic, and political.[1]

While it is true that the availability of CNN worldwide (media), the growth in international organizations (political) and the MacDonald's fast food option in virtually every city (economic/cultural) illustrate the diversity of factors driving globalization, it is also important to recognize that 'globalization' as an issue is linked to the triumph of capitalism in the Cold War. In other words, Robertson had identified some consequences related to the mobility of people around the world. If this was the main cause of globalization, then it would not account for the hostility that globalization has created. Although Robertson is correct to insist that globalization should not be reduced to free-market capitalism, it is important to recognize the centrality of the economic in our contemporary debates about the nature of globalization.

Kofi Annan (the secretary-general of the United Nations) pointed out that when opponents talk of globalization, they see it as 'an ideology of predatory capitalism.'[2] This is precisely what provoked the opposition of the demonstrators at the meeting of the eight industrialized countries at Genoa[3] in 2001. So the International Monetary Fund (one of the most hated organizations) is right to put the emphasis on economics, when globalization is defined thus:

> Economic "globalization" is a historical process, the result of human innovation and technological progress. It refers to the increasing integration of economies around the world, particularly through trade and financial flows. The term sometimes also refers to the movement of people (labor) and knowledge (technology) across international borders. There are also broader cultural, political and environmental dimensions of globalization that are not covered here.[4]

The current extent of the hostility to globalization is one reaction to the Eastern European revolution of 1989. Francis Fukuyama in the summer of 1989 talked about the triumph of liberal democracy as the 'end point of mankind's ideological evolution.'[5] He was not alone; Richard John Neuhaus, the American theologian, saw it as a triumph for the values of capitalism over the dehumanizing tendencies

---

[1] Roland Robertson, 'Globalization and the Future of "Traditional Religion", in Max L. Stackhouse with Peter J. Paris (eds.) *God and Globalization. Volume 1. Religion and the Powers of the Common Life*, (Harrisburg, Pennsylvania: Trinity Press International 2000), pp. 53-4.

[2] As quoted in Max Stackhouse, 'General Introduction' in Max L. Stackhouse with Peter J. Paris (eds.) *God and Globalization. Volume 1. Religion and the Powers of the Common Life*, (Harrisburg, Pennsylvania: Trinity Press International 2000) p. 5.

[3] See http://www.genoa-g8.it/eng/index.html

[4] Taken from the IMF website and a paper on 'Globalization: Threat or Opportunity'. See http://www.imf.org/external/np/exr/ib/2000/041200.htm#II

[5] Francis Fukuyama, 'The End of History?' *The National Interest* 16 (Summer 1989), pp. 3-18.

of communism.[6] The Eastern European revolution was a key step in the perception of globalization as the vehicle for the victory of capitalism over all its alternative ideologies. For this reason the definition of globalization suggested by the International Monetary Fund will be used in this paper.

Hardt and Negri: Empire

Michael Hardt is a Professor in the Literature program at Duke University in the United States. Antonio Negri is currently a prisoner at Rebibbia Prison, Rome. Prior to that, he was a political theorist at the University of Paris and the University of Padua. This book is important because it is the most substantial post-Marxist attempt to explore the problem of globalization.

The argument of the book is simple: globalization is a symptom of the new Empire. The new Empire is a result of the demise of the sovereignty of the nation state. However, 'throughout the contemporary transformations, political controls, state functions, and regulatory mechanisms have continued to rule the realm of economic and social production and exchange. Our basic hypothesis is that sovereignty has taken a new form, composed of a series of national and supranational organisms united under a single logic of rule. This new global form of sovereignty is what we call Empire.'[7] Empire, or globalization, is the latest strategy of the wealthy and powerful to control the weak and powerless. It has a number of advantages over the traditional nation state that it has displaced. First, it has no boundaries. Second, it is attempting to create this myth that it is simply the logical expression of certain economic laws. Third, it wants to shape every aspect of human life. And finally, it shelters behind the rhetoric of peace.[8]

The study makes much of the decline of state sovereignty. It documents with some care the distinctive set of historical and social conditions that gave birth to the idea that a particular people within a particular boundary are sovereign over their actions. It notes that this was often a device that protected a tyranny. Within the nation state, the European powers worked for ethnic purity, while outside the nation state, these same powers worked to suppress and control the other. In other words, the European Enlightenment has strong tendencies towards racism and colonialism.

As national sovereignty declines, however, 'Empire' emerges. Where traditional national sovereignty was grounded in a 'transcendent' ruler (for example, the king over his people), the Empire is now using Capital to operate on the plane of immanence:

> Capital . . . operates on the plane of *immanence*, through relays and networks of relationships of domination, without reliance on a transcendent center of power. . .

---

[6] See Richard John Neuhaus, *Doing Well. Doing Good.*

[7] Michael Hardt and Antonio Negri, *Empire*, (Cambridge, Massachusetts: Harvard University Press 2000), p. xii.

[8] Ibid, pp. xiv – xv.

> In the passage of sovereignty towards the plane of immanence, the collapse of boundaries has taken place within each national context and on a global scale. The withering of civil society and the general crisis of the disciplinary institutions coincide with the decline of nation-states as boundaries that mark and organize the divisions in global rule. The establishment of a global society of control that smooths over the striae of national boundaries goes hand in hand with the realization of the world market and the real subsumption of global society under capital.[9]

Hardt and Negri believe that the socialism of Marx (revolution within the nation state) or the socialism of the 'localization of struggles' are over.[10] Instead globalization (Empire) opens up a new option for struggle. They write:

> Empire creates a greater potential for revolution than did the modern regimes of power because it presents us, alongside the machine of command, with an alternative: the set of all the exploited and the subjugated, a multitude that is directly opposed to Empire, with no mediation between them.[11]

In other words, Empire requires a global alliance amongst the multitude against oppression. They note the irony that although mass communication means that we all know about the revolts and strikes in other parts of the world there is no mutual shared ownership by the oppressed people of the world.

> In other words, (potential) revolutionaries in other parts of the world did not hear of the events in Beijing, Nablus, Los Angeles, Chiapas, Paris, or Seoul and immediately recognize them as their own struggles. . . This is certainly one of the central and most urgent political paradoxes of our time: in our much celebrated age of communication, *struggles have become all but incommunicable.*[12]

Nevertheless, the authors do sketch a political program that would be global in intent and organization. The first political demand would be global citizenship. Mobility of labor is a key condition for capitalism to thrive, yet the millions who do relocate often find themselves as illegal aliens in a foreign land, crudely and ruthlessly exploited. Instead there should be 'Residency papers for everyone', which 'means in the first place that all should have the full rights of citizenship in the country where they live and work.'[13] The second demand is 'a social wage and a guaranteed income for all.'[14] The third is the right to reappropriation, which means 'having free access to and control over knowledge, information, communication, and affects – because these are some of the primary

---

[9] Ibid, pp. 326-332.

[10] Ibid, p. 44f. The latter is the emphasis on the struggle within 'place-based' movements or politics.

[11] Ibid, p. 393.

[12] Ibid, p. 54. (Their italics.)

[13] Ibid, p. 400.

[14] Ibid, p. 403.

means of biopolitical production.'[15] Both Augustine's *City of God*, for spotting how the two Kingdoms of good and evil are mingled together, and St. Francis of Assisi, for insisting on living a life of joy against the abuses of power, are the heroes of the last section of this book.

Although there is much that is perceptive in this book, the major weakness is that it operates with a crude dualism - on the one hand, capitalism and globalization and on the other, justice for the poor. The narrative of the book focuses on power, especially the power shifts from the nation state to global organizations. It takes no account of the argument of those who see that religion (especially, according to Weber, Calvinist religion) is a key factor in generating the capitalist spirit. For Hardt and Negri, the religious component operates in two ways: Augustine provides a framework and St. Francis of Assisi provides an example of counter-cultural living.

However, against this understanding of the relationship between capitalism and religion, we find Max Weber. Weber, in his famous essay *The Protestant Ethic and the Spirit of Capitalism*,[16] argued that it was no coincidence that capitalism evolved in those countries most influence by Calvinism. It was a theological disposition, where one had to live a life of virtue (often interpreted as hard working and frugal) to demonstrate the necessary fruits of the Spirit thereby imparting the self-confidence that one is saved (i.e. part of God's chosen – God's elect), that provided the perfect impetus for capitalism. Now it is not necessary, for my purposes, to accept the details of the Weberian thesis about the role of religion in capitalism. All one need accept is that in amongst the many factors that shaped capitalism there were constructive and good ones. And as it is with capitalism so it is with globalization. To reduce both to the manipulation of resources by the powerful is a crude simplification. Capitalism has generated vast wealth: it has created lifestyle options that previous generations would not have been able to imagine. It has created technological options that can transform life for the elderly and individuals with special needs. Globalization opens up possibilities: it is the result of globalization that an English academic can work in the United States and learn from the insights of Nursi in Turkey.

One further reason to reintroduce religious themes into this debate about globalization needs to be mentioned. At the heart of a market economy are a whole set of virtues. The primary one is 'trust'. The banking system in the West depends on trust: indeed the bank collapses if all savers withdraw their money from the institution at the same time. A contract between the customer and a restaurant is made on the mutual understanding that a healthy product will be served and the customer will pay for the product at the end. V. A. Demant, the English theologian of the 1930s, makes this point well when he writes:

---

[15] Ibid, p. 407.

[16] See Max Weber, *The Protestant Ethic and the Spirit of Capitalism* (London: Unwin University Books 1930).

> The period of capitalism . . . has much else in its economic and social structure besides the free interplay of marketable commodities and services. Underneath that, and keeping society together, were ties and responsibilities surviving from the feudal and local social structure. Underneath it, too, were dispositions and spontaneous social disciplines reared in towns and localities, small enough to constitute what the sociologists call an "assessment group" where every member is under moral and social assessment by his community fellows. That wisest father of modern sociology, Frederick Le Play, and his disciple Emile Durkheim, as well as experts like Karl Mannheim, have made clear that only because of this non-capitalist sub-structure, was the market economy possible on top of it.. There was also much religion and the ethics of Christianity informing persons in the capitalist era.[17]

Capitalism is not simply about power over resources, it is also about the relationship of religion and ethics to economic life.

The danger in this debate about globalization is that we allow our reflections on globalization to be confined to the perspectives of the political left (i.e. those with socialist sympathies) and the political right (i.e. those with capitalist sympathies). To prevent this danger, we shall now turn to the work of Bediuzzaman Said Nursi. If I am right in stressing the religious factors at the heart of capitalism and globalization, then we should expect to learn from Nursi.

Four Themes in Bediuzzaman Said Nursi

Even with great thinkers it is dangerous to expect to apply their thought to problems that they did not experience. The world of Nursi (which means Wonder of the Age) is one that moved from the concluding years of the Caliphate and Ottoman Empire, through the tragedy of the First World War, to the emergence of the Republic of Turkey in 1923 with an initial strong commitment to aggressive secularism. We are all shaped by the world we encounter. For Nursi, he discerned correctly the challenge of modernity to belief and the response was the *Risale-i Nur* (the Treatise of Light), which provided a strong apologetic for the Qur'an.

Although we should not search for the word 'globalization' in the work of Nursi, we do find that there are four themes in Nursi that are relevant. The first is that it is appropriate to build bridges between western, scientific culture and the Islamic world. Nursi had a very strong sense that the best of modernity is both compatible with and anticipated in Islamic thought. So he writes explicitly about certain technological developments that 'Things like the aeroplane, electricity, railways, and the telegraph have come into existence as wonders of science and

[17] V. A. Demant, *Religion and the Decline of Capitalism* (London: Faber and Faber 1952), p. 48. Demant was of the view that capitalism was in decline in the 20th century as the 'state principle' (as he called the growth of socialism) took over. His comments, however, about the relationship of the market to the social and ethical substructure are, I suggest, still true, even if capitalism has proved more persistent than he anticipated. For a good discussion of this irony, see Ronald Preston, *Religion and the Persistence of Capitalism*.

technology as the result of man's progress in science and industry. Surely the All-Wise Qur'an, which addresses all mankind, does not neglect these. Indeed, it has not neglected them'.[18] He goes on to argue that such technological advances are anticipated in the Qur'an. This enthusiasm for the achievements of science underpins his 'natural theology' (i.e. his belief that there are good and decisive arguments for God's existence from the world). He lists the sciences of various disciplines before concluding:

> ...through the certain testimony of hundreds of sciences like these, the universe has been adorned with innumerable instances of wisdom, purposes, and beneficial things within a faultless, perfect order. And the order and wisdom given through that wondrous, all-encompassing wisdom to the totality of the universe have been included in small measure in seeds and the tiniest living creatures. It is clear and self-evident that aims, purposes, instances of wisdom, and benefits can only be followed through choice, will, intention, and volition, not through any other way. Just as they could not be the work of unconscious causes and Nature, which lack will, choice, and purpose, so too they could not interfere in them.[19]

Indeed for Nursi the sciences are part of God's intended purposes for humanity. So he writes:

> The miracles of the other Prophets (Peace be upon them) all indicate a wonder of human art or craft, and Adam's (Peace be upon him) miracle indicates in concise form, besides the bases of those crafts, the index of the sciences and branches of knowledge, and of the wonders and perfections, and urges man towards them.[20]

His confidence that Islam endorses the technological dynamic of modernity (a major feature of globalization) is reflected in this vision of the future. So one writer on Bediuzzaman writes as follows:

> Indeed, as we shall see when examining the Sermon, Bediuzzaman predicted that according to all the signs, Islam and Islamic – or, true – civilization would prevail in the future, and that the majority of mankind would accept and join the religion of Islam. He said: "In the future when reason, science and technology hold sway, that will surely be the time the Qur'an will gain ascendancy, which relies on rational proofs and makes the reason confirm its pronouncements.[21]

The important point is that it is a in a world where reason, science, and technology hold sway, that the truth of the Qur'an will be recognized.

---

[18] Bediuzzaman Said Nursi, 'The Second Station of the Twentieth Word' in *The Words*. From Volume 1 of the *Risale-i Nur* Collection (Istanbul: Sözler Nesriyat, Ticaret ve Sanayi, A. S. 1992) p. 260.
[19] Ibid. Volume 3. p. 408.
[20] Ibid. Volume 1, p. 272
[21] Sükran Vahide, *Bediuzzaman Said Nursi* (Istanbul: Sözler Publications 1992), p. 90. The sermon being referred to is *The Damascus Sermon*.

The temptation for many who are sympathetic to religion is to see the emergence of modernity (and its children – the growth of technology and therefore globalization) as evils that religion must oppose. Bediuzzaman argues very clearly that an attitude would be misguided. The achievements of science, modernity, communication, and therefore globalization need to be recognized. His reasoning is sound: he argues that these achievements represent the best of the human spirit. They demonstrate the creativity of humanity. And they are made possible by the God designed order of the universe.

Themes two to four are much more critical of globalization. The second theme is the need for society to accommodate in a just way the inequalities of wealth between rich and poor. It is interesting to note that he assumes some inequalities are inevitable. However, a 'balance' needs to be realized. So he writes: 'Yes, the upper and lower classes in human society, that is, the rich and the poor, live at peace when in equilibrium. The basis of that equilibrium is compassion and kindness in the upper classes, and respect and obedience in the lower classes. Now, the first phrase has incited the upper classes to practice oppression, immorality, and mercilessness. And just as the second has driven the lower classes to hatred, envy, and to contend the upper classes, and has negated man's tranquility for several centuries, so too this century, as the result of the struggle between capital and labor, it has been the cause of the momentous events of Europe well-known by all. Thus, together with all its societies for good works, all its establishments for the teaching of ethics, all its severe discipline and regulations, it could not reconcile these two classes of mankind, nor could it heal the two fearsome wounds in human life. The Qur'an, however, eradicates the first phrase with its injunction to pay *zakat*, and heals it. While it uproots the second phrase with its prohibition on usury and interest, and cures that. Indeed, the Qur'anic verse stands at the door of the world and declares usury and interest to be forbidden. It reads out its decree to mankind, saying: "In order to close the door of strife, close the door of usury and interest!" It forbids its students to enter it.'[22]

There are two strategies that keep inequalities in an equilibrium. The first is charity, obligated and required of all, but of course required as a greater percentage on those that are rich. And second the forbidding of usury. Even though Christians are not persuaded of the obligation that all forms of usury are forbidden (after all, if we can sell goods and services, then it seems reasonable to permit those who have purchasing power to 'sell' it those who need it). There is an important insight here that we need to accommodate. Economic globalization becomes problematic when the inequalities are not managed. Among the nations there are some that are very fortunate and benefiting greatly from globalization and others that are struggling. As the nations of the world manage these inequalities, this proposal by Nursi has much to commend it. There is an obligation on those that benefit to 'give' to those who are struggling; and there is also an obligation

[22] Bediuzzaman Said Nursi. From Volume 1 of the *Risale-i Nur* Collection (Istanbul: Sözler Nesriyat, Ticaret ve Sanayi, A. S. 1992), pp. 421-2

that when the IMF provides loans to these developing nations the repayments are not prohibitive. The campaign for debt cancellation for the poorer countries of the world is appropriate, especially in the light of the detrimental contracts negotiated in the middle of the 1970s by western financial institutions. The overall point is entirely appropriate: inequalities need to be managed with considerable care.

The third theme is that all wealth and property should be ultimately entrusted to God. Nursi tells a story of a King who has two subjects, one of whom allows the King to hold the property in trust, while the other insists on sole ownership. For the first subject, there are positive consequences; for the second subject, he became an object of pity. The point explains Nursi is this: 'Transient property becomes everlasting. For this waning life, when given to the Eternal and Self-Subsistent Lord of Glory and spent for His sake, will be transmuted into eternity. It will yield eternal fruits. The moments of one's life will apparently vanish and rot like kernels and seeds. But then the flowers of blessedness and auspiciousness will open and bloom in the realm of eternity, and each will also present a luminous and reassuring aspect in the Intermediate Realm.'[23]

This is a fundamental religious insight that should shape very fundamentally our view of globalization. The gift of life is a transitory gift: from the perspective of eternity, it is just a moment. Our attitude to possessions can either be deeply preoccupied with them as an end in themselves or they can be seen as a means to a greater end of serving the purposes of God. If it is the latter, then we are searching for ways to make sure that globalization serves the excluded. Globalization should enable us to bring food to the hungry; knowledge to the ignorant; and hope to the hopeless. To make this the goal of globalization is to entrust our possessions to God, who is after all the source and sustainer of everything that is.

The last theme that is worth noting is that Bediuzzaman is not persuaded that we should see all western achievements as part of the march of progress. There are some very harsh words for those that uncritically support the movement of European progress, especially when it is at the cost of religion.

> O miserable pseudo-patriot who fervently encourages Muslims to embrace this world and forcibly drives them to European industry and progress! Beware, do not let the bonds with which certain members of this nation are tied to religion be broken! If thus foolishly blindly imitating and crushed under foot, their bonds with religion are broken, those irreligious people will become as harmful for the life of society as fatal poison.[24]

Extended discussion of this point is not necessary. Suffice to say, it relates to point three, globalization should not become the goal in itself; it should

---

[23] Ibid. From Volume 1, p. 38.
[24] Ibid. From Volume 3, p. 168.

be the servant of a vision of social organization that allows the spiritual dimension of humanity to grow and develop.

Concluding Reflections

The exercise of exploring Nursi on globalization has been helpful. Unlike the entrenched positions of Hardt and Negri, we find a much more nuanced approach. To simply interpret capitalism as the tool of the powerful to retain control of as much wealth as possible is a distortion of the reality. The capitalist spirit has its roots in certain religious dispositions. It has generated vast wealth. Although there are many dangers, it must be recognized that there are also many possibilities.

As it is with capitalism, so I want to suggest, it is with globalization. Nursi would certainly recognize as good the technological and scientific underpinning of the globalization project. However, he would also want to make sure that globalization is a force that works for good. Crucially and centrally, there need to be strong safeguards against vast inequalities of wealth emerging. He would have, I am sure, been a strong supporter of the campaign for western institutions to cancel the debt burden facing the world's poorest countries. In addition, he would have witnessed to the imperative that the economic life of the world is intended to be means to a spiritual vision for humanity. Generating wealth for itself is madness. Generating wealth so that all people can live full God-directed lives is a vision. Globalization might make the latter a possibility. It is our task to work toward that end.

Bibliography

Abdurrahman, *Bediuzzaman'ın Tarihçe-i Hayatı* (Istanbul, Necm-i İstikbal Matbaası, 1335 [1919])

Ahmad, Israr *Musalman ummaton ka mazi, hal, aur mustaqbil, aur musalmanan-i Pakistan ki khususi zimma dariyan* (Lahore: Markazi Anjuman Khuddamul Qur'an, 1996)

Akşin, Sina (ed.), *Türkiye Tarihi* (Istanbul, Cem Yayınevi, 1989)

Albayrak, Sadık, *Son Devrin İslam Akademisi, Dar-ül Hikmet-il İslamiye* (Istanbul, Yeni Asya Yayınları, 1973)

Algar, Hamid, "The Centennial Renewer: Bediuzzaman Said Nursi and the Tradition of *Tajdid*," in *Journal of Islamic Studies*, 12:3, (Oxford: Oxford Center for Islamic Studies, 2001)

Anwar Ibrahim, The Asian Renaissance, 1996, Kuala Lumpur.

Anwar, Ibrahim, *The Asian Renaissance* (Kuala Lumpur 1996)

Badilli, Abdülkadir, *Bediuzzaman Said Nursi, Mufassal Tarihçe-i Hayatı* (Istanbul, Timaş Yayinlari, 1990)

Bakar, Osman, *Islam and Civilizational Dialogue*, (Kuala Lumpur, 1997)

Brinton, Crane, *The Shaping of the Modern Mind* (New York: Mentor Books, 1950)

Canclini, N.G., *Consumers and Citizens*, translated G. Yudice, (Minneapolis: University of Minnesota Press, 2001)

Casanova, Jose, "Private and Public Religions," in *Social Research*, 1992, vol. 59, Issue 1

Davie, Grace, *Europe: The Exceptional Case* (London: Darton, Longman, and Todd, 2002)

De la Gorce, Paul-Marie, "Bombing to Control" *in Le Monde Diplomatique*, March 2002

Demant, V. A., *Religion and the Decline of Capitalism* (London: Faber and Faber 1952)

Dunn, John, *Modern Revolutions* (2nd ed.; Cambridge: Cambridge University Press, 1989)

Dunya, Ibn Abi, *Al-Sabr wa-'l-thawab 'alayhi* (Beirut, 1418/1997)

Düzdağ, Ertuğrul (ed.), *Volkan Gazetesi* 1908-1909 (Istanbul, İz Yayincilik, 1992)

Easterbrook, Gregg, *The Progress Paradox* (New York: Random House 2003)

El-Seyyid Salim, Islam and Asian Civilizations, 1995, Seoul Bediuzzaman.

Fackenheim, Emil L., *The Religious Dimension in Hegel's Thought*, (Bloomington: Indiana University Press, 1967)

Firinci, Mehmed, in Şahiner, *Son Şahitler Said Nursi'yi Anlatıyor* (Istanbul: Nesil Basım Yayın, 1999)

Fromkin, David, *A Peace to End All Peace. The Fall of the Ottoman Empire and the Creation of the Modern Middle East* (New York, Avon Books, 1989)

Fukuyama, Francis, 'The End of History?' *The National Interest* 16 (Summer 1989)

Fukuyama, Francis, *The End of History and the Last Man*, (New York: The Free Press, 1992)

Giesbrecht, Martin, *The Evolution of Economic Society* (W. H. Freeman and Company: San Francisco, 1972)

Han WOO'Keun, *The History of Korea*, Seoul, 1970.

Hardt, Michael and Antonio Negri, *Empire*, (Cambridge, Massachusetts: Harvard University Press 2000)

Hee-Soo, Lee, *The Advent of Islam in Korea* (Istanbul Mohammad, 1997)

Heisenberg, Werner, *Physics and Philosophy: The Revolution in Modern Science* (New York: Harper ' Row, 1958)

Hick, John, *Faith and Knowledge* (London: Fount, 1957)

Hoffer, Eric, *The True Believer: Thoughts on the Nature of Mass Movements* (Perennial Library Edition, 1966; New York: Harper ' Brothers, 1951)

Husain, Mir Zohair, *Global Islamic Politics* (New York: Harper Collins Collage Publishers, 1995)

Ibrahim Canan, "Bediuzzaman Said Nursi's View of Civilization" Panel 1: Bediuzzaman Said.

Jah, Omar, *Globalization and Socio-Cultural Change in the Muslim World*, Unpublished Paper, 2001

Javed, Malik, *Dawah Highlights*, Vol. XII, Issue – V, May 2001

Karpat, Kernal, "Nursi, *Sheykh* Badi' al-Zaman Sa'id," in *The Encyclopedia of Islam*, 2nd edition, vol. VIII

Khatami, Mohammad, *Hope and Challenge* (Binghamton University 1997)

Kung, Hans, *Theology for the Third Millennium*, Trans. Peter Heinegg (New York: Doubleday, 1988)

Lasswell, Harold D., "The World Revolution of Our Time," (Essay originally published in 1951 by Stanford University Press) *in World Revolutionary Elites: Studies in Coercive Ideological Movements*, ed. Harold D. Lasswell and Daniel Lerner (Cambridge: The M.I.T.Press, 1965)

Leaman, Oliver *Brief Introduction to Islamic Philosophy* (Oxford: Polity, 1999)

Leaman, Oliver, "Nursi's Place in the *Ihya* Tradition," in *The Muslim World*, Vol. LXXXIX, No. 3-4, July-October, (Hartford: The Duncan Black McDonanld Center at the Hartford Seminary, 1999)

Lee, Hee-Soo, The Advent of Islam in Korea, 1997, Istanbul Mohammad.

Mallaby, Sebastian, "The Reluctant Imperialist" *in Foreign Affairs*, March-April 2002

Mardin, Şerif, "Nurculuk," *The Oxford Eneylopedia of the Modern Islamic World*, ed. John L. Esposito (New York: Oxford University Press, 1995)

Mardin, Şerif, "The Nakshibendi Order of Turkey," in *Fundamentalisms and the State*, ed. Martin E. Marty and R. Scott Appleby, (Chicago: University of Chicago Press, 1993)

Mardin, Şerif, *Religion and Social Change in Modern Turkey, The Case of Bediüzzaman Said Nursi* (New York, SUNY Press, 1989)

Markham, Ian, *Plurality and Christian Ethics*, (Cambridge: Cambridge University Press 1994)

McCarney, Joseph, *Routledge Philosophy Guidebook to Hegel on History*, Ed. Jim Crane, (London: Routledge, 2000)

Mohammad Khatami, *Hope and Challenge*, 1997, Binghamton University.

Neuhaus, Richard John, *Doing Well. Doing Good*, (New York: Doubleday, 1992)

Northrop, F.S.C., "The World's Religions at Mid-century: An Introductory Essay," in *Religions and the Promise of the Twentieth Century*, ed. Guy S. Metraux and Francois Crouzet (New York: New American library, 1965)

Nu'mnni, Muhammad Manzur, *Ma'arif al-hadith*, Vol. 1, (Karachi: Dar al-Isha'at, 2001)

Nursi, Bediuzzaman Said, *Emirdağ Lahikası* (Istanbul, Sinan Matbaası, 1959)

Nursi, Bediuzzaman Said, *The Flashes Collection* [Engl. trans.] (Istanbul, Sözler Publications, 1995)

Nursi, Bediuzzaman Said, *A Guide For Youth* [Eng. trans.] (Istanbul: Sözler Publications, 1991)

Nursi, Bediuzzaman Said, *İki Mekteb-i Musibetin Şehadetnamesi veya Divan-ı Harb-i Örfî ve Said-i Nursî* (Istanbul, Sözler Yay., 1975)
Nursi, Bediuzzaman Said, *Isharat al-I'jaz fi Mazann al-Ijaz* [Tahqiq: Ihsan Qasim al-Salihi] (Istanbul: Sözler Yayinevi, 1414/1994)
Nursi, Bediuzzaman Said, *Kastamonu Lahikası* (Istanbul, Envar Neşriyat, 1994)
Nursi, Bediuzzaman Said, *Letters* 1928-1932 [Engl. trans.] (Istanbul, Sözler Publications, 2nd. ed., 1997)
Nursi, Bediuzzaman Said, *al-Mathnawi al-'Arabi al-Nuri* [Tahqiq: Ihsan Qasim al-Salihi] (Istanbul, Sözler Yayinevi 1994)
Nursi, Bediuzzaman Said, *Mesnevi-i Nûriye* [Turk. trans. Abdülmecid Nursi] (Istanbul, Sözler Yayinevi, 1980)
Nursi, Bediuzzaman Said, *Muhâkemat* (Istanbul, *Sözler* Yay., 1977)
Nursi, Bediuzzaman Said, *Nur'un İlk Kapısı* (Istanbul, Sözler Yay., 1977)
Nursi, Bediuzzaman Said, *The Rays Collection* [Engl. trans.] (Istanbul, Sözler Publications, 1998)
Nursi, Bediuzzaman Said, *Sikke-i Tasdik-i Gaybî* (Istanbul, Sinan Matbaası, 1960)
Nursi, Bediuzzaman Said, *Şuâlar* (Istanbul, Envar Neşriyat, 1994)
Nursi, Bediuzzaman Said, *Sünûhat* (Istanbul, Sözler Yayinevi, 1977)
Nursi, Bediuzzaman Said, *Ta'liqat 'ala Burhan al-Galanbawi fi'l-Mantiq* (facsimile edn.) (Istanbul, Sözler Yayinevi, 1993)
Nursi, Bediuzzaman Said, *The Words* [Engl. trans.] (Istanbul, Sözler Publications, new ed., 1998)
Osman Bakar, Islam and Civilizational Dialogue, 1997, Kuala Lumpur.
Raschke, Carl, "Fire and roses, or the problem of postmodern religious thinking," in *Shadow of Spirit: Postmodernism and Religion*, ed. Philippa Berry and Andrew Wernick (London: Routledge, 1992)
Reischauer, Edwin O. and Marius B. Jansen. *The Japanese Today: Change and Continuity*, Harvard University Press, 1995. pp. 203-204.
Robertson, Roland, 'Globalization and the Future of "Traditional Religion", in Max L. Stackhouse with Peter J. Paris (eds.) *God and Globalization. Volume 1. Religion and the Powers of the Common Life*, (Harrisburg, Pennsylvania: Trinity Press International, 2000)
Robinson, Richard D., *The First Turkish Republic: A Case Study in National Development* (Cambridge: Harvard University Press, 1963)
Russell, Bertrand, *Mysticism and Logic* (London: Longman, 1919)
Şahiner, Necmeddin, *Said Nursi ve Nurculuk Hakkında Aydınlar Konuşuyor* (2nd edn.) (Istanbul, Yeni Asya Yayinlari, 1979)
Şahiner, Necmeddin, *Bediüzzaman Üniversitesi, Medresetü'z-Zehra* (Istanbul, Timaş Yayinlari, 1996)
Şahiner, Necmeddin, *Bilinmeyen Taraflariyle Bediüzzaman Said Nursî* (12th edn.) (Istanbul, Yeni Asya Yayinlari, 1996)
Şahiner, Necmeddin, *Haşır Risalesi Nasıl Yazıldı?* (Istanbul, Zafer Yayınları 1997)
Şahiner, Necmeddin, *Bilinmeyen Taraflarıyla Bediüzzaman Said Nursî* (Istanbul: Nesil Basım Yayin, 13th edn. 1998)
Sakr, Naomi, *Satellite Realms: Transnational Television, Globalization and the Middle East*, (London: I.B. Tauris, 2001)
Salih Özcan in Şahiner, Necmeddin, *Son Şahitler Bediüzzaman Said Nursî'yi Anlatıyor* (Istanbul, Yeni Asya Yayınları, 1986)
Salim, El-Seyyid, *Islam and Asian Civilizations* (Seoul Bediuzzaman, 1995)
Short, John, *Global Dimensions; Space, Place and the Contemporary World*, (London:

Reaktion Books, 2001)
Smith, Wilfred Cantwell, *Islam in Modern History* (Princeton: Princeton University Press, 1957)
Stackhouse, Max, 'General Introduction' in Max L. Stackhouse with Peter J. Paris (eds.) *God and Globalization. Volume 1. Religion and the Powers of the Common Life*, (Harrisburg, Pennsylvania: Trinity Press International 2000)
Sungur, Mustafa, in *Son Şahitler* (New ed., 1994)
Tamimi, Azzam, *The Origins of Arab Secularism*, in Azzam Tamim and John Esposito, (eds.), *Islam and Secularism in the Middle East* (London: Hurst & Company, 2000)
The World's Great Religions, Time Incorporated. New York, 1957, pp 73-95.
Thomas, Lewis V., "Recent Developments in Turkish Islam," *Middle East Journal* 6 (1952): Reed, Howard A., "Revival of Islam in Secular Turkey," *Middle East Journal* 8 (1954)
Vahide, Şükran, *Bediuzzaman Said Nursi* (Istanbul: Sözler, 1992)
Vahide, Şükran, *The Author of the Risale-i Nur, Bediuzzaman Said Nursi* (2nd edn.) (Istanbul, Sözler Publications, 1998)
Waters, Malcolm, *Globalization* (London: Routledge, 1995)
Weber, Max, *The Protestant Ethic and the Spirit of Capitalism* (London: Unwin University Books 1930)
Weiker, Walter F., *The Turkish Revolution, 1960-1961* (Washington: The Brookings Institution, 1963)
Woo'Keun, Han, *The History of Korea* (Seoul, 1970)
Yahya, Abu Zakariyya b. Sharaf, *Riyad al-Salihin*, 1st Ed., Hadith No. 1822, (Riyadh: Dar al-Salam, 1996)

Index